LISTENING INTO OTHERS:
AN ETHNOGRAPHIC EXPLORATION IN GOVINDPURI
TRIPTA CHANDOLA

Theory on Demand #36
Listening into Others: An Ethnographic Exploration in Govindpuri
Tripta Chandola

Editing: Geert Lovink and Sepp Eckenhaussen
Supervision of previous versions: Dr. Jo Tacchi and Dr. Christy Collis

Production: Sepp Eckenhaussen
Cover design: Katja van Stiphout

Publisher: Institute of Network Cultures, Amsterdam, 2020
ISBN 978-94-92302-63-2

Contact
Institute of Network Cultures
Phone: +31 20 5951865
Email: info@networkcultures.org
Web: http://www.networkcultures.org

This publication is available through various print on demand services. EPUB and PDF editions are freely downloadable from our website: http://networkcultures.org/publications/.

This publication is licensed under the Creative Commons Attribution-NonCommercial-NoDerivatives 4.0 International (CC BY-NC-SA 4.0)

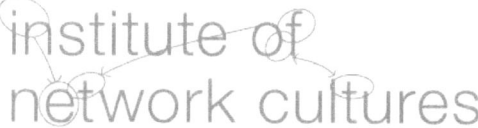

CONTENTS

PREFACE: FOR BITIYA	6
HOW TO USE THE BOOK	8
FACT SHEET	13
1. IN SEARCH OF THE NEVER-LOST SLUMS: ETHNOGRAPHY OF AN ETHNOGRAPHER	31
2. LISTENING: AN ETHNOGRAPHIC EXPLORATION	45
3. AN 'OBSCENE' CALLING EMOTIONALITY IN/OF MARGINALIZED SPACES: A LISTENING OF/INTO 'ABUSIVE' WOMEN IN GOVINDPURI	61
4. THE SUBALTERN AS A POLITICAL 'VOYEUR'?	75
5. COLLABORATIVE LISTENING: ON PRODUCING A RADIO DOCUMENTARY IN THE GOVINDPURI SLUMS - WITH TOM RICE	92
6. I WAIL, THEREFORE I AM	100
7. SONIC SELFIES: EQUALIZING THE ENCOUNTER WITH THE OTHER - IN CONVERSATION WITH JODI DEAN AND GEERT LOVINK	108
8. REVISITING THE HOUSING QUESTION	123

9. TO WHOM DO YOU 'BEAUTIFULLY' BELONG? THE SLUMS' RESPONSE (IF INDEED THEY WERE ALLOWED THE TONGUES): OR, THE RITE OF PASSAGE TO THE RIGHT OF THE CITY: BUT WHERE IS THE SELF OF THE SLUMS?   128

10. THE SHRIEK: A POETIC INTERLUDE   139

BIBLIOGRAPHY   142

ACKNOWLEDGMENTS   146

ABOUT THE AUTHOR   149

PREFACE: FOR BITIYA

> Things last longer than men. Who can say whether the story ends here; who can say they will never meet again. – J.L. Borges, The Encounter.

In a flat city, or flattened by the many who walk it, the hilltop of an illusion allowed for a sense of height and depth. It was a clear, early winter morning, and I was looking at my crisp best, dressed as the jaded travelers are: collar-down coat, black of course, a roll-on case with no untidy edges and a distant look. However I was not yet at the airport. It was not only the look that was distant, but the look that had rendered a distance to everything immediate – as is a tactic with those who spend hours in the in-between spaces (of the airports), dreaming (or obversely, dreading) of faraway lands. The reverie was broken by the announcement of a white van with blaring red lights. I was starkly reminded of where I was; blame it on the cinematographer's abuse, I had imagined a more dramatic setting.

I was at the entrance of the Safdarjung Mortuary awaiting Bitiya to arrive. We had serious business of the dead for the living to resolve. She was always on her way, never on time. And I found myself distracted from the matters at hand to one hot, summer afternoon years back.

In those times I was an earnest researcher in search of the subjects in the lanes of Govindpuri. I was led into a tiny room, thick with darkness. It was a relief, even though it took me a couple of minutes to find my bearings and the faces of the people present. A huge wooden bed was the only furniture occupying most of the space in this six by four feet room. On it lay a young woman about whom the first thing I remember is her hair; they were spread out like sleeping rivers. The presence did not need any announcement. Baby, my companion, introduced me to an older woman who was squatting at one end of the bed. She was the lying young woman's mother, Salma. Between the two of them, mostly the lying woman, there was very little space on the bed to offer me a seat. She was nudged. Her stillness was absolute. Baby in a high pitched tone informed her that I was there to interview people about their lives; that I was interested in hearing it all. A spark struck. She turned around, though still lying, shifting towards the wall to make space for me, reached for my hand, sat me next to her, and without any courtesies of formal introductions or establishing the intent of my so-said questioning, set out on her soliloquy; my hand merely a prop. For the next hour, and then some, she narrated at length, at once despairing and delighted, about her affair with her lover, Bitiya, of last seven years with whom she recently had yet another altercation.

Her performance was relentless. The interruptions of tea being made in one corner of the room, served and partaken; first, Baby and then Salma excusing themselves on account of reaching their respective place of work as domestic workers, did not deter her. Before leaving, both, Baby and Salma, had tried to intervene and disrupt the performance in which they reckoned I was entrapped as an unwilling audience. In continuing to allow her to hold my hand I assured the two departing women that no coercion was being exercised; they had eventually left, slightly bemused. And thus it was the lying young woman, who had by now gathered herself in a squat, her spread out hair and sparkling eyes.

In spite of the agonies of her affair, every once so often she would break into a childlike enthusiasm about the accessories I was carrying: my bag, the pouch in which I carried my rolling tobacco and the perfect cigarette I was rolling. Half an hour later I had to bid her farewell to keep another appointment. It finally dawned upon her that no formal introductions had been made: She introduced herself, Bitiya. And asked the intent of my visits. I told her. Before I departed she once again reached out to my hand and sought a promise: "You are writing the story of this place, right? Will you write about my love story? I want the world to know that no one can love like me". I told her there were many other stories I had to consider as well, but of course I will. She left me standing at her porch, her hair swaying, loudly announcing after me that I should make my next visit soon; she hadn't told me anything yet.

That afternoon was almost a decade back. But in the now and here, Bitiya had arrived, effervescent, her brown-eyes sparkling ahead of her and slight jump in her walk. Considering the matter at hand, I wanted to reach out to her and seek apology for not having accompanied her here when she had to come the first time: two-years back in the middle of the night and eight-months pregnant. But together we had seen, felt and grown enough to know that such courtesies were not required between us. Of course notwithstanding the situation and the setting, Bitiya remarked on the tardiness of my roll-on case, which she later did take to pack to her satisfaction.

The first time, in the middle of the night, Bitiya was accompanying Dimpy's – the love of her life - brutally stabbed dead-body to the morgue. Having heard her wail on the phone, I had not the courage to be there for her then. But in the now and here, we were at the office which maintained the records to claim what Bitiya reckoned was rightfully hers: the dead-man's name as hers.

As the tales of listening into the others, but not the task of it, folds onto itself, Bitiya and I have a web of the etching of the lanes of the Govindpuri slums, where we laughed, loved, fought, cried, mourned and steadfastly held on to each other, bearing its testimonies on ourselves, poetics and politics. We also have a seven-year old between us, Myshkin, who is putting us to the task of compelling and challenging the practice of our politics, a battle which we had reckoned we had already won. He is our anchor, ensuring that for no seductions and sirens shall we let our politics and poetics of our practice be compromised.

बितिया यह तेरे लिये [Bitiya, this is for you]:
तुम्हि मेरी नग्मा
तुम्हि मेरी नाज हो।
कोना और आगार हो।
सनाटा, शोर और सेहर,
तुम्हि हो।

Postscript:
As I shared these recollections with Bitiya, she claimed the book by demanding that an inscription of her own to be inserted for Dimpy, the love of her life, '*I miss you, Dimpy*'.

INTRODUCTION: HOW TO USE THE BOOK

This book is an invitation to listen into the everyday lives of the Govindpuri slums listened into over a span of almost two-decades. Slums lie on the margins of the state and society. However, unpacking the casual spatial/geographical reference is integral to locating the position of the slums in the city as it is revealing of the complex materialities and modalities of executing this marginalisation. More often than not, slums do not geographically lie on the margins of the city; in fact, historically, across continents, cities and cultures, the growth and evolution of the slums is intricately linked with the development of the cities, and thus, more often than not, they are located in the heart of the city. And it is precisely this centered-ness of the slums in the city which causes anxiety between the two entities – geographically, historically, theoretically and in the everyday practice. The centrality and visibility of the slums is after all a stark reminder that the 'modern, world-class' city around it is not a result of the fantastic imagination of the precious few, who have access to the glittering city, but rests on the histories of efforts and exploitation of the many who only experience it in its cold, clinical reality of steel and mortar structures.The presence of the slums in the city is undeniable, solid, and typically evokes strong reactions. Most city-dwellers harbour the sentiment that the reality of the everyday of the slums is in 'any respect unfit for human habitation' and that slums 'are detrimental to safety, health and morals'.[1]

The essays in this book intend to enliven the lives and practices of living in the slums beyond these simplistic, distant assertions by undertaking the task of 'tuning the ears'. These imaginations of the slums, arising from a limited, tenuous and more often than not biased engagement with their reality, is what populates the intellectual and political environment from which issue the multiple institutional investments in the city, including urban development policies, legal actions and political priorities, as well as the social–cultural responses to the slums and its residents. The protagonists of this book are the residents of the slums of Govindpuri. The book begins with the assertion and acknowledgment that slums are unsettling sights in the city. In this case the city of New Delhi; but in any city its slums are, metaphorically, testimonies of its unsettlement. Yes, slums are indeed unsettling sights. They are dirty and congested. The houses, permanent and semi-permanent, appear to have no logic, each being incestuously woven with its neighbours, and the dwellings from a distance seem to be precariously balanced on the edge of a precipice.

The book, however, takes issue with the category of assertions made in expensively produced official reports and by the mainstream media. These are the same assertions made loudly and sanctimoniously by the city's middle classes. To wit, that the living conditions of slums, that make them unsettling sights, are also the making of their inhabitants. The book unveils the 'anxiety of proximity' that fundamentally informs where the slums are in the city's present,

---

1   The *Slums Areas (Improvement and Clearance) Act* (1956) declares an area as a slum when the buildings: (a) are in any respect unfit for human habitation; or (b) are by reason of dilapidation, overcrowding, faulty arrangement and design of such buildings, narrowness or faulty arrangement of streets, lack of ventilation, light or sanitation facilities, or any combination of these factors, are detrimental to safety, health or morals.

but also where they will be in its past and future — geographically, politically, philosophically, socially, culturally and imaginatively.[2] Besides the denial of structural and systemic rights, and the othering of their residents, this signification of the slums also denies them a position in the history of the city itself, and thus denies them their own histories.

By insisting on the *listening,* and engaging with the everyday lives in the slums through its soundscapes, the narratives here highlight the creative, contested and political manner in which the marginalized negotiate the multiplicities of urban living, revealing their selves and their others, instead of only being regarded as the other. These experiences reveal that the slums-dwellers not only exercise a strict code of conduct to engage with others within the settlement based on caste, communal, gender and moral, amongst other considerations. Moreover, the slum-dwellers identify the city and its middle classes as their others, using similar vocabularies and frameworks to those used by the mainstream to other slum-dwellers. In doing so, the book inserts parallel and alternative narratives of the engagement of the urban poor with the hegemonic networks. These negotiations highlight the intersections and overlaps of lives on the margins with the existing formal structures and networks.

Whilst a key focus of the book is to insist on the self of the residents of the slums as it expresses itself in and through sonic assertions, the book critically sets the everyday negotiations of the residents of the Govindpuri slums against the discourse of othering and violence that they encounter. The book begins with the dual premise that slums are othered spaces and that their residents encounter othering and violence at an everyday and structural level in the city. The disenfranchisement and marginalisation of the residents of the slums, and thus their limited claim on the 'right to the city', are in fact the starting point for this book. The spectres of precarity, illegality and limitation haunt the past, present and future of slums in the city. Following Judith Butler, the book recognises that the structural and systemic denial of 'social and economic support, housing, health care, employment, rights of political expression, forms of social recognition, and conditions of political agency' persist because *slums* are considered 'un-liveable' and the lives of its residents 'un-grievable'.[3] As much as it is the intent of the book to portray the space and every day of the Govindpuri slums, its task is steadfastly to unfold the macro-political, theoretical and intellectual agenda at work around 'the slum' and to rehabilitate slums as, in fact, 'liveable' spaces where lives are 'grievable'.[4]

The book has been almost two-decades in the making. During this time, I have been immersively embedded in the emotional, political, social, economic and cultural landscapes of the slums. At this juncture of reckoning of sorts, the book is as much about the residents as it is about its interlocutor, the ethnographer. During this time, I have spent more afternoons and

---

2   Slavoj Žižek, 'Human Rights and its Discontents: The Logic of the Stalinist Show Trials', *Olin Auditorium, Bard College,* 16 November, 1999.
3   Judith Butler, *Notes Towards a Performative Theory of Assembly,* Cambridge, MA: Harvard University Press, 2015, p. 198.
4   Butler further elaborates that within specific constructions 'life is established as tenuous, precarious, and in that sense not worthy to be protected from injury or loss, and so not grievable' (198) and raises questions of biopolitical import as, 'Whose lives matter? Whose lives do not matter as lives, are not recognizable as living, or count only ambiguously as alive?' (196).

evenings in the Govindpuri slums than any other place in the city. The Govindpuri slums have at once been a space which made me question assumptions about self, other, being: an ongoing research engagement; the site of my doctoral thesis; but most significantly, a space whose particular and peculiar materiality, enlivened by the lives of those who inhabit it has shaped and refined my politics and poetics. At the risk of compromising objectivity and exposing sentimentality, I have no hesitation in admitting that in the lanes, intersections, corners, roof tops, carefully organised meagre houses and amongst people living precarious lives, I feel at home, a sense of belonging and becoming. It is a matter of deliberation – a political act, if you must – for me, as an ethnographer, to not only remain inserted and immersed in the stories of lives from the slums, but also not to retrospectively extend a sophistication of intent and agenda in the engagements that were sustained. But most importantly in retaining the anxiousness, the intent is to insist on the *messiness* of the researcher-researched encounters, especially when this relationship is predicated within the precise mainstream-marginalised (middle-class researcher and slum residents as the researched) positionality which the book questions and attempts to reflect on, if not alternate but simultaneous negotiating possibilities within this praxis.

Following Foucault, I locate transgressions as the enactments of challenging the boundaries.[5] When performed, claimed and enacted on the margins and by the marginalised the *transgressive acts* do not simply remain a matter of furthering one's horizons, in more ways than one. Here, these *transgressive acts* assume a political and poetic currency as inherent in and to these acts is the possibility of an alternative, or at least a simultaneity, of, with and within the normative discourses and practices. In that, underlying the perusal of the narratives and experiences from the slums is taking into cognizance the complexities and the upsetting, de-stabilising and disruptive capacities of the *transgressive acts*. Here the intent is to unveil the 'text-ility' of the texts (those instituting the dominant narratives, others offering critique, alternatives and affirmations, and the lived realities) to attempting a suturing, 'as in invisible mending' to weave the multiplicities of the reality of the 'real' and its 'myth' not in a linearly progressing narrative structure culminating in a neat resolution, but precisely to disrupt and displace the epistemological, political and cultural practices which attempt to distil (and thus consolidate) these complexities into a perverse static singularity of a problem to be met with a definite set of solutions.[6]

In the meanderings of the essays in the book, whether this ambitious task has even barely achieved its agenda and intent remains to be seen. However in these meanderings, at first intuitively and then with more theoretical and political mandate, the intent has been as outlined by Spivak 'to make the anthropologist construct her object as a teacher for a different end, learn to learn from below, from the subaltern, rather than only study him (her) [...] Not to study the subaltern, but to learn'.[7]

---

5 Michael Foucault, 'A Preface to Transgression', trans. Donald Bouchard and Sherry Simon, in Donald Bouchard (ed.) *Language, Counter-Memory, Practice: Selected Essays and Interviews*. Ithaca, NY: Cornell UP 1977.
6 Gayatri Chakravorty Spivak, 'Scattered speculations on the subaltern and the popular', *Postcolonial studies* 8.4 (2005):483
7 Gayatri Chakravorty Spivak, 'Scattered speculations on the subaltern and the popular', *Postcolonial*

In these essays, I make the point for listening as methodological framework, political intervention and poetic expression to 'learn to learn from below' and expose the dense multiplicities and lifeworlds of the subaltern employing the grammar and vocabularies as articulated by them, instead of rendering the experiences from below into explicable phenomenon within the hegemonic narrative.

The essay *In Search of the Never-lost Slums* explores the potential of the transgressive working of the hyphen to actualize the project of learn to learn from below. At the risk of exposing the limitations of my own research practice and praxis, which should not be an embarrassment but an acknowledgement of the learning from below, I discuss at length the anxiety of undertaking research in the slums, outside of my middle-class comfort zones of convenient theories and frameworks. The essay intends to rupture the revered position of the anthropologist and the ethnographer as a neutral, apolitical observer. In the essay, *Listening: An Ethnographic Exploration*, I propose listening as a methodological framework to first and foremost 'learning' from below but also to insist on listening as a critical imperative in acknowledging the 'self' of the others, here the residents of the slums. I thus listen into the listening of the self from within the interiority of the slums.

The essays *An Obscene Calling* and *The Subaltern as a Political Voyeur* put to task listening as a methodological framework. In the former, the anxiety, perils, tumultuous terrains of the experience, experiencing and expressions of love and loving through the narratives of Baby and Bitiya. Inscribed on their selves – bodily, emotionally, spatially and socially – is the double whammy of othering as woman and as residents of the slums. These inscriptions, I argue, for the subaltern, those on the margins have the consequences of their emotionality and thus the selves remaining unacknowledged. In *The Subaltern as Political Voyeur* I present the listening into the political lifeworlds of the residents of the slums. This essay is dedicated to the memories and learning from Saroj, who passed away a few years back. The conversation with Tom Rice is an attempt to further the disciplinary boundaries and practice of listening as a research framework and the potential of soundscapes to engage with lifeworlds particularly of with those on the margins and whose 'self' remains unacknowledged within the hegemonic modalities of knowledge production.

Listening as a methodology necessitates, first and foremost, the muting of the hegemonic self. As a political intervention, it demands the ontological praxis for the *others* to listen into their *self*, and that this *listening* accrues the validity and veracity of and as robust knowledge-systems within which when the *other* speaks, it is not reckoned to be in tongues. The denial of the *listening(s)* onto/into themselves, the hegemonic self intends to 'neutralize listening within himself, so that he cannot philosophize' having thus denied the others most fundamental claims to the structure of the self, the hegemonic self then extends its willing ears - insists that it is *all ears* which in fact 'belongs to a register of philanthropic oversensitivity, where condescension resounds alongside good intentions; thus it often has a pious ring to it'.

---

studies.

In insisting on the *listening(s)* by the others of their other, the essays in the book attempt to engage in the politics and praxis of *othering* as practiced by the identified others. It is in the processes and practices of *othering* that the self of the other is to be recognised. In the othering, as is evidenced by the manner in which the hegemonic self encapsulates the complexity of the others into a singularity solely premised on the former's reflexive and referential *listening* of the latter, the others' landscapes of reflexive and referential of making meaning of the self are to be unveiled.

The book ends with a few provocations towards this mandate. In a displaced dialogue with Jodi Dean and Geert Lovink, I discuss the possibilities of technologically mediated possibilities of 'equalizing the encounter with the others' in *Sonic Selfies*. In *I Wail, Thus I Am*, the disruption to the hetero-normative, hegemonic narratives, however temporarily, the sonic assertion of wailing women create. In *Revisiting The Housing Questions* and *To Whom Do You Beautifully Belong*, I locate the denial of the self and silencing of the slum-dweller in the hegemonic narratives and imaginations as being both strategic and an impediment to actualize the project of the 'right to the city'. *The Shriek* is a poetic interlude awaiting the presences of the identified others to be listened into.

Thus the essays in the book, recognize and insist that that *slums* are not anathema to the city, whether one speaks of the city's history or its present or future. Rather, that the *slums* as civic and social spaces are in fact a by-product of the violent, inequitable and exploitative processes of urbanisation. Through these essays the intent then is to act in whatever limited way to encourage the ethics of cohabitation across spaces, communities and ideas between spaces as the slums and its middle-class neighbours. And lastly, to provide a response to the everyday othering of the slum-dwellers by 'listening to, and recording, the details of the story the other might tell, letting that story become part of an undeniable archive, the enduring trace of loss that compels the ongoing obligations to mourn'.[8]

And thus the sounds of the ethnographic lives, of the *Others* I engaged with and the *Self* as their interlocutor slowly start humming.

From where you are, listen with me.

References

Spivak, Gayatri Chakravorty. 'Scattered Speculations on the Subaltern and the Popular', *Postcolonial Studies* 8.4 (2005): 475-486.

---

8   Judith Butler, *Notes Towards a Performative Theory of Assembly*, Cambridge, MA: Harvard University Press, 2015, pp 202.

FACT SHEET

The Matters of Definition

The Slum Areas Act, 1956, act declares slums areas as settlements which '[…] by reason of dilapidation, overcrowding, faulty arrangement and design of such buildings, narrowness or faulty arrangement of streets, lack of ventilation, light or sanitation facilities, or any combination of these factors, are detrimental to safety, health or morals'.[1] In Hindi, the slums are translated as *jhuggis* and *jhoparis*. The official departments as the Delhi Urban Shelter Improvement Board (DUSIB) and Delhi Development Authority's (DDA) Slum and *Jhuggi Jhopari* Rehabilitation extend the official designation, recognition and nomenclature to slums as such. Collectively and popularly referred to as the Govindpuri *jhuggis*, the settlement I am concerned with in this book is located in South Delhi and consists of three different camps: Jawaharlal Nehru Camp (referred to as abbreviated Nehru Camp in everyday use, and the nomenclature followed in the book), Navjeevan Camp, and Bhumiheen Camp. Adjoining the jhuggis is an authorised, legal colony known as Govindpuri, from whose referential location the camps also acquire their name in the popular usage. The three camps fall under the Kalkaji constituency, which is one of the seventy Vidhan Sabha (Legislative Assembly) constituencies of the National Capital Territory.[2] The total area the slums cover is 103896 sq m (Nehru and Navjeevan camp=103896 sq m and Bhumiheen camp =35156 sq m) with 6706 households (Nehru and Navjeevan Camp = 4578 and Bhumhiheen camp = 2128) in the three camps, according to the Delhi Urban Shelter Improvement Board List of 675 JJ (Jhuggi Jhopdi) Bastis.[3]

The official definitions of the slums enters the everyday imagination and translations in such a manner that the structural factors are employed to exert practices of othering on the residents of the jhuggis, with implications of social, physical, cultural, financial, emotional and political discrimination, denial of agency, and claims and rights as citizens. And thus residing in a jhuggi and thus being a jhuggi-walah, slum-dweller, significantly limits the spaces, services and rights one can claim in the city. Throughout the course of the essays, particularly when insisting or highlighting the narratives and experiences of the residents, I use the self-identified term which is either jhuggis or the specific camps to refer to their homes, which also marks their official addresses. In their usage, jhuggi, first and foremost, is the site and space of their settlement, habitation and belonging. When used in singular usage, jhuggi refers to

---

1   Delhi Urban Shelter Improvement Board, DUSIB, The Slum Areas (Improvement and Clearance) act, 1956, http://delhishelterboard.in/main/wp-content/uploads/2011/12/SLUMACT_14FEB17.pdf
2   Govindpuri's immediate neighbourhoods are Kalkaji Extension, the three camps, and Govindpuri Extension. The nearby middle-class residential areas are Chittaranjan Park, a middle-class, predominantly Bengali, residential settlement, and Alaknanda, an upper-middle class/middle-class residential area with several apartment blocks. In the vicinity of the slums, across the road from Navjeevan camp, are the apartment blocks, Konark and Kohinoor. And Bhumhiheen camp shares its boundaries with the neighbourhood of Tuglagabad (and its extension).
3   Delhi Urban Shelter Improvement Board, http://delhishelterboard.in/main/?page_id=3644., List of 675 J Bastis, last updated on (Updated 03-10-2019) http://delhishelterboard.in/main/wp-content/uploads/2019/10/JJBastisList675.pdf.

a house, when evoked in the plural, jhuggis, it is in the collective sense of referring to the entire settlement. Whilst I do acknowledge that the inherent othering which the 'naming' is laden which needs to be dissipated, I also remain astutely cognizant of the fact that whilst dealing with the issues of rights (particularly in regards to demanding judicial interventions, by the way of stay order on sudden, and often violent, demolitions and evictions, but also claims to resettlement in case of such a predicament and other services) the evocation of this particular 'naming' - slums, and its associated disenfranchisement also accrues weight and validity to the arguments.

In the essays, I use the terms of slums and jhuggis interchangeably, without laden prejudices and politics of othering. As deems most suitable to the particular narrating of experience and experiencing, I also either refer to the camps in their specificity or to the collective of the slums, which I often choose to take the liberty of referring to the 'slums of Govindpuri' and for the sake of convenience also abbreviate to GP.

Unless asked or agreed upon threat perceived, the names of individuals, groups and communities in the essays have not been anonymized. The decision to be known, written and referred to by their real names was in deliberation with the residents of the slums, and should be insisted on as a position of self-assertion by the slum-dwellers. Whilst conducting my doctoral research to fulfil the criterion of meeting with all the rules and regulations of the ethics committee, I had to seek consent from the people I was interviewing and hanging about. One of the assurances I had to extend amounted to ensuring that their 'names will be anonymized, and their identities not be revealed so as to not invite any harm towards them'. I always found making introductions or following the intense conversations about one's lives with the clause of anonymity rather trite and lacking in merit of truth. During one of such conversation, when I was repeating the whole consent form for the benefit of the recorder and to record the participant's response as a record of her consent (the verbal, record consent had to be sought as most of the participants were not formally educated and the literate, written compulsions needed to be circumvented), a fiery woman in her 30s lashed out at me, however lovingly, to say, 'we are telling our stories because we want them to be told. What is this nonsense of not writing our real names, I want the world to know this is who I am and this is what I think. And don't worry about our safety, it is my challenge to anyone from, use my name and if you have the gumption, find me in these lanes. And if you do find me, I will be here to take you on'.

Since then I have followed the wisdom and claiming of not only one's lifeworlds and spaces these are unfolded within and only annonymized names when have been asked for. I do however leave out the address within the lanes of the slums of Govindpuri, almost in perverse pleasure, for someone to take on the fiery woman's challenge of finding them with the name as a maker in these lanes and take her own.

The Spread of and around the Slums of Govindpuri

In the map, the slums of Govindpuri are marked out in red, defining their boundaries. For those venturing into this space via this aerial, zoomed out perspective, if the slums appear like a patch-work pattern weaving into the broader spread of the neighbourhood that is because they are. GuruRavidas Marg is the main arterial road along which the slums are located, which leads towards Tughlakabad Extension on one end and at the intersection of another main arterial road, Ma Anandmayi Marg, lies the Govindpuri Metro Station. The Govindpuri Metro station was opened in 2010 to coincide with the inauguration of the Commonwealth Games. It falls on the violet line of the coloured-code Delhi Metro Map.

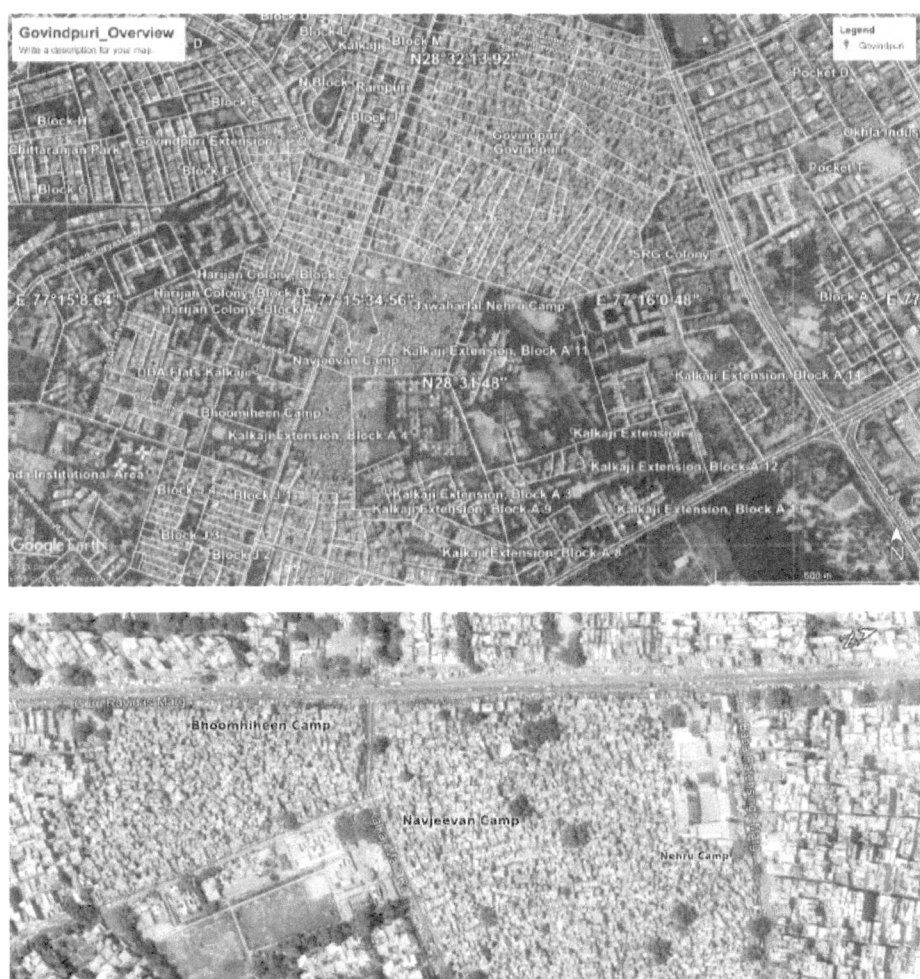

Figures 1 and 2: Overviews of Govindpuri and its three camps.

In my initial years of conducting research in the slums, I rarely used the public transport systems. The buses were erratic and demanded long waits and longer, convoluted routes to where I lived in the city, in its Northern end. I either used auto-rickshaws or made use of my then partner's bartered old red Maruti. In fact it is only in the last few years after the connectivity of Govindpuri Metro with other intersections were operationalized that I have started using the metro service regularly. To avoid making a knee-jerk acquaintance with the slums of Govindpuri, I propose a walk from the Govindpuri Metro Station wading through the neighbourhoods of the slums to insist that in their make, materiality and markets the slums are woven into the spread out the larger settlement, perhaps as a patchwork, but still held together by the fine threads of shared histories, spaces, contestations and alliances.

At the intersection, as one sets about on the GuruRavidas Marg towards the slums, across from the metro station, stands the Masjid Govindpuri. In my initial days of researching, I had created my own mapping of the neighbourhood depending on the availability of and access to toilets, especially if I were on a rare chance was using the public transport system. Adjoining the mosque, facing the main road, is a workshop which specializes in amplifying horns volumes, tunes and sounds for different vehicles. Tom Rice and I interviewed him for the BBC documentary Govindpuri Sounds, and even though it has been years (2013) and I do not recall much of the conversations, but the sounds of the amplified horns and the man's delight in giving us a demonstration and our own pleasure in it seem like an afternoon from yesterday.[4] Alongside the road, on both sides, push-cart eateries offering all kinds of street-food indulgences are offered and of course tea-stalls. Here, I often make pit-stop for the snack, tea and smokes. Next to the metro station, on the GuruRavidas Marg, is a small settlement of about 30 families displaced and evicted from settlements in the city. The main preoccupation is playing drums, *dhol,* at social and cultural events, and are colloquially referred to as the *Dhol Basti*. Considering the eviction and the subsequent settlement here happened fairly recently (post 2010, the exact year is not known to me), the settlement is not registered in the list of slums and JJ clusters and thus not eligible for any resettlement claims.[5] Even though in the few years since the settlement started forming its bearing here, I have interacted with a few of its residents, mostly children, hanging about the roadside and during my snack/smoke/tea breaks I have never conducted deliberate research here.

Giri Nagar is the first marked out residential area which falls on this route. The development of this neighbourhood witnessed sustained growth from the mid-1960s when Okhala Industrial Area for small and medium scale industries operationalized and started drawing traction. At the following intersection, down this road, where an inner road cuts through, starts sprawling the neighbourhood of Govindpuri from whose referential proximity the slums draw their colloquial name as a collective. Govindpuri is a mix of middle-class, lower and working class, and a high migrant labour rental residential population. It is marked out along 16

---

4   Tom Rice, 'Govindpuri Sounds', *BBC*, https://www.bbc.co.uk/programmes/p02hm1rx. The documentary was commissioned by BBC for its The Documentary program and was aired on 2 February 2015. More information here, https://ore.exeter.ac.uk/repository/bitstream/handle/10871/34775/Tom%20Rice%20 Govindpuri%20Sound%20REF%20document.pdf?sequence=4&isAllowed=y.

5   For eligibility criteria, Delhi Urban Shelter Improvement Board, Present Policies & Strategies, http://delhishelterboard.in/main/?page_id=128.

parallel, intersecting *galis* (literally, lanes) with residential quarters and building across the lanes. Govindpuri has witnesses resettlement in phases, first post-1971, India Bangladesh war, and 1984, post the assassination of the then prime minister, Indira Gandhi, and the riots targetting the Skih community that followed. Owing to its proximity to Okhala Industrial Area and Nehru Place, from the early 70s, Govindpuri emerged as a strong hub and neighbourhood for the emergence of small-scale industries running out semi-residential until 2000 when Supreme Court ordered the closure and relocation of all 'non-conforming industries' operating in the urban area of Delhi.[6] The combined pull factors of availability of jobs and cheap rental arrangements, along with the overwhelming prospect of hacking it out in the city, significantly contributed to drawing migrants from across the country, particularly its northern states – Bihar, Uttar Pradesh, Rajasthan - here.

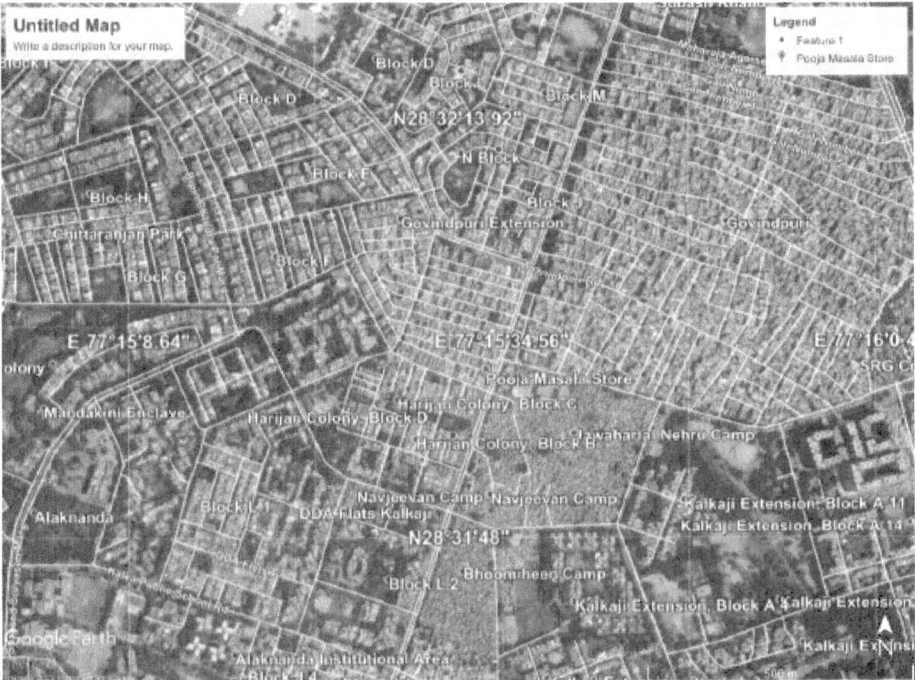

Figure 3: Pooja Masala.

At the intersection of GuruRavidas and Baba Fatehsingh road, lie the slums of Govindpuri. Opposite the fifteenth street, across the road, is the encroached Govindpuri - slums of Govindpuri, as they are termed in popular usage. Nehru camp is the first camp on this layout, followed by Navjeevan camp and separated by a drain, which in the present day is not easily visible. Across Govindpuri, and its 16 lanes, lies the middle-class settlement, Kalkaji and its extension, leading all the way up to the DDA flats in Kalkaji opposite to Bhumhiheen camp in

---

6   Aditya Nigam, 'Industrial Closures in Delhi', https://www.revolutionarydemocracy.org/rdv7n2/industclos.htm.

the slums. On that route, pursuing the Ma Anandmayi Road, at the intersection from the DDA flats of Kalkaji on one side and Bhumhiheen camp on the other, the Tuglagabad Extension neighbourhood is marked out.

Amongst the residents of Govindpuri and the slums, more immediate, authorized markers are used to refer to the three camps. While the Nehru camp camp and Navjeevan camp are the slums *of* Govindpuri, Bhumhiheen camp is evoked in reference to the slum *of* Delhi Development Authority (DDA) flats, as this camp is opposite these flats. Pooja Masala, something of a landmark of a grocery store falling along the Kalkaji Extension neighbourhood, is a common reference and meeting point for the residents of the slums and the neigbourhoods. Pooja Masala, as a landmark, is evoked to map spatial, temporal and social markers: *I am 15 minutes away from Pooja Masala; the lane into the jhuggis bank opposite Pooja Masala is where I will be waiting for you;* and, *she is doing well for herself, now she has rented an apartment only a few lanes away from Pooja Masala.*

Nehru camp was one of the first slums in the area: as mentioned, settlement here started from the early 1970s. Most of the initial settlers were migrant labourers who rented in legal Govindpuri. At that time, the rent was quite reasonable, INR 8–12 per month (Jiyo Devi, Local head) with the development of Okhala Industrial Area offered livelihood options. With the setting up of small-scale and other industrial units here, the rents shot up dramatically from INR 8– to INR 20–25 per month as Govindpuri became the outpost for this industrial area. Thus the migrants started arriving in Govindpuri in the late 1960s to work in Okhala Industrial Area and the upcoming small-scale industries, the land area wherein the slums are now situated was a large, unoccupied, infested with overgrown thorny shrubs. In the MasterPlan for Delhi, 2001 and 2011, this tract of land is marked for residential use. In the Master Plan for 1962, the land area is marked but it is not clear for what purpose. In the shared, local historical recalling by the long-term residents, this was a barren tract of land meant to be a park. Recounting from these narratives, the shift from the lanes of Govindpuri to the barren, shrub infested area was obvious and logical. The rentals in Govindpuri were not proportionate to the earnings as manual labourers, and lacking any social security systems to absorb the simultaneous shift to the city and supporting the families in the villages, the shift to tame the uninhabited, barren, thorny area to save on rents and other overheads was a logical decision. The task of taming this bareness – or as it is reckoned as encroachment in official records and popular reckoning – was by no means an easy feat.

It was then that the people started to move in and set up their makeshift houses in the barren tract of land. The period between the 1970s and the late 1990s was favourable to the current and prospective slum-dwellers and the three camps saw steady inflow of migrants in the camps: government had assured resettled land plots of 12.5 square metres; and the *Olga Tellis case* of 1985 had categorically identified slum-dwellers' right to live, safeguarding them against evictions, which 'contributed to their sense of security'. However, the 'real reassurance for this sense of security [...] came from no major evictions taking place after 1977 until 1997–98'.

In this scenario, most of the initial settlers did not mind shifting their base from legal Govindpuri to the slums, given the economic hardships they could avoid along with the promise of a resettled plot in the future. For this particular group of slum-dwellers, their shift from lower middle-class status to that of slum-dwellers is a testament of the lack of social, financial and allied support and security systems for the urban poor. The majority of this section of the urban population essentially subsidizes the everyday and sustained living of the middle-classes in the city by providing cheap, menial labour and also being critical in value-supply chains where they work in highly exploitative, precarious conditions. Whilst the promise of the resettled plots and a life of dignity in the city, and an urban futures for their families, was a compelling factor, they have to endure loss of social, cultural, political and emotional capital and capacities. During the initial years of the research (2004), the shift from Govindpuri and other parts of the country into the slums was a constant reference on two accounts: I was pursuing the line of questioning and because of the recent closure of the small-scale industries in Govindpuri, which had left a significant section of the population jobless.

The first phase of the research was a humbling experience, during which I had to *learn* how to conduct research in and about sonic cultures. In that sense, the problem was not the inability of the residents to engage with my research questions regarding engagement of the everyday through its soundscapes. It was the limitations of my ability to articulate my research agenda and aims – a methodological concern of sensual scholarship raised by Paul Stoller in *The Taste of Ethnographic Things*. By insisting on humbleness as a much-needed perspective and personal trait, Stoller highlights the phenomenal task that lies ahead in building a robust epistemological, academic and intellectual tradition for sensual scholarship. Senses, and here soundscapes, as *ethnographic objects* are tenuous and delicate. Senses as *ethnographic agendas* are complex and overlapping. Senses as ethnographies, not surprisingly, demand humility. It is not merely a matter of 'describing the way things look or smell in the land of others'.[7] A sensual scholar needs to surrender to the world of senses – their meanings, their connections, their articulations and aspirations – humbly and patiently, without preconceived notions and prejudices. A sensual scholar needs to have the sensibility to sense the senses as they are sensed in its context. In short, making sense of *senses* is not an undertaking without its moment of sensorial-intellectual-methodological numbness, deafness and blindness.

The constant mention of factories and construction sites to recount the Govindpuri slums' sonic past, which in the initial phase had exasperated me, in fact provided important sonic references for further listening. It was in these factories and construction sites that the residents found their main source of income. The persistent humming of machinery lent a sonic temporality to the everyday. After the factories were relocated in the early 2000s, due to the Delhi government's drive to curtail sources of pollution – noise amongst others – the residents recalled the place feeling 'eerily silent'. This silence was not literal, as even without the machineries the soundscape of the Govindpuri neighbourhood and the slums is very dense. This silence was the social and cultural articulation of exasperation at a 'loss of livelihood' and the anxieties that surrounded it.

---

7   Paul Stoller, *The Taste of Ethnographic Things: The Senses in Anthropology,* University of Pennsylvania Press, 1989, p. 9.

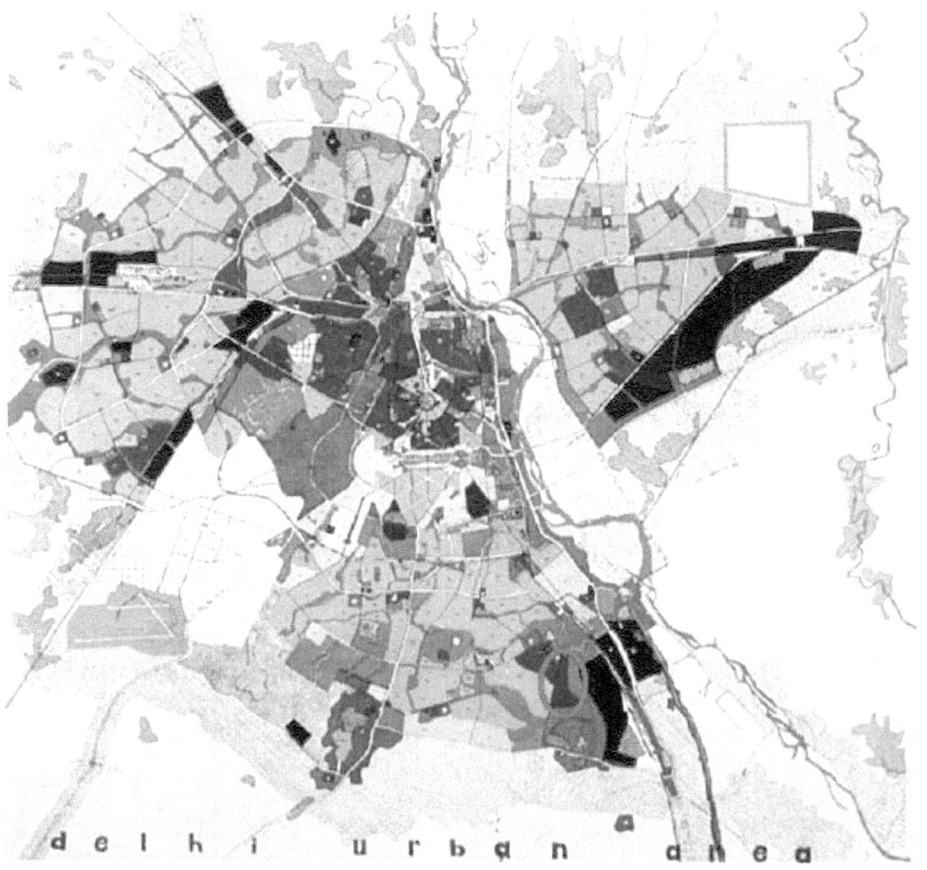

Figure 4: The Dehli Urban Area Master Plan, 1961.

Figure 5 (opposite page, top): The Dehli Urban Area Master Plan, 2001.

Figure 6 (opposite page, bottom): The Dehli Urban Area Master Plan, 2021.

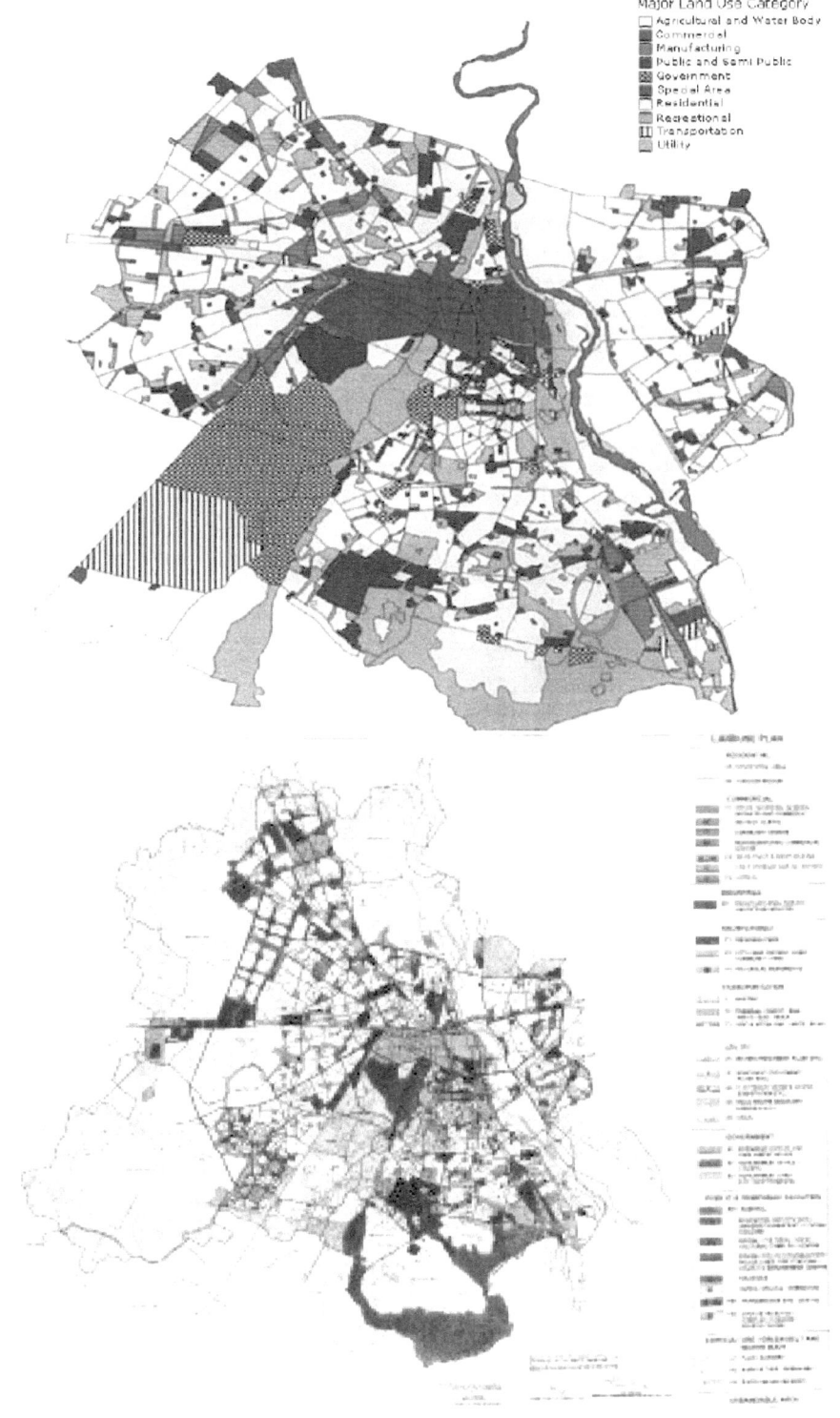

MASTER PLAN FOR DELHI - 2021

The settlement patterns in the other two camps were similar, except that Navjeevan camp was the last to be settled on account of a lack of basic amenities – water and electricity. Unlike the other two camps, Navjeevan camp does not share close proximity with any Lower Income Group (LIG) -Middle Income Group (MIG) settlements, which made it almost impossible for the residents to tap into their networks for these resources as Nehru and Bhumhiheen camps could. Most of the residents of the Govindpuri slums hail from small towns or villages – primarily from the states of Uttarpradesh, West Bengal, Haryana, Rajasthan, Madhya Pradesh and Maharastra, where the social, cultural and moral climate is rigid, conservative and restricted, based on strictly demarcated and defined caste, class and gender roles with prescribed responsibilities. As recounted by the residents during the course of my doctoral research, in the context of their villages, it was not possible for men and women to break social and cultural barriers and undertake jobs outside of their prescriptive caste, class and gender roles. Slums, however, offered a possibility to negotiate these barriers and roles. For instance, many residents of the Govindpuri slums – mostly women but also men – work in middle-class households as cleaners or cooks, an economic undertaking they would not have been able to pursue in their hometown or village on account of social-cultural pressures. Also, for many upper-caste men and women, it allows a move beyond caste hierarchies and roles and enables them to take jobs otherwise not allowed; these include, but are not limited to, working in leather factories, or working as cooks and domestic servants. This is not to suggest that Govindpuri slums have no caste, class and gender hierarchies. The compulsion to earn a livelihood, along with the distance, social, spatial, cultural, moral and psychological factors carried from their native homelands, allows the residents of the Govindpuri slums to negotiate around such issues.

In the later years, when the residents of the slums and I had negotiated anxieties and lens of engagement with the *other,* we rarely spoke about the past or evocation of the villages as a reference point. Instead we remained, as we still are, indulged, intrigued and exasperated by the fate of our beloved city, Delhi, and what how its fate and ours our intricately linked and our ambitions, aspirations, desires, dreams and dreads about the collective futures.

The Markets and Materiality of the Govindpuri Slum

The three camps Nehru, Navjeevan and Bhumhiheen, are distinct from each other – though this is not necessarily obvious to an outsider. An open drain separates Nehru camp from Navjeevan camp, while a main road divides Navjeevan and Bhumhiheen camps. One of the key distinctions between the three camps are highlighted by their markets. Each camp specialises in certain markets, which lends it a particular materiality while revealing the community, religious and caste affiliations specific to each camp.

All the camps lie alongside a main road connecting south Delhi to southwest Delhi. Most of the LIG and MIG settlements are located across this road. Most of the local markets of Govindpuri slums are strategically situated alongside this road, as they cater both to the local Govindpuri as well as the LIG-MIG population.

Nehru camp is closest – spatially, socially and culturally – to legal Govindpuri and the Okhala Industrial Area, where 'sweatshop'-type production houses thrive. These sweatshops provide an important occupational engagement for the residents of this camp. The camp is divided into three communal affiliations: lower caste communities who are professional cleaners/ sweepers; fortune tellers from Maharastra; and fruit sellers from Uttar Pradesh, comprising both Hindus and Muslims. The fruit sellers do not set up their stalls in the camp, but in a daily *haat* – vegetable market – that is held across the road. There are a few tea stalls catering to the workers in the production houses. Within and outside the camp, the two communities of cleaners and fortune tellers are socially and culturally ostracised on the basis of caste, and implied cultural decadence and moral bankruptcy. Even the social workers operating in this space do not venture into these areas until and unless absolutely necessary, evoking 'alcoholism, crime and dirt' as the main hindrances. The lack of markets in this camp is attributed to the presence of these communities: 'Even if we wanted to set up shops, no one would come. It is the better for us to explore into other territories.' (M, 40, tea stall owner)

Navjeevan camp, on the other hand, has a thriving market specialising in meat products and plastic goods – sheets, containers, and so on. A significant percentage of Navjeevan camp's population is Muslim, a group that traditionally deals in meat products – which explains the concentration of this business in the area. The density of the plastic market is remarkable to an outsider, middle-class sensibilities; it is an important element of Govindpuri's materiality.

Two kinds of housing that are prevalent in Govindpuri : *pucca* (concrete) and *kaccha* (makeshift). The materials used for *pucca* houses are bricks, cement and iron. The *kaccha* houses, on the other hand, use bricks, wood, bamboo and plastic sheets, which are used to shield the houses from both the sun and the rain. Plastic is affordable and durable. The plastic containers – usually having the capacity to hold 20 litres as a minimum – are very important aspects of the landscape of the Govindpuri slums. A shortage of running water means residents have to constantly evolve ingenious ways to store water. The plastic containers serve this purpose while also being used for storage of other kinds as well. Each household has at least one, if not more, of these plastic containers. These containers are also often used to hold up a wall or boundary. They are also in demand to serve the needs of the production houses in legal Govindpuri , as well as the storage needs of LIG-MIG residents, as water is scarce in these areas as well.

The plastic market of Navjeevan camp is a very profitable business. Most of these shops, however, are not owned by the residents of the camp,

> A few years back all the shops were demolished. Those whose shops were demolished were entitled to resettlement and a lot of them got plots either in Kondli or Narela. However, as the pressure of the authorities started to ease, most of the families came back and once more built their shops. Most of them sold their resettlement plots, bribed officials for fake I-cards [ration cards] to become eligible for resettlement in the next lot of demolition as well. They have shifted out of the slums into legalised colonies but they still want to retain control over this space on two accounts:

first, the business is profitable over here; and second, they will be able to claim resettlement plots yet again. (Male, 32, shopkeeper, Gandhipuri camp)

Bhumhiheen camp is the most prosperous camp in the slum cluster. Its population base is distinctly divided amongst Bengalis (immigrants from West Bengal and Bangladesh after the Bangladesh Liberation war) and non-Bengali settlers. The latter comprise families mainly from Uttar Pradesh, but also from Haryana and Rajasthan. There are limited interactions between the two communities at an everyday level. Bhumhiheen camp has several market pockets specialising in different commodities. On the main road, the vegetable market is held daily. This market caters to the local as well as a significant LIG-MIG population. As the vegetable market shares proximity with the slums, the prices of the vegetable are considerably lower than in other middle-class areas, attracting customers from this area. It is not easy to set up a stall in this area. One has to bribe local police personnel, acquire consent from local politicians and other important parties, and pay rent to the shopkeeper in front of whose shop the stall is set up. These shops alongside the road specialise in bamboo and woodwork. Most of these shops are owned by people from Uttar Pradesh, a northern state in India, where shopkeeping is a traditional professional for many communities. As mentioned earlier, these shops cater to the architectural needs of the local residents, as bamboo is an essential architectural feature of houses in all camps. It also provides bulk orders to other slum areas in the city.

Bhumhiheen camp is also distinct from the other camps in that it has a thriving market *within* the camp. This is called the Bengali Market. It is an organised and formal market controlled by the Bengalis, who form a significant proportion of the population of this camp. This market is further demarcated into specialised units offering specific commodities catering to the needs of Bengalis within and outside the camp. There is a specialised fish, jewellery and cloth market. One of the nearby MIG settlements, Chittranjan Park, has a high population of Bengalis, who patronise this market at an everyday level, contributing to the prosperity level of the Bengali community within Bhumhiheen camp. In 1991 a major outbreak of fire gutted most of jhuggis in Bhumiheen Camp, and which is often evoked as reference point whilst charting out the camp's history, as following which the camp received both state and non-state investment to construct *pucca* houses.

Each of the camp is popularly referred to and mapped out in individual and collective geographies and memories by its markets. In the initial years, when the lanes of the slums still bewildered me and I had not the confidence to lose myself to find the ways, if Pooja Masla was the landmark for me to keep appointments with the residents of Nehru Camp; the plastic-ware shop at the corner of Kalkaji Main Road in Navjeen and the fish market in Bhumhiheen camp were the rendezvous points. There is significant mobility between the three camps, but community members in each camps have their own biases and marking of socio, cultural, emotional and spatial othering. I have detailed these practices whilst discussing the water routes and other negotiations in my doctoral thesis.

Besides the peculiarity of the markets, the material fabric of the Govindpuri slums is strikingly uniform. Most of the housing types, as mentioned above, vary between the *pucca* and *kaccha*. The construction of these, however, depends on the location. Most of the constructions on the main road are up to three to four levels, used both for residential and commercial purposes. These are usually *pucca* constructions that use bricks, concrete, plastic, bamboo and wood for framing purposes. The tallest of these constructions, despite having three floors, is no more than 7 metres. As these lie on the main road, which is just over 3 metres wide, though congested with the markets around, they give a sense of space compared to the interiors of the slums.

The inside of Govindpuri is a very different reality. Most of the constructions inside the camps cannot be strictly categorised as *pucca or kaccha*, reflecting an ingenious usage of materials and optimisation of space. The streets are narrow, no more than 1 metre to 1.3 metres, in most instances. The tallest of the constructions inside of the camps is just over 3 metres. The houses are not only incestuously woven into each other but are *in* each other. The lack of space and the density of population necessitate architectural innovations, with a house's roof serving as makeshift rooms for others, or several households having to share a common entrance. Drains, flowing or blocked, marked the trajectories on the space. With the exception of Bhumhiheen camp, none of the other camps has a dense concentration of a market, though there are intermittent shops, dealing in a variety of merchandise, spread across the camps.

Unlike other slum settlements in the city, the three camps of Govindpuri have not witnessed spates of demolitions in the heart of the cluster, though there have demolitions on the fringes undertaken by the Delhi Development Authority to clear the passage on the main road. Considering the markets open on to the main arterial road, Guru Ravidas Marg, the clearance drive to move back the push-carts and temporary shops as they extend on the road is still quite common. These clearance drives are piecemeal and not directed at the peripheral roads in the slums. In 2008, the slums of Govindpuri witnessed one of the only coordinated demolitions, though on the fringes, across all the camps. The demolitions however were not towards evictions and clearance of the land area, but in response to the Public Interest Litigation (PIL) filed by the members of the Residential Welfare Associations (RWA) to seek 'a solution against encroachment of roads and services by slum residents'. The High Court responded to this demand by the 'construction of a five-foot wall to divide a slum cluster from neighbouring middle-class colonies' as a '[...] a temporary arrangement to offer protection to flat owners'.[8] The demolition is discussed further in the essay, *I Wail, Therefore I Am*.

And thus whilst the narratives of being and belonging are replete with speculations about resettlement prospects, the threat of demolitions is not as pronounced as in other accounts. The slums of Govindpuri also stand apart from most other slum settlements in the city in regards to the proposed in situ resettlement project. In 2008, the Delhi government announced the construction of 14-storey with 3,024 apartments in the same area, about 1.5 Kilometres away from the slum settlement, Nehru camp being the closest . It has been 12 years since the announcement, and the promise of the resettlement in the 'flats' has constantly been evoked in elections manifestos, claimed by every contesting parties.[9] The residents of the

---

8   Preeti Jha, 'Great Wall of Kalkaji', *Indian Express*, 05 April 2008.
9   See: https://www.thehindu.com/news/cities/Delhi/When-their-aspirations-of-owning-a-home-hit-a-brick-

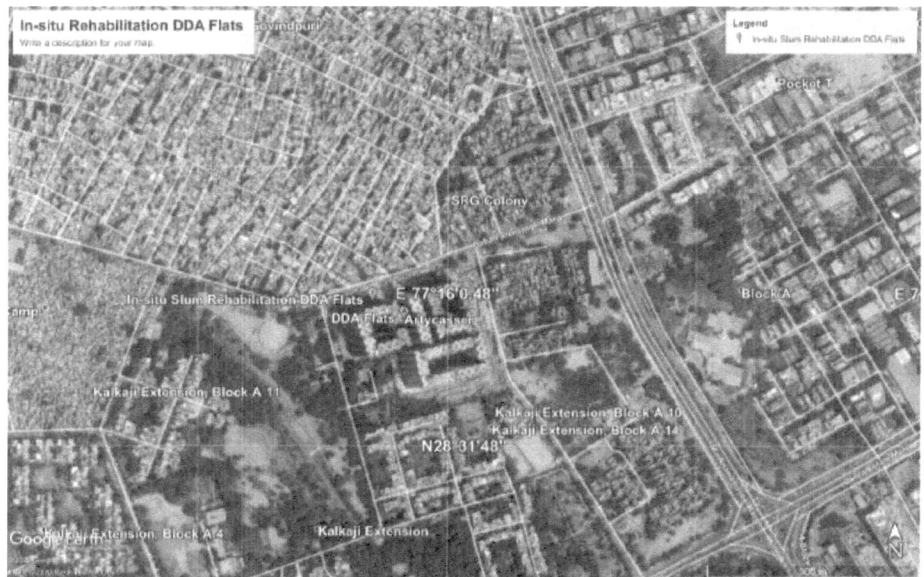

Figure 7: Rehabilitation DDA Flats.

slums remain unconvinced of the promise being actualized, particularly considering there are only 3,024 flats available and no clear idea about on what basis these will be allotted. 'Of course we will apply for the flat, and will shift into it or claim it, if we are the lucky ones', Babu Lal from Navjeevan camp commented, 'but we don't know whether it will ever happen'. A real estate agent from Govindpuri contextualized the future of the resettlement project in mid-2018 by when they were almost ready:

> The apartments do not look like in situ or resettlement project. They have the feel of other apartment blocks. My sense is that, even if the jhuggi-walahs are allotted the apartments, they will not able to afford it as the down payment is estimated to be around 2 lacs. What will happen is that they will sell their allotments to those who can afford it in the black, and along with the apartments, the parking spaces will be really coveted! Even if they can afford the apartments, how are they going to pay for the maintenance of the building, which the residents are supposed to collectively contribute towards…

Whilst discussing the prospect of allotment and living in the apartment block, the concerns of the apartment being 14-storey and the maintenance is constantly raised, how are the elderly supposed to climb up the 14-storeys?', 'what if the lift if not working, and who is going to pay for the lifts and for the power-back, if there is no electricity?'. And then more compelling concerns about how the 14-storey apartment living is going to correspond to the lives in the

wall/article14028514.ece., and https://www.dailymail.co.uk/indiahome/indianews/article-2632029/Around-3-000-slum-families-set-new-homes-thanks-DDA-project.html.

lanes, '[…] the sexual and romantic encounters and affairs are just going to increase; here, at least we have some control, in the apartments, they will be making out in the lifts and on the roof'. The shift from lanes to the 14-storey apartment block is also evoked in apocalyptic predications of the fate that shall befall during violent altercations, 'here, we are still in the lanes, I am telling you, when the same fights break out there [in the apartments], people will be throwing each other from that high!'. The fact that the Govindpuri Police station is adjacent to the apartment site is not appealing to some of the residents, 'right now, there are places to navigate about in the lanes, which we know well, but in the apartments, the cops will know exactly where to find us'.

These are speculative conjunctures of the residents regarding the life in the apartments, however it must be insisted that none of the residents I have spoken to over the years have expressed any desire to continue to live in the slums, perchance their name comes in the allotment list and they have the resources to pay for the downpayment, 'of course, we will like to shift, live in the apartments, not be jhuggi-walahs anymore'.

Across the 14-storey, DDA resettlement site lies the Transit Camp, as is popularly known. In official records, this settlement is called the Shri Rajeev Gandhi Colony. In 1984-85, several slum settlements across the city where demolished and people allotted land as a transit arrangement, and thus the name. In its materiality, the transit lies somewhere between the lower-income class houses of Govindpuri and the slums of Govindpuri. Whilst most of the houses are pucca, they lack the solidity of the houses in Govindpuri. The residents of the Transit camp[10] and also the local politician[11] have made suggestions for DDA to convert the land use marked in the master plan 2021, from 'Green Area/District Park' to Residential Area, which will make their claims for in situ rehabilitation stronger. Whilst there are strong links of mobilities between transit camp and the slums, the residents of the transit camps insist on maintaining a clear distinction lest they are also considered to be jhuggi-walahs also owing the proximity to the slums, sharing the similarities in nomenclature and the material conditions.

Owing to the proximity of the industrial area, the concentration of the migrant labourers to provide subsided labour for the small-scale industries in Govindpuri, the phases of re-settlement that the neighbourhood went through, even though the slums appear as a patch-work pattern, there are very strong, geographies of everyday, historical, cultural, emotional, financial, cultural, romantic and sexual exchanges, transactions and mobilities between these spaces. I do not intend to romantize the landscapes of these alliances between the neighbourhoods, of which the slums happen to be one. The relationships are fraught which tensions and contestations which manifest in particular kinds and practices of othering directed at the identified other, for instance, the residents of the slums for the middle-class neighbourhood and the newly arriving migrants and the *kothi-walahas* for the slum-dwellers.[12] However, the dominance of the resettled, migrant population in the neighbourhood, the materiality and the

---

10   See: https://dda.org.in/planning/suggestions/Dy.%20No.%202790%20DDA%20MPR.pdf.
11   See: https://dda.org.in/planning/suggestions/Dy.%20No.%202792%20DDA%20MPR.pdf.
12   Kohti, literally translates as bungalow, however both the houses and apartment blocks in which the residents of the slums work in different capacities are referred to as the same.

spilling out markets of each of their neighbourhoods compels practices of ethical co-habitation between the different groups. And herein lies the promise of political alliances and spaces of ethical co-habitation being actualized, perhaps the accommodation of the identified other emanates from compulsions but the fact that these practices *in fact* exist titillates and excites the possibilities of shared, democratic and equitable political urban futures.

As late as early 2020, when I last visited the slums of Govindpuri to hang around with some of the crew there – Akki, Pooja, Sonia, their kids, partners, lovers – the living conditions of the slums have significantly improved since the early 2004, particularly sanitation, sewage and water facilities. In all of the three camps, both on the fringes and in the insides of the lanes, prominent, robust and well-built religious structures are prominent. The building practices have become more robust with people paying attention to the foundational structures, and the use of marble-flooring and tiling has increased. A few of these houses I have seen transform over the years indeed look very handsome. Baby of Navjeevan camp, who is one of the protagonist in the essays, often teases me about the sale-deed of one of her jhuggi's she was tempting me with and which I was very keen on but for lacking resources (or living off my savings in that moment), reasons I cannot precisely recall now, I could not finalize, 'you should have taken then, now see how it has all developed, and maybe you would have gotten an apartment too'.

After almost two-decades of ins and outs in the lanes, lives, dreams, despair of the residents of the slums of Govindpuri and also spending equal amount of time engaged in discussions about the future of the slums, the best resettlement practices, the deliberations of in situ rehabilitation, it is my political duty and responsibility to summarize what the slum-dwellers really want, and here I present a consolidation of many voices resounding over several years:

> We don't to go from here, we have created these lanes and this settlement. We don't want to have newer, safer houses to live here, these houses are as safe as they can be, at least three-generations of families have safely grown up here. Earlier, yes, there were issues with water, sanitation, garbage disposal…these have been sorted out, we really have no issues, they could be better. If something is really to be done for us, stop humiliating us, exploiting us, denying us chances because we are jhuggi-walahs. We are proud to be living in the jhuggis, we have after all built these houses, these roads, these buildings, lives here. Just don't treat us like 'kheede-maukede' (insects-spiders) […] just we because we live in the jhuggis, living and material conditions, which are beyond your experience does not mean we do not feel, we do not have self-respect, we do not desire to be treated to with dignity…all the problems of the jhuggis they keep talking about will vanish – poof – if they stop treating the jhuggi-walahs like sub-humans.

A woman working as a domestic help in the nearby apartments whilst talking about the way her employer treat her and others who work for them was narrating the manner in which these working bodies are reckoned to be beyond pain and hurting (this was specifically in regards to not allowing her to use hot water to do the dishes during the bone-chilling Delhi winters), '*saala, unko lagta hai unka badan mom ka, hamara momjam ka hai.* (Bastards, they think that they have wax bodies and ours are made of cheap plastic).

Babu Lal who has been in Navjeevan camp since the early 80s, has worked as a mason and contractor with several builders across the city, is a repository of the history of the Govindpuri's social, political, infrastructural and architectural layout in the slums, and is also keenly involved in the political landscape. Presently he lives with his wife, son, daughter-in-law, a granddaughter and a dog in a three-story, marble -tiled floor house with a resplendent roof in the same lane. His astute analysis, evaluation and resolution for the slum problem, *yeh jhuggi ki samasya,* is as following (if someone in position of power indeed wants to listen, he added):

> This land is marked as residential land, and so in some ways we are ahead of the fight which the Transit camp people are fighting about. So, half the battle is won. The only thing that is required of those in power is to just take out the jhuggi-jhopdi reference in the official records. They will have to give us land somewhere, why not this area? I am telling you, once the name is changed in the official records, over a period of things will change. These camps will be like any other settlement, most of the problem is being treated demeaningly as jhuggi-walahs.

These the lived experiences and accrued knowledge of their lifeworlds, aspirations and histories of the urban poor (as articulated by Babu Lal and others), more often than not, fail to find way into policy framing and considerations. I identify this tendency as symptomatic of the 'denial of the self' to the urban poor, slum-dwellers, and those on the city's urban and margins. This 'denial of the self' of the urban poor is strategically imbricated within the capitalist, neo-liberal, hegemonic logics to keep this constituent population bound in exploitative relationships to extract maximum profits from them. By denying them real and active participation, the urban poor within this imagination are thus relegated only as data sets and markings on the maps which need to be cleaned, cleared and tamed towards the beautification and smooth running of the city.

The essays in the book present the fact of the matters as listened into and learned from the lived experiences of the residents of the Govindpuri slums. This task of deep, engaged, and dialogic listening into these realities, experiences and life-world of the residents of the slums is just a modest step towards the ambitious project of 'urgent utopia' and 'right to the city', theoretical, philosophical and political projects which are premised on an ongoing, dialogic interactions and encounters across all citizens of the city, including and especially those on the margins.

References

Nigam, A. 'Industrial Closures in Delhi', *Revolutionary Democracy,* 7.2 (September 2001): https://www.revolutionarydemocracy.org/rdv7n2/industclos.htm

Stoller, P. *The Taste of Ethnographic Things: The Senses in Anthropology,* University of Pennsylvania Press, 1989.

1. IN SEARCH OF THE NEVER-LOST SLUMS: ETHNOGRAPHY OF AN ETHNOGRAPHER

Hear this: clanking of utensils; water filling plastic bottles; tender bottoms being slapped; grown-up cheeks struck; raucous laughter in the corners; coins being sorted; technologies of communication, communicating—phones, televisions and amplifiers, creating, collapsing and distancing words and lives; sellers of wares, necessary, unrequired, and varied, dangling their goods through the prowess of their throats; children otherwise told to 'shut up' in the classrooms frolicking about imitating the tongues elders speak—I will fuck your sister, you are a cunt; the elders making claims to the fucking—of mothers, sisters, daughters—with more intent and lost innocence; aazaan on the loudspeaker from the mosque in the corner defining the day for many; the same loudspeaker announcing the find of a young Hindu boy, who if not claimed timely enough will be converted; the precious touch of the hand to the bells in the temples nearby, ting-tong, tong-tong, tinging; the hum of the city passing by; the vehicular conversations, honkingly undertaken; confidences of the most delicate sorts shared across corridors, lanes, and lives; songs of yearning penetrating through; a young girl on the roof remembering the cities she is forbidden to visit; an old man spinning yarn of the lives he has not lived to everyone in general and no one in particular.

The Interrogation

It was a Delhi summer afternoon on its deathbed. The evening promised the colours, but not respite from the heat. I was walking along the main road (Baba FatehSingh Marg) which separates Nehru Camp from the legal lanes, 15 in all, of Govindpuri. The distance to Nehru Place, the site of my first unwitting ethnographic research, was only a matter of a couple of kilometers but I could not wait to get there fast enough. The long-delayed, and now much-desired, smoke and a glass of cold beer felt like a deserving indulgence after the hours I had spent in Nehru camp.

Here, I had spent the last few hours interviewing residents of this camp, mostly women, about their everyday. Perhaps interviewing is misleading as it suggests an engaged, informed inquisition on my part. I had in fact spent these hours merely hurdled in a corner, of whomsoever was generous enough to allow me that space, listening to them live their everyday. Even with little or nothing to contribute to these conversations, I felt a day's work well done.

At a few meters distance from the main road, from where I meant to hail an auto, I was stopped by a doctor with whom I had casual acquaintance and who ran a little clinic from a *jhuggi* in Nehru camp. He invited me to his clinic for a conversation which I found difficult to decline. After all, I reckoned, it was important for me to establish as many contact points in the slums as possible. I had never been inside his clinic. The *jhuggi* coupling as a clinic was only different from the others I spent time in with its lack of an overwhelming bed, a refrigerator in the corner and a precariously perched television set. The presence of a not-so-white coat, a stethoscope and an array of unmarked bottles with little pills extended respectability to his self-proclaimed profession. There was nothing (by the way of framed certificates) or no one (in the form of ailing patients) to corroborate his claims. But he nevertheless proceeded in a precise and clinical manner to inquire about my reasons for spending time in the slums.

'I am doing my doctoral research, I am interested in understanding how the poor live', I muttered almost as an apology, slightly taken aback by not knowing the answer myself in its entirety'.

The doctor, unfazed by discomfort, continued with his prognosis:

> You do not have to come here everyday to know about that. I can tell you all there is to know about the poor, these slum people, the jhuggi-wallahs. People like you come here every once so often, for a few months, and think you know it all about the poor, how they are suffering, how miserable they are, what small houses they have, no jobs, and wonder what to do about them, right? But you are mistaken, these people – the jhuggi-wallahs – are the scum of the earth. They are all pretending. Of course I am not one of them, I am only here to help them, but are they interested, no, they are not. They have become used to doing nothing, and living off charities, making a fool of people like you. You think you come here, they are nice to you, do not be fooled. Come here in the evening, the same people – these men – saying madam, madam, to you will not think twice about ripping your clothes, mounting you violently, raping you collectively, laughing at you all the while and leaving you to rot on the corner of the road.

When I came to the main-road again, the evening was firmly set but I was bereft of a sense of accomplishment and assuredness of a while back. The doctor's violent sermonising about my fate at the hands of the jhuggi-wallahs had left me rattled. I abandoned the collected composure, which became of me during my visits to the camps, frantically hailed an auto and hurried towards the intoxicants, no longer as an award but as a refuge.

In short, I was scared were such a fate in fact to befall upon me; after all, what did I know about '*these jhuggi-wallahs*'? Doesn't everyone speak of 'them' as being morally and otherwise corrupt, violent and decadent? Why ought I be spared? I found myself overwhelmed, emotionally, but also in the same instance intellectually and politically compromised. After all, in the comfortable confines of one living-room or another, and ensconced within the walls of JawaharLal Nehru University, the bastion of left-leaning politics and teaching, had I not proclaimed about the rights, and denial of dignity, to the poor, marginalised and disenfranchised? Had I not patronisingly chided at those who expressed their reservations about these others?

Now, almost 15 years later, I not only claim an intimate relationship with the people and corners in the slums of Govindpuri, I am also actively invested in its politics, culture and the everyday. However, I would not only be compromising truth but also allowing myself undeserved due if I presented this intimate proximity in and with the spaces of Govindpuri to have come to me naturally. The first encounter with the slums of Govindpuri, nothing less than a 'touristic' adventure, was a recce of sorts, to finalise a site of study for a research project.

A Pervert's Guide to Slumming

In 2004, I was appointed as researcher assistant to Dr. Jo Tacchi for a project ethnographically exploring the role of information communication technologies in poverty alleviation in two sites in India, one rural and an urban. The slums of Govindpuri were decided upon as the urban site. The decision was not arrived at on account of the existing, or potential, networks in the slums but solely on the promise of the assured, obvious poverty levels in the slums derived from an extensive secondary research about the state of the slums in the city. Having arrived at the decision, I asked my then partner, B., whose office was in the neighbouring middle-class settlement of Kalkaji, to take Dr. Tacchi and I for a recce of the area before we set out for our fieldwork the following day. B., a straight-sorta'-fella, was not much amused by the prospect of I visiting the slums every day, or at least as frequently, for the next 18 months. His knowledge of the slums at that time was as academic as mine, but I only recall his anxiety. He complied with our wishes, driving us around the slums of Govindpuri, all the time recounting incidents amounting to cautionary tales about taking the proposed undertaking. Dr. Tacchi and I were amused, but determined.

As a final, desperate, bid to make us change our minds, B. proposed that if we indeed were so adamant on selecting a slum as our research site, there was one right next to his office. He added, almost as an incentive, that way, him and I could get to work together, everyday. The offer demanded an evaluation, and we agreed to give his slums a chance, which were basically four makeshift shanties for workers in a nearby private construction site. The firm silence that occupied the car informed B. of our decision. Over the years, in lighter moments, I took to recounting this incident with all its sassy details, B.'s anxiety, his feeble attempts to keep me away from the slums and offering one of his own to insist on his apathy, trite middle-class-ness and for being a straight-sorta'-fella. After all, I would always add as a dramatic climax, B.'s slums were a few thatched huts by the side of the road, they were a rather insipid offering compared to the squalid, spectacular poverty on display of the slums of Govindpuri. It never failed to evoke uncomfortable laughter.

With this personal narrative, the intent is no longer to embarrass my then partner B., but to admit to my own anxiety in establishing terms of engagement with slums as a concept and the reality of the slums of Govindpuri, in particular, which has dominated my research, political and intellectual undertakings. By adopting the tactics of deflection, I shifted the onus of the anxiety on to B.'s, indeed a cheap attempt to distract attention from mine. But I was the one who visited the slums of Govindpuri, a few times a week during the period of the research project, and the knot in my stomach, so to say, to make sense of moving across the materialities of the slums back to my middle-class confines left me distressed.

The encounter with the doctor, I started with, not only exaggerated the sense of anxiousness but also compelled a methodological, intellectual and political catharsis. If I were to be so fearful of the other, so much so to dread my safety and violation, how could I ever argue for an equitable, ethical cohabitational space (politically, intellectually and culturally) with and for the others – not only slum-dwellers, but also individuals and communities situated on the praxis on account of their caste, communal, sexuality and gender affiliations? I was left distraught.

A paralysis of sorts overwhelmed me, I knew I had to revisit my own prejudices, position and politics. I took a sabbatical from the field to identify the core from where these anxieties were emanating from and in what ways to resolve the same, agreeing that if I could not arrive at an identification or a resolution, I will abandon the project in the slums and instead take the research to more known, comfortable settings.

From the Academic to the Lived: De-coding Slumming

'*What is it that you really want to know?*' was a refrain which I had to constantly negotiate during my initial research engagements within the Govindpuri slums. I had approached the slums, hesitantly, in early 2004 as a potential research space for a project I was involved in. Till then, my experience and exposure of the slums in Delhi was through a primarily middle-class, educated, urbane lens which essentially meant that whilst I was aware of the violence and rhetoric of displacement and resettlement vis-à-vis the slums in popular mainstream media and academic discourse, I had never experienced the space first hand. I had no understanding of the dynamics of the space about which I had attended more than a few illustrious talks and conferences.

Over the years, I had helps coming into my house to accomplish the assigned tasks from different slums depending on which part of the city I was residing in at that moment. During my conversations with the helps, I rarely could locate the geographies of the spaces they inhabited. Occasionally, I would try to follow the maps that were being unfolded for my benefit. I would, however, always lose my way somewhere in between hopelessly convincing myself that nothing was lost as '*there wasn't much difference from one such place (slum) to another*'. All slums in Delhi, for me, were a homogenized space living the rhetoric of displacement and resettlement. In my acquired knowledge of the same, there was no scope for a multitude of experiences and dimensions or, narratives beyond those of lacking and longing. My initial engagements, then, were burdened by the guilt of middle-class upbringing which I naively assumed offered choices denied to the others out of this realm.

The constant refrain, *what is that you really want to know,* with shifting emphasis, depending on what I was being interrogated about by whom - my intent, my identity, my personal situation - significantly contributed towards my education of the spaces and lives of and within the slums. In the initial years, my middle-class positionality framed the engagements with the participants. More than the middle-class identity, and what it represented, it was the agenda of my proposed research which was constantly questioned and scrutinized. From whatever little I knew of conducting research in marginal spaces - from personal accounts of researchers, academic, and other texts - I was not prepared for such an interrogation. In these texts and accounts, what was presented was a clean, linear, one-sided engagement with the residents of marginal spaces, wherein the researcher in question rarely, almost never, recounts the questions that were asked of her. And thus over the years, in negotiating the refrain, the roles of the subjects and the ethnographer were constantly challenged and, more often than not, reversed.

The Politics of Poverty Performance

Years after the relationship with the residents of the slums, across the three camps, had moved beyond the strict researcher-researched equation, one afternoon, I was sitting in one of the lanes, a few women and I were catching up with what was happening in our respective lives. I had recently returned after a longish stint in Australia in mid-2014, and there was much to update the friends with, including but not limited to an intense breakup. The women were regaling me with their on-goings: gossip about new and broken relationships; travels; debts; judicious loans and the manner in which they were paid; the gold which was bought, and that against which loans had been secured. All the while tea, snacks and smokes were being shared with a generous amount of teasing, laughs and occasional reprimands.

Our reverie was interrupted by a group of earnest young girls. They were huddled together, and their hesitance was obvious. They introduced themselves as students of the Delhi School of Social Work and informed us that they were conducting a survey about the living conditions in the slums. The gathered women, almost in chorus, spoke about the difficulties of living in the slums; the lack of water; the deplorable sanitation facilities and so on so forth. As they left, after a while we all burst into a cackle of being on in a shared joke. Though nothing was evidently said, it was obvious that the women (and with them, I) were revelling in the performance just brilliantly pulled off. The performance in question is in tune with the mandate informing the agenda and the praxis of engagements, inadvertently, subtly and insidiously, of most researchers, activists, non-governmental and governmental agents visiting spaces as the slums: *the poor can only perform and live in poverty.*

Slums as spaces, witness interventions from agencies, organizations, and individuals assuming the role of interrogators. These interventions are on account of varying agendas: state initiatives to conduct surveys, activities facilitated by social groups operational in the area catering to specific needs (health, sanitation, education, among other), and academic-social research. My interactions with the space and its residents fall in the last category. In the last three-decades of the settlements' existence, the Govindpuri *slums* have continually experienced encounters with different and diverse researchers, agents and agencies. The residents are acutely aware of the benefits these encounters accrue for them, whether these be in regards to being enrolled in governmental records, which attracts subsidies in different forms, or being beneficiaries of different non-governmental schemes. And at once, as is evidenced from the performance of poverty in the aforementioned incident, the residents are astutely cognizant of the fact that the interrogators only want to hear narratives and experiences of lacks, poverty and *being poor.*

In 2005, during one of my trips in Navjeevan camp, I was walking around with a group of young adults from the local school which is run by a prominent NGO in Delhi. There was no fixed agenda for interviews or group discussions and we were wandering around the camps, recording conversations and discussions, and clicking pictures. In one of the streets, the students initiated a conversation with an old woman who was sewing clothes for an export house. The students were interested in the patterns she was sewing and a discussion about the volume of her assignments per week, how she finishes it, and the remuneration for it, followed. Around this time, two old men joined the discussion. They were not actively participating in the discussion but would occasionally make a comment. Interpreting this as their willingness to join the discussions, I asked one of the men, directly, a question about the penetration of small-scale industrial units in the camps and its benefits to the residents when he suddenly burst out into an angry retort. He accused me of being an agent of the NGO, which supported the school, to perpetuate its agenda:

> They [the NGO] are only interested in showcasing poverty so they can get funds from the big companies from abroad. They are not bothered about us. What do you know about us? They want more and more people in the camps to become dependent on them so that they can have us as figures in their files [...] What do you know about poverty, anyway?.

Not prepared for such a retort, I conveyed to him that I was not affiliated with the specific NGO in question or any such organization for that matter. On hearing this, he calmed down commenting that, 'he was tired of people coming and asking the same questions over and over again [...] how poor are you? How do you manage, etc.?' The two men agreed that it was a humiliating experience for them, their space and other residents, to be put through such an interrogation, over and over again, just to avail a few benefits (and sometimes not even that) in return.

Undertaking research in spaces such as the slums is a politically and ethnographically messy affair. In the initial couple of years of my research inroads in the slums of Govindpuri - hesitant, anxious, unsure of the vocabularies and the grammar of the everyday in the slums - I was doing my own kind of performance. Usually adorning only jeans and t-shirts in my everyday and professional spaces, I promptly visited one of those swanky stores catering to expats and bought two pairs of *salwar-kameez* and a few scarves. This is one of the most common attire for young women in the country, and is considered to be a modest wear compared to the more 'Western and attention-drawing' jeans and skirts. A heavy smoker I would not light up whilst in the slums, and in spite of being a drinker of some merit, a fact which I would otherwise proudly claim, even if not asked, I would maintain a stern silence about it. I also at times found myself blatantly lying, particularly when questions regarding my romantic status or the income levels were asked of me.

The encounter with the doctor, with which I opened the essay, and the subsequent sabbatical from the field I took were pivotal in me sophisticating my own practice and politics of undertaking ethnographic research (not only in the slums of Govindpuri, but also in any other site the assignment took me to) and in my endeavours of 'working the hyphen'.

Negotiating the Anxiety of Researching Anxious Spaces

Before undertaking ethnographic research in Govindpuri, I had conducted a yearlong research in Nehru Place, South Asia's largest second hand electronic hardware market and the hub for software piracy. Owing to the nature of male dominated trade practices in Nehru Place, electronic retail, repair, and piracy, the space has a very masculine character. Whilst conducting research in Nehru Place, I had to negotiate the masculinity of the space. The shops were I usually interviewed people were amidst narrow lanes and the shops themselves congested places populated predominantly by men. My presence would demand that the shopkeepers make unhindered space for me, which more often than not was disruptive to their activities. However, after the initial hesitation, the interactions were devoid of the gender politics as for most part, I was also a potential customer. In addition, the conversations, more often than not, were around trade practices. Once the trust was established, most men freely engaged in detailed discussions even those of illicit nature, particularly since we were discussing the value supply chains of pirated software, which is a criminal offence. During this period, I had also established a relationship of mutual exchange wherein I would bring them CD's of the latest Open Source software whilst they offered substantial discounts on the purchases I made. The nature of the interviews and interactions in Nehru Place did not by any means challenge or threaten the position of the men, socially and culturally.

The ethnographic engagements in the Govindpuri slums, on the other hand, plunged me into the politics of space and its everyday from the very start. The site of my research had changed from a neutral market place complex domestic space with multiple political, social, and cultural complications and prejudices. Unlike the space and scope of engagement in Nehru Place where the interactions where transactional in nature and did not involve pursuing sensitive discussions about social, cultural, political and emotional opinions and conflicts; in the Govindpuri slums it was precisely in and around these issues that the research was framed.

In retrospect, I realized that my research engagements in the two spaces, Nehru Place and Govindpuri slums, differed because of the manner in which I approached these spaces through the prism of what my middle-class identity represented. The uncomfortable edginess I could not resolve in the slums was not because the space was volatile or the residents hostile. In my initial engagement with the Govindpuri slums, I realized, much to my dismay, that I was relying too heavily on the constructions of the slum-dwellers perpetuated by the narratives in academic discourses, popular media, and everyday middle-class dialogues. In doing so, I was unconsciously, romanticizing the slum-dwellers by engaging with them only through the prism of lacking and poverty. In addition, even though subtly, I was convinced that the slum-dweller would not be able to understand my middle-class status, background, identity and its realities.

In short, I realized, I was denying them the capacity to engage and understand any other reality than their own. In my framing, I was approaching them as the other.

Encountering the Self of the Other

Gulabo is a widow who lives in Nehru camp with her 13-year-old son. I first met her in 2003 whilst conducting research for the Department For International Development, UK Government, on the 'Role of ICT's in Poverty Alleviation'. The agenda of the project was such that I had to inquire, at length, about the income, expenditure, and consumption patterns of each household at length. Such inquisitions are very common in the Govindpuri slums, undertaken at the beset of either state agencies or other non-governmental organizations and, more often than not, have promise of some direct benefit (loans, subsidies, etc.) associated with them. Whilst conducting the research, my intent of collecting data of this nature was constantly questioned. Not surprisingly, considering the precarious relationship the slum-dwellers have with the state, there is an apprehension vis-à-vis the state interventions. Though I would constantly reiterate that the data I was collecting was for purely academic purposes, there would be persistent requests for extending some kind of help, mostly monetary, to the families.

During the DFID research, Gulabo as a research participant offered significant insights in the gender politics and its direct association with income-expenditure patterns in the Govindpuri camps. She lives in a two room, very meticulously decorated house. Her house is part of what initially was one large slums. The initial settlers, over the years, sold out parts of it to two other families to meet their financial needs. When I initiated my research in Govindpuri, three families, including Gulabo's, formed this cluster. The entry to all the three houses is common and owing to the lack of space the interactions between the families at an everyday level is very intense and intimate. During the conversations, Gulabo always evoked her widowed status and, more often than not, analyzed situations, income-expenditure patterns, her everyday interactions, through this prism. Her narrative was shrouded with the difficulties she had to endure being married to an alcoholic and the subsequent struggles when he passed away. Though her living conditions appeared to be comfortable and she was getting her son educated in a private English medium school, a rarity on account of the financial burden the family has to bear, she always denied having any regular income and evaded questions about her financial support systems. A few months in the year, she set up a roadside kiosk to sell home cooked eateries in the area. Besides that, she never mentioned having any other source of income. It was a chance encounter which revealed to me the complexity of the gender politics and the networks of financial systems in the slums.

One afternoon at the clinic which I mentioned at the beginning of the essay, and before the encounter with the practitioner, Gulabo came into the clinic. She did not immediately register my presence. The medical practitioner and she were discussing some rent arrangement and subsequently, the medical practitioner handed some money over to her. Interested in this transaction, I inquired about its details. Gulabo, realizing my presence, tried to evade the topic. However, the medical practitioner mentioned that he has to pay Gulabo a monthly rent for using this space. Gulabo had never mentioned that she owned any other property in the slums except the house she lived in. Sensing her discomfort, I did not pursue the matter further. After that day, Gulabo would be very reticent in my company. In another incident of a similar kind, I went to Maya's (her neighbor and initial owner of the entire cluster) house during a hot Delhi-summer afternoon. During these times, the heat is so oppressive that most people withdraw into their houses, especially when the power situation permits running water coolers. By this time, it had already been a year since I had been visiting these families and I had established a relationship outside of the strict researcher-researched praxis. Maya, her daughter-in-law, and I were sharing lunch when we heard some men call out for Gulabo. The spatial layout of the cluster is such that all conversations, if not carefully contained, can be overheard. We could hear a transaction in negotiation. The men wanted to purchase some liquor bottles and Gulabo was quoting a price for the same. Overhearing this conversation in Maya and her daughter-in-law's presence was disconcerting. In the last year, Gulabo or any of her neighbours had not even hinted at Gulabo being involved in the illicit liquor trading business. Maya, who usually withheld any comments about Gulabo said:

> […] we know she does it. We don't approve it. My late husband was strongly against it as such activities invite all kinds of people at different hours. But, well, she is all by herself. She does not have anyone to look after her. Her husband was an alcoholic. He always beat her up. Her in-laws constantly tried to appropriate whatever little she has.

Over the next few years, I maintained my research and personal relationship with Maya's, Gulabo's, and Shishir's (the third family in the cluster); however we never discussed Gulabo's networks and systems of generating income. By then, once every so often, she would hinted that she has sources of income which she cannot disclose and respecting her desires, I never pursued the inquisitions. Gulabo's is an extreme case in point. There were many instances in the Govindpuri camps where individuals and families did not offer information about their income-expenditure patterns and I, sometimes, discovered some unrevealed sources or networks, accidentally. This was on many accounts. On some occasions, the individuals being interviewed did not have knowledge, especially women in the households. Besides these, there is a prevalent threat of being brought under scrutiny by state agencies if involvement in the networks other that the legitimate ones was offered. Lastly, these threat perceptions were heightened by my own middle-class identity. My position was constantly under scrutiny vacillating between being a state agent to representing a non-governmental charitable organization with the potential of extending substantial help.

Zameela, an employee at a prominent NGO operating in the Govindpuri camps, was an important cultural translator whilst also getting me introductions to diverse groups of people in the camps. One of her assignments is to facilitate community micro-finance activities. She primarily works with women groups assisting them in setting and running Self Help Groups (SHG's). Whilst visiting the groups with her, I realized that in spite of my presence, both the men and the women would freely discussed the income-expenditure patterns divulging in detail the nodes, networks, and systems in which they had either invested or in which their savings circulated. After many such meetings, one day I had the following conversation with Zameela to understand the manner in which 'money' and poverty levels were articulated:

> Tripta [T]: When we go together, the residents do not hesitate to discuss, even in front of me, the details of their investment, etc.? Why is that?

> Zameela [Z]: What do you mean? When do they say, when you ask them about it?

> T: They do not lie. I am not saying that. I am just saying they do not discuss it as openly. However, when I am with you, they do not hesitate but also ask for your advice.

> Z: Have you ever been asked how much money you earn in a month?

T: Yes.

Z: And, do you always tell me the exact amount? Or about the savings you have? Or the gifts you receive from your parents, etc.?

T: No [...] I usually avert the question.

Z: It's the same thing only a bit more difficult for people in the slums. After all these years, they know that the representatives who come (either state agents or NGO's) want to hear that they are poor. If they do not find enough indications of poverty, the general sentiment is that the victimization will increase and, also, the benefits to be derived in terms of loans and subsidies cut down. When they discuss the finances with me openly even in front of you that is not because they suddenly trust you but because they trust me, I am one of them.

Gulabo, I realized, could not discuss the finances with me at length not because she wanted to hide anything but because there were only that many vocabularies available to her to discuss these matters with the outsiders. She was expected within the constructions through which the slum-dwellers are approached to constantly evoke the narrative of widowhood, lack of income and fragile social support to garner support and help from different agencies. The financial systems in the Govindpuri camps cannot be evaluated through the strict prism of income and expenditure; multiple nodes and networks at formal, informal, illicit and interpersonal levels are involved. The navigation through these networks to optimize them is very significantly dependent on the social, political, cultural, and moral agency the individual, family, or group can exercise within this space. Gulabo's status as a widow, within the Govindpuri camps, allowed her concessions to engage in illicit liquor trade, an engagement socially denied to women. However, the same status and her involvements made her highly vulnerable when negotiating with the outside agencies, namely, the police.

Once I was visiting a research participant's house not because an interview was scheduled but because I needed to take a break from the research. During visits as such, the conversations were not strictly research driven and, more often than not, I would be asked to give updates about my own life, marriage, holidays, etc. Shortly after my arrival, a few of the research participant's relatives from the village paid a visit to her. The research participant introduced me as a friend who was working in the Govindpuri camps. Tea and snacks were organized. The conversations that followed amongst them were pertaining to a family wanting to purchase a newborn baby from someone the research participant knew. The rates were being negotiated. Soon, the relatives left. The research participant had sensed my discomfort whilst the conversation was taking place:

Research Participant [RP]: Did it disturb you? Haven't you ever heard of babies being sold?

Tripta [T]: I have but I have only read about it. It has never been discussed in front of me. Can't I do anything about it?

RP: Like what? Stop the sale of the babies? Why?

T: Well, it just does not seem the right thing to be able to sell and buy babies like this.

RP: The women who are selling it, at least most of them, are not doing so by choice. There are women who have made a business practice out of it, mostly, women who are migrants from other states. That is also because they need the money to feed the rest of the family. What can you do? You can inform the authorities, the police, but do not think they already don't know. They do. They will take some action while you are pursuing it and then? What will happen to the women?

T: But what happens to the children? There should be some way to ensure that they are not sold for child labour or prostitution. Is that not a possibility?

RP: It is, a very strong possibility. However, childless couples or those desiring a son also adopt many of these children. They give them love, affection and care their own parents would have never been able to afford. What about that?

I did not have enough arguments. My middle-class, educated sensibilities were demanding me to undertake an action. However, at the same time, I had mixed feelings. I was aware that I could not ignore the matter whilst at the same time I knew I could not report it. I told the research participant that I would have a conversation about these practices with a social activist working with women in the area. Not with the intent that those involved in this practice, especially the women, are brought under scrutiny but so that they can be informed about proper channels and options if they did not want to go through with the deal. The research participant gave her consent to approach the social activist. When I asked her whether I could use our conversation as part of my thesis, she only relented after I assured that in the narrative, I would not mention any names, locations within the Govindpuri camps, or communities involved.

As an ethnographer, from a space outside of the one being researched, I realized, that certain cultures and practices, however dehumanizing they might appear, need to be situated within the larger matrix of the materiality of the space. Being a widow in a slum settlement allowed Gulabo to sustain her livelihood through illicit liquor trade. These networks would have been very difficult for her to penetrate, if not entirely accessible, if she were living in a legalized colony. Most of her clients are from the neighboring lower-middle class legalized settlement which allows her to bargain the price for the liquor. It is the networks which the slums allow, owing to their illegal nature, to flourish that trade practice around sale of new-born babies can be undertaken.

Working the Hyphen[1]

Unlike many of the ethnographic studies in different anthropological traditions which romanticize the subjects and sites, Jorge Luis Borges, anything but an anthropologist, in The Ethnographer romanticizes, and in the process complicates, the position of the ethnographer. The protagonist who had 'nothing singular about him' sets out to learn the 'esoteric rites of the west' on the persuasion of his college professor who convinces him that 'when he came back he would have his dissertation, and the university authority would see that it was published'. The protagonist spends two years on the prairie, learns to unlearn his urban-research ways and is eventually told the tribe's secret doctrine. However, on his return, he refuses to reveal the secret forgoing the promising career he could chance upon by the revelation. He explains this to his rather indignant professor by stating '[…] the secret is not as important as the paths that led me to it. Each person had to walk those paths himself'. He, Borges informs us to end the tale, is now 'married, divorced, and is now one of the librarians at Yale'.[2]

This brief text, The Ethnographer, played a pivotal role in initiating a self-reflexive exercise in evaluating my own position as an ethnographer in different contexts. At different times in varying context, I have been humbled and equally perplexed by the insights, political, cultural, and personal, which the subjects have offered without malice or agenda. I have in the same vein as the protagonist of Borges's text had several moments of crisis during my research. The boundaries between what was purely research material and secrets revealed to me for I had 'walked the paths' were very fluid and blurred. I have often contemplated over categorizing interactions as interviews, discussions, data, and conversations of personal nature. Moreover, through these different categories of interactions evaluate my own shifting position as an ethnographer or an unwelcome intruder. More often than not, these categories collapse.

After a research sabbatical and evolving my own frameworks of participation in the research space, I made new entries into the space acknowledging that the everyday reality of the slums would never fundamentally constitute part of my every day and vice versa. This, however, did not mean that either the slum-dwellers or I could not evolve dialogic praxis within which we could attempt to understand, respect, and appreciate the realities we represented and lived. However, the important breakthrough in the research praxis was to acknowledge, and critically engage with the subtleties of representations, which I as an ethnographer or the slum-dwellers as subjects, constantly evoked and employed to establish certain inroads (including, but not limited to, research data) for me or derive benefits for the residents of the slums.

As a middle-class ethnographer, my position was uncertain. The production of knowledge of and about the space, given these constraints, could not have achieved at by establishing an economy of trust. The trust, I speak of here is not limited to revealing their lives or the secrets as was the concern for Borges's protagonist but also involves extending respect for the matter of choice for the lives the residents I was interacting with led. It also meant allowing

---

1 Fine, Michelle Fine, 'Working the hyphens' in *Handbook of qualitative research*, Thousand Oaks, CA: Sage, 1994.
2 Jorge Luis Borges, *Collected Fictions*, trans. Andrew Hurley, New York: Viking, 1998.

me to be interrogated without any apprehensions. This trust is established over a period of time, when both the parties involved have tested and tried the limits of the other. Once this trust was established with individuals, families, and communities in the Govindpuri camps, it also meant that I, as an ethnographer, had to not question and be judgmental about certain practices which were prevalent in the Govindpuri camps.

Here, I want to involve and engage the position, articulated and projected, of the ethnographer as an important element of the ethnography itself. The experience of the ethnographer cannot be distanced from the ethnography that emerges for the ethnographer negotiates, questions, imbibes, and treats preferentially, consciously or unconsciously, covertly, overtly, and subtly, certain categories of experiences than others. The ethnographer is not a neutral agency of observation. Or articulation. And in presenting these, the aim is to initiate a dialogue on the creation, sustenance, projection, and the articulation of the other. The importance of contextualizing the position of the ethnographer is accentuated in the context of the present study as it located in the slums where the everyday is constantly examined, articulated, and represented through different categories of other.

Ethnography as a methodological tool is not devoid of its politics. George E. Marcus and Michael M. J. Fischer address the problematic and politics of ethnographic practice within the larger anthropological body of work in *Anthropology as Cultural Critique: An Experimental Moment in The Human Science*. Enumerating on the role of an ethnographer in producing cultural texts, they state:

> In fact, what gives the ethnographer authority and the text a pervasive sense of concrete reality is the writer's claim to represent a world as only one who has known it firsthand can, which thus forges an intimate link between ethnographic writing and fieldwork.[3]

It is *this* authority, which is vested in an ethnographer, in me, through the methodological tool one employs that one needs to constantly not only be conscious about but also question it constructively. And I was consciously aware of this predicament. The ethnographer, in essence, should acknowledge the implications of the authoritative engagement and representation with a researched space. As an ethnographer working in the slums, I entered into the space as an outsider as I am not a resident of the space. I have not lived the space. That, however, does not mean that I cannot engage with the space. But the manner in which an ethnographer, I, interact characteristically determines the representation of the space in the larger domain. Most of the texts about the slums, academic and otherwise, reflect an edgy nervousness while discussing their subject matter. This uneasiness, first and foremost, comes from the inability to articulate the anxiety of being present in the slums. Even when the researchers are informed by the most radical theoretical and political intent and agendas of the right to the city for the *jhuggi-walahs*, the act of being *present* and to *engage* uninhibitedly in their

---

3 George E. Marcus and Michael J. Fischer, *Anthropology as Cultural Critique: An Experimental Moment in The Human Science,* Chicago: University of Chicago Press, 2014.

everyday is an anxious ridden prospect as it challenges (and perhaps also threatens) to reveal their own class, caste, communal informed practices and politics.

Whilst I was negotiating with my own anxieties, I reached out to academic texts to find resonance with other researcher's negotiating with similar dilemmas. I was seeking out in these texts an assurance that indeed *it was OK to feel unsettled in these living conditions; that I really did not like certain people – both men and women in the slums – for their politics, or their particular personalities and that I was finding myself drawn to a few people, especially women, with whom I was not only breaking the researcher-researched biases but forming emotional relationships.* In the academic texts I had sought refuge in, I was however left wanting for any confidantes articulating similar anxieties.

All the dilemmas and issues which the city faces, 'crime, dirt, filth, immorality' in its spread-out territoriality and temporality are consolidated in the confines of the slums. In that sense, the slums are magnified and amplified versions of what that city could be if it was not as controlled and constricted. It is important to consider that the problems concerning the slums are not a classic situation of the slums, per se, but prevalent in the city as well.

Within the schematic of this research, which requires establishing an engaged relationship with the slums, I attempted to deal with the prejudices at the conceptual, practical and personal level. In this intent, I realized that my middle-class-background constantly informed the lens through which I made entries into the space. However, I also realized that differences necessarily are not a negative entry point to build relationships, research and otherwise. Until the time the differences are respected and acknowledged, one cannot aspire for a relationship and interactions on the same plane. In particularly recognizing ethnography as much a political intervention as a methodological tool, the task of constantly negotiating difference, not towards resolutions but sustained dialogue continues to inform my research practices and my engagements with the residents of the slums in Govindpuri.

References

Borges, Jorge Luis. *Collected Fictions*, trans. Andrew Hurley. New York: Viking, 1998.

Fine, Michelle. 'Working the Hyphens' in *Handbook of qualitative research*. Thousand Oaks, CA: Sage, 1994.

Marcus, George E., and Michael MJ Fischer. *Anthropology as Cultural Critique: An Experimental Moment in the Human Sciences*. University of Chicago Press, 2014.

2. LISTENING: AN ETHNOGRAPHIC EXPLORATION

> A self is nothing other than a form or function of referral: a self is made of relationship to self, or of a presence to self, which is nothing other than the mutual referral between a perceptible individuation and an intelligible identity (not just the individual in the current sense of the word, but in him the singular occurrences of a state, a tension, or, precisely, a "sense")-this referral itself would have to be infinite, and the point of occurence of a subject in the substantial sense would have never taken place except in the referral, thus in spacing and resonance, at the very most as the dimensionless point of the re-of this resonance; the repetition where the sound is amplified and spreads, as well as the turning back [rebroussement] where the echo is made by making itself heard. A subject feels: that is his characteristic and his definition. This means that he hears (himself), sees (himself), touches (himself), tastes (himself), and so on, and that he thinks himself or represents himself and strays from himself, and thus always feels himself feeling a "sels" that escapes or hides as long as it resounds elsewhere as it does in itself, in a world and in the other. To be listening will always, then, be to be straining towards or in an approach to the self (one should say, in a pathological manner, a fit of self: isn't [sonorous] sense first of all, every time, a crisis of self?).[1]

Listening is a political act. It can only be enacted from a position of power, but it is precisely on this account, that this act is also laden with the possibilities of disrupting, challenging and dismantling the mesh of the intersectionalities of the performative, and eventually insidiously existing, hierarchies of power relationships. In its enacting, the task of listening compels acknowledging and accommodating the grammar, vocabulary and the structures of the s*elves* which constitute the identified *other*. But more fundamentally and significantly, the 'act' of listening, as a constitutive practice of the identified o*ther,* and as a philosophical punctum, political rupture, and poetic interruption allows the identified o*ther's* interiority to resound in its loudness or perform itself in its firm silences. The o*ther* is at once denied 'silence' as a state of being and subjected to 'silencing' as manner of becoming. The identified o*ther,* across the spectrum and landscape of power negotiations and particular constructions, is always imagined in is hollowness.

This book fundamentally makes a call for *listening* as a methodological praxis and political intervention to engage with the self of the others and acknowledging the others of the identified other. In the act of *othering,* the essays in the book identify the assertion of extending 'meaning to oneself'. Whilst the essays, interrogate, highlight and problematizes the strategic manners in which the identified others are othered along the axis and intersections of social, cultural, political and emotional, among others, disenfranchisement; in denying the identified *others* the capacities of *othering,* the hegemonic self unleashes (or at least attempts) the ultimate erasure of the ontological Self of the Other. Is the 'self', after all, '*nothing other than a form or function of referral*'?

---

1   Jean-Luc Nancy, *Listening*, trans. Charlotte Mandel, New York: Fordham University Press, 2007, 8-9.

Thus: Listening as a methodology necessitates, first and foremost, the muting of the hegemonic self. As a political intervention, it demands the ontological praxis for the *others* to listen into their *self*, and that this *listening* accrues the validity and veracity of and as robust knowledge-systems within which when the *other* speaks, it is not reckoned to be in tongues. The denial of the *listening(s)* onto/into themselves, the hegemonic self intends to 'neutralize listening within himself, so that he cannot philosophize' having thus denied the others most fundamental claims to the structure of the self, the hegemonic self then extends its willing ears - insists that it is *all ears* which in fact 'belongs to a register of philanthropic oversensitivity, where condescension resounds alongside good intentions; thus it often has a pious ring to it'.

In insisting on the *listening(s)* by the others of their other, the essays in the book attempt to engage in the politics and praxis of *othering* as practiced by the identified Others. It is in the processes and practices of *othering* that the self of the other is to be recognised. In the othering, as is evidenced by the manner in which the hegemonic self encapsulates the complexity of the others into a singularity solely premised on the former's reflexive and referential *listening* of the latter, the others' landscapes of reflexive and referential of making meaning of the self are to be unveiled.

> When two people are conversing with one another, however, a third is always present: Silence is listening. This is what gives breadth to a conversation: when the words are not moving merely within the narrow space occupied by the two speaker, but comes from afar, from the place where silence is listening. That gives the words a new fullness. But not only that: the words are spoken as it were from the silence, from that third person, and the listener receives more than the speaker alone is able to give. Silence is the third speaker in such a conversation.[2]

Thus, Max Picard identifies central and critical to the task of a conversation, a validation of the act of speaking is silence. Furthermore, Foucault, in drawing out his self-portrait in conversation with Stephen Riggins, insists on 'silence [as] a specific form of experiencing a relationship with others', which he 'believe[s] is really worthwhile cultivating' and he is in, 'favor of developing silence as a cultural ethos'.[3] In the same interview, Foucault whilst recognizing certain silence for fostering 'deep friendship, emotional admiration, even love' also attributes it the potential to imply 'very sharp hostility'. For Picard whilst silence is the third speaker, if not punctuated with 'speech' - an exchange, silence is rendered meaningless retaining its 'wild pre-human monster' form. It is through the act of 'speech' that silence 'is transformed into something tame and human'.

In making a call for listening as a methodological framework, political intervention and theoretical praxis, particularly to engage with the identified Other, it is not without deliberation that I begin with a rumination on silences. There is an inherent anxiety in talking about *listening* as an embodied auditory experience and methodological intervention motivated by definite

---

2 Max Picard, The World of Silence (Vol. 6067), *Chicago, IL: Henry Regnery, 1952, pp -9*.
3 Michel Foucault, *Politics, Philosophy, Culture: Interviews and Other Writings, 1977-1984*, Routledge, 2013.

political ambitions. And here lies the tension: unless not compelled by considerations of *paracusis* of varying orders *listening* as a function of a 'healthy' body is an involuntary act. Because: the ears, they don't close. And thus when I make a call for listening with its methodological and political deliberations, is there not implicit an assumption of deafness in these regards, of the closing of the ears, so to say?

Oliver Sacks in *Seeing Voices* meticulously disrupted the notion of 'world of utter, unbroken soundlessness and silence' which both the deaf, suffering from the pathological, and deaf, as a cultural symptomatic, live in.[4] The silence I draw attention to, whilst insisting on listening, is the one which in both Picard's and Foucault's reckoning is pregnant with possibilities at once of ethical cohabitation - an equitable exchange - and oppressive obliteration of the self. Silence as social, cultural, political and emotional act is denied to the others. The self on the other hand desires and demands *silence* as a revered state of consciousness and a right to inculcate its finer tunings; to nurture its solidness; to have undisrupted reflexiveness; to reverate silence as a meditative path to higher unfurling the higher selves. But silence as a right is denied to the other: however much the self dreads the noise of the other, its silence is even more demonic. The noise of the other is evidencing of its industriousness geared to serve the purpose of the self, to constantly be in service of sustaining the silences which the self insists on. Moreover, even in its persistent humming, even though causing discomfort, the other is accommodated; in doing so, it is after all but a rambling, incoherent entity incapable of ruminations and thus also lack the agency to demand a dialogue. The only silences permissible to the other are in its real and figurative obliteration. The denial of silence to the other is a strategic ploy by the hegemonic ideologies, insidiously at play, changing a note here and there, never the entire operatic scale, to evoke the incoherence of the other as a foundational premise to not initiate a dialogue, and in doing so, sustaining the 'monologue of power'.[5] The listening to the others in the essays in this book is punctuated by silences, ruminations, ramblings and ruptures towards dialogues, not always conciliatory and comforting, but definitely to ever-so-slightly change the notes in the 'monologue of power'.

Sonic Strategies of the Self: The Political Instrumentality of Listening

> A voice means this: there is a living person, throat, chest, feelings, who sends into the air this voice, different from all other voices. A voice involves the throat, saliva, infancy, the patina of experienced life, the mind's intentions, the pleasure of giving a personal form to sound waves. What attracts you is the pleasure this voice puts into existing: into existing as voice; but this pleasure leads you to imagine how this person might be different from every other person, as the voice is different.

This is a quote from Italo Calvino's *A King Listens,* a story in which the position of the king, literally and figuratively, depends on 'listening into', and here, 'the palace is the ear of the

---

4   Oliver Sacks, *Seeing voices: A journey into the world of the deaf,* Pan Macmillan, 2009.
5   Jacques Attali, *Noise: The political economy of music.* Vol. 16, Manchester University Press, 1985, pp. 9.

king'.[6] This ability to hear into the palace, which gives the king his power, also leaves him restricted to his throne – if he moves, even briefly, there is a danger he will miss something significant – maybe sounds of rebellion or deceit. He listens not only because he is 'condemned to listen' as 'we have no ear lids', but because he has to keep his 'ears open' to maintain the status quo and his power.[7] Owing to the inherent disembodied and thus un-containable – *detached from the solidity of things* – of the *voice*, the burden of listening which the King in this tale has to endure, forgoing even his carnal and other sundry pleasures, almost evokes sympathy. But, beyond and besides, the burden, the *listening* is not only integral but essential for the King – and by that extension the State, and those in dominant, hegemonic roles – to maintain their position. And herein lies the real tension, and thus the anxiety: in its inherent *un-containability* the *voice* has the potential to transgress boundaries – of spaces (physical, political and intellectual) – lending it its obscene disruptiveness so dreaded by those in power. I will do so by making a categorical distinction between hearing and listening to specifically identify the sites – the ears, so to say – where the moralising politics and containing of the sounds are enacted.

Hearing is the encounter with the ubiquity and ephemerality of soundscapes; while listening is the experiencing of soundscapes, informed by one's social, cultural and moral leanings. It is a matter of deliberation to draw this distinction between hearing and listening. I argue that it is between this encounter and experience that the politics of production, performance and articulation of sounds unfolds. While everyone translates the encounters with soundscapes into organised experiences, I further argue that not all and everyone's experiences – and, thus, listening(s) – accord legitimacy to the organisation of sounds as noise, music and silence. It is in asking questions, such as the following, that these forms of politics can be teased out: whose experiences of soundscapes – that is, listening – are given preference and whose listening is not?; how and where is such listening desired and demanded?; how does the character of space, cultural contexts and soundscapes alter and transform with impositions of certain kinds of listening?; and what are the ways in which non-recognised listening(s) filters in and out of these soundscapes?

Within this framing, the city–slum relationship can be presented as one unfolding within listener – hearer praxis. And within the everyday materiality of the Govindpuri slums, these positionalities are also constantly negotiated. There is a highly paternalistic, moralistic, infantilizing tendency informing the ethnographies on and of the slums, they rarely acknowledge the contestations and negotiations of power as manifest in the hegemonic self (city) - muted others (slums) within the life worlds of the slums. In doing so, these undertakings continue to the task of contributing and consolidating the notion of the other as a rambling, incoherent entity, thus both denying them their silences as also the claims and agency to demand a dialogue.

---

6   Italo Calvino, 'A King Listens', trans. William Weaver, in *Under the Jaguar Sun*, San Diego, New York, London: Harcourt Brace Jovanovich, 1988, pp. 31-64.

7   Murray Schafer, 'Open Ears', in Michael Bull and Les Back *The Auditory Culture Reader*, New York: Berg, 2003, p. 25.

From within the interiority of the Govindpuri slums, listening into its pulse, here I narrate some of the highly fluid, dynamic, political and contested sonic strategies of obscene, perverse performance of the self vis-a-vis the identified other.

The 'Noisy' Other

The Totas form a prominent community in Nehru camp. This community hails from Maharashtra, and has South Indian lineage. They are fortune-tellers who use parrots as an aide; thereby the name 'Tota', which literally translates as parrots. This is their livelihood. P. Nagaraja in *South Asian Folklore*, details the manner in which fortunes are told using parrots by this community:

> These fortune-tellers go around the streets announcing their presence, or wait along footpaths or in front yards of busy buildings like temples or offices. Usually wearing a Maharashtrian cap, the parrot astrologer carries a cage of parrots and a bag of cards, a book, and a few remedies for misfortune, such as stones or talismans […] The fortune teller "reads" the figure and the fortune in a peculiar Marathi dialect mixed with syncretic forms of other South Indian languages in a catchy shrill voice and emphatic pronunciation. For "elaboration" upon the reading he "consults" the book he carries with him. Usually clients are offered "remedies" for evil eye or other misfortune, first in the form of a prescription and later from the various objects in the bag.[8]

The interaction of this community with others is limited in Nehru camp. They are uncouth, loud, and immoral in the articulations of the dominant groups. Women and children are not allowed to interact with them. I was also advised to exercise caution when interviewing them. In the dominant narratives, the main reason for their ostracisation was their loud habits, coarse language, and 'emphatic pronunciation'. These, along with their magical powers, make them highly vulnerable to scrutiny.

Members of the Tota community, aware of these prejudices, have their own reasons for maintaining a distance:

> We are fortune-tellers. Whether you believe it or not, we have the ability to predict the future. In some cases, even avert misfortunes. The parrots are not just props. It requires years of practice to master the skill. We are a very close community because we have to pass this knowledge from generation to generation to keep the tradition alive. We cannot compromise with that. We cannot share our secrets with those who are not part of the group. Most people think we do nothing but sing, dance, and drink – yes, we do – but all of this is part of the learning process. We also sing and dance because we want to. There are others in these camps who are involved in far more deplorable activities than us – selling drugs, prostitution, alcohol – but they are

---

8   Peter J. Claus, Sarah Diamond, and Margaret Ann Mills, *South Asian Folklore: An Encyclopedia: Afghanistan, Bangladesh, India, Nepal, Pakistan, Sri Lanka,* Taylor & Francis, 2003, p. 231.

not targeted. It's us. We enjoy what we do and, yes, we do make money. If they don't want to talk to us neither do we.

The position of the Tota community in Nehru camp, in relation to other dominant communities, is that of the hearer. The Totas are excluded from social and cultural interactions. By eliminating the scope of a dialogue, the Totas are denied a voice. The sonic practices of the Totas, however, complicate this positioning. The dominant groups in the Nehru camp have established a very strict sensorial code of conduct to interact with the Totas. As hearers, any sonic production and performance of Totas is articulated as noise by other dominant groups.

Commenting on noisy Totas, a senior member of the local administrative body for Nehru camp said:

> It is irritating. It gives us headaches. Sometimes they continue playing music late into the night as well. But, what can we do except warn them at times? We cannot call the police that Totas are disturbing us [...] they will not listen to us anyway. For them, we all are one. And, how can one regulate it? There is no way you can say, there, that is the person who is responsible for it; you cannot keep targeting the entire community. If we can identify one or two persons we might take action. But if it's the entire community we are against, who we know is not going to single out people, we cannot do much.

The voiceless Tota community in the existing hegemonic structure assumes a 'loud' character owing to the peculiarities of sound production, performance and articulation. It is quite a common practice in the Govindpuri slums for communities to play loud music, however, not all music is categorised as noise, nor all its producers regarded as uncouth.

In conversation with the members of the Tota community, I raised the issue of the 'loud' music:

> We are surely not the only ones who play loud music. We are a very close community. Unlike other communities in the camp we do not tell on each other, fight with each other [...] we are like a big family. We like to do everything together and that includes singing and dancing. Also, some of the music we play is important for our children to learn the trade.

For the members of the Tota community, playing loud music is not only an act of deliberate resistance, it is a community-building exercise. Loud music as *noise* consolidates the position of the Tota community on two accounts: first, the collective production and consumption of music represent a strategy to reiterate the sense of solidarity amongst the community; and second, it allows them to extend their territoriality beyond the social, cultural and moral landscape where their interactions are limited. While the loud music as *noise* gives the Tota community a sense of solidarity, confidence and security, it challenges the authority of the dominant group by compelling them to *hear* the presence of the Totas, even if the dominant group wants to ignore them.

The collectivity of soundscapes from the slums, including those of the Totas, is articulated as noise by the middle classes. The dominant groups in both instances – communities who ostracise the Totas within the Govindpuri slums and the middle classes who ostracise the entire slum settlement – refuse to *listen into* their soundscapes and afford them acceptable sonic meanings. While the sonic production and performance of disempowered groups – in this case, *Totas* and slum-dwellers – allow them to have a distinct sonic presence, its articulation as noise by dominant groups only aggravates the processes of othering through which they are further discriminated against, segregated and excluded.

Silencing, Silence and Unlistening

Meena is Diya's sister-in-law. Since 2004, Diya has been living in her paternal home, along with her son, following an altercation with her husband's family. This eventually led to a breakdown of communication between the two families and any chance of reconciliation between Diya and her husband are slim. Her parents initially supported Diya and acknowledged the mental and physical torture she had to endure in her marital home. However, with the passing of years, her presence is seen as a financial burden and a matter of social shame for the family. This leads to frequent altercations between her, her brothers and parents. Meena is married to Diya's eldest brother, who constantly abuses Meena, emotionally and physically. Even though both Meena and Diya are sympathetic and supportive of each other's predicament, they can do little for each other. Neither of them gets any support from the family. Both employ different sonic strategies to negotiate their disempowered position. They both are hearers.

Diya has, over the last few years, assumed a 'loud' temperament. She openly criticises her parents, laments their failure to initiate reconciliatory dialogue with her husband, and bemoans the limited resources made available to her. This sonic performance usually happens in the street. In her house, she is denied such permissions. When I first tried establishing an acquaintance with her, I was constantly informed that she was 'mad'. Every time I would approach her to initiate a conversation, her neighbours – mostly women – would join the conversation, uninvited. They would talk over Diya's conversation and offer testimonies of her life, totally ignoring her presence. She is consistently silenced. Her sonic productions and performances were denied any validity, and thereby an acceptable articulation, because of her projected madness. Even though she was heard, she was not listened into. Her loud behaviour, which openly challenged the dominant familial roles, was articulated as a sign of definite madness. She has no history of clinical insanity.

Meena, on the other hand, assumed a different sonic strategy to negotiate her position. In the initial years, she tried to engage her in-laws and her neighbours to address her abuse. Her 'loudness', she mentioned, would only lead to more abuse. Eventually, she stopped having any sonic interactions with others. By maintaining a silent sonic presence, she not only refuses to acknowledge and engage with the sonic hierarchies established by her family, she does not allow them any scope to either validate or negate her sonic performances. She listens to herself, she said, and finds peace in it as she knows no one else knows what she is listening into. Indeed, her family is much intrigued by her silence, often articulating it as an act of defiance; however, the instances of abuse against her have decreased as her silent demeanour is considered 'threatening', according to her mother-in-law.

Slum-dwellers who have sustained engagement with the middle classes, as domestic servants, drivers, guards and gardeners, have to follow a highly prescriptive code of conduct in the extended sensorial realm. Sonically, they are *silenced* and expected to perform *silence*. This is most exaggerated in the case of drivers, who share intimate space with their employers and often overhear their conversations, interactions and engagements. Men from the Govindpuri slums who work as drivers in middle-class households have a sonically dominant position in their immediate sonic realm, yet they are disempowered in their extended sonic realm by their inability to either engage or define sonic practices. Moreover, in this realm they have to take orders from middle-class women, which further challenge their position. In this extended sonic realm, men have to sonically perform *unlistening*, which in their immediate sonic realm women – as hearers – tend to rely on as a sonic strategy.

The soundscape of the Govindpuri slums abounds in its multiplicity. In their sonic interactions with men, specifically, women as hearers do not have the legitimacy to engage or influence sonic practices. Men, enjoying the liberties they have, use abusive language, and discuss sensitive matters of financial, social and moral importance openly and loudly. They rely on *unlistening* as a strategy to negotiate this predicament.

A young woman who moved into the settlement with her husband, after her marriage found the use of abusive language increasingly disconcerting. In her immediate sonic realm, she was not used to men openly expressing abuse in front of women and found it very offensive. When she confronted her husband, he severely reprimanded her for *listening into* his private conversation. She has been in the settlement for the last eight years now, and she can both perform and pretend to perform *unlistening* as the situation demands:

> There are times when you just stop listening, you zone out but at other times it is convenient to pretend that you are not listening, especially when financial matters are discussed. This way I can at least keep some tabs on him.

Unlistening as a sonic performance is employed by different disempowered groups across the Govindpuri slums to maintain sonic balance, which men working in middle-class households have to assume as well. Even though disempowered groups – women in the immediate sonic realm and men in their extended sonic realm – perform *unlistening* and *silence* and are *silenced*, they attempt to subvert these social hierarchies by relying on gossiping and eavesdropping as sonic strategies.

Gossiping

Gossiping is not harmless, social bantering. It is an effective sonic strategy subvert dominant social and cultural positions. Aruna is a 25-year-old petite, confident woman. I first met her not in Navjeevan camp, where she resides, but in the office of a nearby organisation that provides free legal counselling to Govindpuri residents in Bhumhiheen camp. She was seeking advice regarding her divorce and child custody. During the period of my research, I volunteered in this organisation once a week to help the counsellor with filing and other administrative needs. As we discussed her case, it became evident that the separation was acrimonious and on more than one occasion her husband had been physically abusive. Mrs Dave, the counsellor, advised her to take immediate action – a report was filed in the nearby police station and the women's cell. Over the next few weeks, her husband – who did not live in the Govindpuri slums – was restrained from visiting Aruna and their daughter in Navjeevan camp. The husband was incensed by this decision. Soon afterwards, unknown to Aruna or her family, he started making visits to the prominent tap areas along Aruna's water route; everyone knew him as Aruna's husband. While spending time at the tap areas, he started telling 'stories' about Aruna, including but not limited to her involvement in prostitution rackets and the ways to solicit her. The multiple conflating soundscapes in the tap areas were exploded by the sonic sensation this information generated. The events to follow took a very unfortunate turn. Aruna was persistently harassed by rowdy men, who propositioned her when she moved around the camps, making even the most basic of movements unsafe for her. Eventually, Aruna's family took serious action and her ex-husband was put behind bars for three months. This did not mean that 'stories' about Aruna stopped circulating in and around her neighbourhood; however, people started questioning their validity since her husband, the main perpetrator, had been jailed. For most, this was a definite sign that he was lying. Aruna was not very optimistic about this turn of events. She expressed her distress about having to shift from the Govindpuri slums in the near future. When I inquired about the reason for the move, considering that her family lived in the slums and she had a strong support network, she said it was on account of her daughter:

> Right now, she is young, she doesn't understand. There are people who will come outright and say my husband was wrong, he was spreading rumours, etc. but that doesn't stop the rumours and gossip. People will keep talking even years later. I don't want my daughter to grow up listening to stories about how I was abandoned by my husband for being a prostitute. I find peace in the fact that he is in the prison but he will be released soon; I, on the other hand, am caught for life in this story he has created.

After their separation, Aruna's husband was well aware that he would not be welcome in Aruna's family home, nor those of neighbours or relatives. However, he managed to tap into the volatile water route and networks, through which he knew he could harm the reputation of Aruna and her family, as it is one of the most important means to transmit information, gossip and news in the locality. He was aware that here, people – even those who did not approve of him – would listen to his stories.

Within the soundscapes of the Govindpuri, gossip allows women as hearers to assert their sonic selves, otherwise denied to them, as most of these networks are controlled by older women. While the younger women in the Govindpuri slums are under constant scrutiny and are required to maintain a strict sensorial decorum, age allows the older women permission to forgo these restrictions. In certain instances, they tend to assume a very 'masculine' decorum. Bodily noises, which the younger women have to find ingenious ways to mask, are nonchalantly performed in public by older women. They abuse as obscenely and as loudly – if not more so – than the men. During the day, in the absence of the men, these older women, matriarchs, control the sonic networks. There is usually one matriarch in a community who exercises absolute control. She has an extensive network of *listeners* who inform and update her about the sonic performances of others. These are then articulated – either validated or denied – within the gossip networks.

In one instance, a family settled in Navjeevan camp permitted their daughter 'unprecedented' freedoms, including college education and mobile phones. These freedoms implied 'mobilities' denied to others. The matriarch did not approve of the freedoms given to this girl, believing it would only encourage other girls also to waver from the path and assume loud, uncouth practices'. This young girl was under constant sonic scrutiny. Not so surprisingly, the girl was apparently *heard* having romantic conversations over the phone. A communal meeting was called for, the girl and her parents were summoned, her phone records were validated, and it was established that the girl was having an 'affair'. The parents were strictly reprimanded for this digression and threatened ostracisation if they did not impose restrictions on their daughter. She had to give up her education and, obviously, no longer had access to the mobile phone.

The slum-dwellers, men and women, working in middle class households also use *gossiping* as an effective sonic strategy to subvert and challenge their disempowered position in the extended sonic realm. Even though these gossip tactics do not have the same impact as gossip within the slums, on many occasions they have managed to create tensions and rifts amongst middle class families by transferring information from one network to another. The middle class, well aware of these gossiping tactics, try to maintain the sonic distance by conversing in English, a language most slum-dwellers do not understand, in the presence of their domestic servants. These sonic strategies of the self from the interiority of the slums exhibit a strong 'sonically ordered sense of self' of the slum dwellers.[9] Second, it highlights the definite sonic strategies employed by dominant and disempowered groups (both within the slums and slum dwellers collectively *vis-à-vis* the middle classes) to reiterate and circumvent social, cultural and political hierarchies.

The Sounds of Slumming (Or, Matters of Sonically Slumming)

By *reading* the city as text, where 'ordinary men' are scribes, *walkers*, 'whose bodies follow the thicks and thins of an urban 'text' they write without being able to read it', Michel de Certeau privileges sight as the sensual anchor to experience as well as produce space and its dynamics.[10] Indeed, de Certeau's city is Western, visual and masculine; however, in his readings he resolutely acknowledges the agency vested in the common people – the silent majority – to displace the rationality of urban space, 'brutally lit by alien reason'. The hier-

---

9   Tom Rice, 'Soundselves: An Acoustemology of Sound and Self in the Edinburgh Royal Infirmary', *Anthropology Today*, 19.4 (2003): 4-9.
10 Michel De Certeau, *The Practice of Everyday Life,* trans. Steven Randall, California: University of California Press, 1984, pp. 93-105.

archical and semantically ordered 'surface of the city' transforms into 'liberated spaces that can be occupied' by these movements. Beyond its cartographic moment, space transforms into an experience that is not singularly visual in its orientation. It is populated by the calls, murmurings, voices, tastes, smells and touches; in short, it is a sensual experience in which each sense – hearing, smelling, touching, seeing, tasting – defines, broadens or limits the scope of how the space is practised, consumed, articulated, experienced and represented. Space transforms into a 'social experience' through the 'mingling of the modalities of mingling' of the five senses.[11]

In the Indian context, specifically in the case of the Govindpuri slums, it is difficult to articulate space as compartmentalised pockets, each maintaining their own homogeneity. According to the 2001 census, the population of all the three camps together was recorded as 370,665, spread over an area of 41.85 acres. In terms of distribution of space, this means 900 people per acre. The density of the space does not allow for segregated spatial entities. Porosity of the city, which Benjamin and Lacis evoked for Naples, defines the essence of everyday reality in the Govindpuri slums.[12] The walls are literally built in each other and the roofs share an incestuous relation with the others of their kind. The architecture has a perplexing unpredictability to it. One never knows when one room will open into another courtyard or kitchen. Everyday, personal lives are constantly performed in the public eye. However, this is not to imply that there is no sense of privacy, and no claims or authority over space. The manner in which these are exercised has distinctly evolved within the materiality of the site. The associations with space are not within the strict conceptual framework of propertied claims, but are constantly negotiated within the existing socio-cultural fabric. In the popular narratives, a displaced sense of claims to property and its ownership emerge. The ownership is not established in the present, temporally and geographically, but projected in a distant future where the demolition of the existing slum settlement will entitle slum-dwellers to land in a legal resettlement colony.

The exploration of sonic practices of space in the Govindpuri slums furthers the embodied, temporal and interconnected understanding of how space is created, consumed and projected. This embodied experience provides a framework to articulate everyday life in the slums (as well as city–slum relations) outside the hegemonic, illegal–legal binary. The everyday reality of slums, 'animated through sound', reveals a complex interplay and overlap of identity and space which significantly determines the mobilities and positions within the immediate–extended–imagined realm.[13]

It is within these theoretical frameworks of understanding space that the slums, in the given context, can be understood as a representative not of the 'marginalised' spaces in the city, but rather the *process* of marginalisation of spaces in the city. The lived realities and association

---

11   Steven Connor, 'Michel Serres's Five Senses', Birkbeck College, May 1999, http://www.stevenconnor.com/5senses.htm.
12   Walter Benjamin and Asja, 'Journal de Naples', 1925.
13   Constance Classen, *Worlds of Sense: Exploring the Senses in History and Across Cultures,* New York: Routledge, 1993, p. 121.

of the slum-dwellers cannot be understood simply within the prism of 'mobility' and 'movement' across 'one-directed abstraction of time and space'. The cities inhabited, created and consumed by slum-dwellers have to be understood as 'a site where multiple spatialities and temporalities collide', and where 'the city contains living and moving bodies, but they are not bodies moving through space-time, they are performing it and making it'.

The city and the slums constantly evaluate (and pre-empt) trajectories of interaction with each other through similar cultural constructions and categories. From the narratives in the Govindpuri slums, it emerges that the slums' residents view the city in the same manner as the city represents them: as a space of moral bankruptcy. The residents who venture into the city are advised to exercise caution. If the slums are the other for the city, the city is also the other for the slums. However, as the city dominates and determines the tropes through which city–slum relations are evaluated, slums are denied a sense of self, and the practices by which they exercise a deliberate distance – social, cultural and spatial – from the city are denied vocabularies, and hence an agency. Space in the Govindpuri slums is not only sonically consumed, but sonically constructed and represented as well. The sonic interaction amongst communities is determined by the relative positioning of the self in the immediate–extended–imagined sensorial realms *vis-à-vis* the other. Sonic articulations are significant in determining social, cultural, sensual and spatial engagements with a space. The sonic practices of space highlight these negotiations.

Drawing from these insights, instead of stating a broad hypothesis or a set of main questions, I introduce this essay as a narrative woven around the thematic of *other and othering* of the spaces of slums in the discourse of the city and the articulation of sound/soundscapes as an urban experience. In evoking the thematic of 'other and othering', there is an inherent danger that this body of work might be approached as consolidating the position of 'slums' and 'sonic experiences' as an oppositional 'other' category vis-à-vis the mainstream, the city, and the visual (an integral referential point to explore the urbane/city). However, it is precisely this oppositional consolidation of these categories, slums and sound, in the everyday experience, mainstream media, and academic discourse that this body of work aims to rework and challenge by exploring the process of 'othering' bringing to the forefront the nuances and the lacunae of the same. The intersection of slum and sound studies, both bodies of work which at different occasions find position in urban history, historical accounts, social discourse, media and cultural studies, and the field of sensory perceptions, was by no means an easy one to navigate whilst conducting the study or framing it within a theoretical discussion.

With all their distinctions, slums and sound studies, share the predicament of being on the fringes, so to say, of academic-mainstream discourse as well as experiential articulation. The situation gets further complicated within the Indian, third world and Global South scenario, where the narrativization of and on slums is being reworked in languages suiting to the needs of new middle class sensibilities as well as the burgeoning impetus to sanitize the metropolitan cities to make them amenable for the global-western experience. In regards to sound, the discussion is picking up momentum, albeit only within the framework to implement more effective noise pollution regulation in tune of sanitizing the city, particularly aimed at 'silencing' the identified noisy and noises.

In that sense, bodies of work on slums and sound in the Indian context are shrouded in an ominous silence, which pushes them further into the domain of the 'other', both academically and experientially. It was this shared predicament of these two bodies of work which allowed for this present work to formulate a theoretical discussion around them within the thematic of 'other and othering'. In the Indian context, there is an intellectual gap in the manner in which slums are approached and perceived. The academic tradition leans towards highlighting the lacks at administrative, infrastructural level whilst the everyday middle class narrative is shrouded in the language of moral, social, and cultural decay. In the recent years, there has been some research undertaken which attempts to move beyond these positions but these take into account the national and state level developments, economically, socially, politically and culturally, to enumerate the perception and position of slums within the same. The discourses within the field of social activism calling for better conditions and rights for slums dwellers in the city strongly resonates with the rhetoric of displacement and lacks, which inadvertently further calcifies the position of the slums and its residents as the 'other'. None of the works, within the field of study, understand to examine the instance of slum settlement in its own right, materiality and politics, and the experience of the space of slum outside this dichotomous position vis-à-vis the state or the city. It is in this regard that this body of work intends to make a departure. At the core of my work lies an attempt to produce an ethnography of lived, everyday, aspirational interactions, insidious and obvious, within the *jhuggis,* and between the city and the slums, in order to locate the slums and their materiality within a larger discursive and experiential scope than it is usually attributed to. Soundscapes and the politics of production, circulation, and articulation of the same, are evoked as the reference point to understand and explore these dynamics. J*huggis* are not anathema to the city, whether one speaks of the city's history or its present or future. In fact, the dominant reckoning, interventions and reflections on the slums contributes towards obliterating the memory of the slums in the present but also denying them any historicity. The *jhuggis* are civic and social spaces that are a by-product of the violent, inequitable and exploitative processes of urbanisation. Through my essays the intent then is to act in whatever limited way to encourage the ethics of cohabitation across spaces, communities and ideas between spaces as the slums and its middle-class neighbours. And lastly, to provide a response to the everyday othering of the slum-dwellers by 'listening to, and recording, the details of the story the other might tell, letting that story become part of an undeniable archive, the enduring trace of loss that compels the ongoing obligations to mourn'.[14]

Concluding Remarks

By asking the question, 'Can the subaltern speak?' and answering it in the negative, Spivak lend to the recognition of 'voice' as a potent political agency for the marginalised.[15] Since then the attempts to extend this 'voice' has had overlapping and intersecting implications, variously articulated both in popular and political reckoning in regards to its significance in the rights/

---

14   Judith Butler, *Notes Towards a Performative Theory of Assembly,* Cambridge, MA: Harvard University Press, 2015.
15   Gayatri Chakravorty Spivak, 'Can the Subaltern Speak?' in C. Nelson and L. Grossberg (eds.) *Marxism and the Interpretation of Culture,* Urbana: University of Illinois Press, 1988, pp 271–315.

identity/space the subaltern can assert and claim. In interventionist initiatives – especially, political and developmental – this inability of the subaltern to 'speak' is often translated literally. And thus the sustained efforts to extend a space (real, virtual, mediated by technologies) to the marginalised to 'speak' out and thus have a voice.

However: most of these readings, and the subsequent interventions, in fact misread Spivak's evocations, and not surprisingly leapfrog – or completely miss out – on an a stage/situation/ modality integral in translating (validating) the act of speaking into voice as a matter of political agency. And that is the consideration of listening. So: we have the matter of the act of speaking translating into affective *voice* with listening as a practice providing the necessary punctum - the turntable, so to say, which when tuned well emanates sounds filled with robustness and *solidity*. And whilst there is a demand, urgent and immediate, to tune into these frequencies of theoretical considerations for definite political actions, there is an equally compelling, perhaps even more so in its practice, task to open our ears, systematically and systemically, to recognise the multiplicity of the acts of speaking.

I argue that the denial of the acts of speaking to the other is deliberated within the logics of sustaining economic, social and political alienation such that the other always remains an 'unactualized' self: rambling, incoherent and in need of disciplining. The fate of the other, who only speaks in tongues, is thus relegated to either being silent or silenced. Critical and central to this othering project is the denial of emotionality to the other firmly situated in the practices of unacknowledging the acts of speaking of the other, and rendering all the utterances of the other as cacophony. I identify the emotional self as the availability of grammar and vocabularies to nurse, cherish, indulge the self, to indeed have reflexive spaces and interlocuting acts of of speaking to call out the pain, anguish, the crushing of the soul, the injustice, violence, marginalization within the broader matrices of class, caste, communal, spatial, gendered negotiations. But also for the self to have the emotional capacities to announce themselves in their full bloom. The other is strategically denied any structures to inhabit and claim their emotionality, and in doing so, they are then denied any structures of defiance. Sans emotions, and emotional capacities - a self which suffers, but also loves, cries in joy, dances in abandon, gives in to desires, makes flippant choices, endures heartbreaks and has poetic inflections - the other is a two-dimensional, cardboard equivalent of merely a receptacle with no depth to evoke reaction and respond.

Deliberating on a distinction between hearing and listening in this essay has been to highlight the manner in which encounters with spaces, cultures and bodies translate into experiences informed by sensorial, social, cultural and moral backgrounds. I argue that it is within, and without, the field of force between the encounter and its translation into an experience that politics of space, identity and gender manifest themselves and abound in multiplicities in everyday materialities of transforming urbanities, especially in the global South. I have also argued that this deliberation does not limit itself to experiencing sounds, but stretches to the body in space and the space of the body. The body of the slum dweller in the city is considered to inhabit illegal space thriving with informal practices. This accords her position in the urban discourse, and her right to the city, an anxiety, on account of either being lamented as a crisis or celebrated as 'heroic entrepreneurship'.[16] What adds to this anxiety is the agenda of the state to implement its projects and policies, through which these spaces will 'eventually be integrated into a modern and manageable economy', which, in turn, can be a blow to the informality in this economic situation. Informality as an idea, practice and population set has been instituted as anathematic to the projected aspiration of a 'world-class city' in the global South.[17] The tensions in the transforming urban materiality of Delhi – a city with ambitions and aspirations to become a world-class city – to accommodate these informalities is further exaggerated by the role these spaces, specifically on account of being informal and illegal, play in wider transformations. They extend the cheap, readily available menial labour necessary to ensure and erect a world-class, international city.

The sensorial and moral regimes of othering, as executed by the deliberate un-listening and silencing, are attempts at fixing the position of slum dwellers as the other – socially, legally, sensorially and morally. This framing allows the state the rhetorical legitimacy to oust them from a formal city structure when deemed appropriate, as also to institute regimes of disciplining their bodies, individually and collectively. Further, within this framing, the predicament of these spaces and their residents as slums that are informal and, thus, 'un-modern and un-manageable', is increasingly being framed as a moral limitation of the spaces and the residents themselves. However the potential of the un-containability of sounds – and thus the potency of voice as a political agency – is not completely lost to the residents of the slums, marginalised spaces as the following essays evidence. In these, the subaltern loves, wails, waits, argues, and shrieks; the subaltern indeed does speak, but denied a listening – the validations of its acts of speaking – is caught in the cul-de-sac of sublaternity in perpetuity.

References

Ahmed, Waquar. 'Neoliberal Utopias and Urban Realities in Delhi', *ACME: An International E-Journal for Critical Geographies,* 10 (2011).

Attali, Jacques. *Noise: The Political Economy of Music,* Vol. 16. Manchester University Press, 1985.

Butler, Judith. *Notes Towards a Performative Theory of Assembly,* Cambridge, MA: Harvard University Press, 2015.

Calvino, Italo. 'A King Listens', trans. William Weaver, in *Under the Jaguar Sun,* San Diego, New York, London: Harcourt Brace Jovanovich, 1988, pp. 31-64.

---

16   Hernando De Soto, *The Mystery of Capital: Why Capitalism Triumphs in the West and Fails Everywhere Else,* Civitas Books, 2000.
17   Ananya Roy, 'Urban Informality: Toward an Epistemology of Planning', *Journal of the American Planning Association,* 71 (2005): 148. Waquar Ahmed, ' Neoliberal Utopias and Urban Realities in Delhi', *ACME: An International E-Journal for Critical Geographies,* 10 (2011).

Certeau, Michel De. *The Practice of Everyday Life,* trans. Steven Randall, California: University of California Press, 1984, pp. 93-105.

Walter Benjamin and Asja, 'Journal de Naples', 1925.

Classen, Constance. *Worlds of Sense: Exploring the Senses in History and Across Cultures,* New York: Routledge, 1993, pp -121.

Connor, Steven. 'Michel Serres's Five Senses', Birkbeck College, May 1999, http://www.stevenconnor.com/5senses.htm.

Foucault, Michel. *Politics, Philosophy, Culture: Interviews and Other Writings, 1977-1984,* Routledge, 2013.

Nancy, Jean-Luc. *Listening,* trans. C. Mandell, New York: Fordham, 2007.

Peter J. Claus, Sarah Diamond, and Margaret Ann Mills, *South Asian Folklore: An Encyclopedia: Afghanistan, Bangladesh, India, Nepal, Pakistan, Sri Lanka,* Taylor & Francis, 2003, p. 231.

Picard, Max. *The World of Silence,* 6067, H. Regnery, 1952.

Rice, Tom. 'Soundselves: An Acoustemology of Sound and Self in the Edinburgh Royal Infirmary', *Anthropology Today,* 19.4 (2003): 4-9.

Roy, Ananya. 'Urban Informality: Toward an Epistemology of Planning', *Journal of the American Planning Association,* 71 (2005): 148.

Sacks, Oliver. *Seeing Voices: A Journey into the World of the Deaf,* Pan Macmillan, 2009.

Schafer, Murray. 'Open Ears', in Michael Bull and Les Back eds., *The Auditory Culture Reader,* New York: Berg, 2003.

Soto, Hernando De. *The Mystery of Capital: Why Capitalism Triumphs in the West and Fails Everywhere Else,* Civitas Books, 2000.

Spivak, Gayatri Chakravorty. 'Can the Subaltern Speak?' in C. Nelson and L. Grossberg (eds) *Marxism and the Interpretation of Culture,* Urbana: University of Illinois Press, 1988, pp 271–315.

3. AN 'OBSCENE' CALLING EMOTIONALITY IN/OF MARGINALIZED SPACES: A LISTENING OF/INTO 'ABUSIVE' WOMEN IN GOVINDPURI

The Calling

And thus does Zizek expound on the 'traumatic dimension of voice' by focusing on *The Exorcist* in *The Perverts' Guide to Cinema*:

> Voice is not an organic part of the human body. It is coming from some where in between your body. Whenever we talk to another person there is always this minimum of ventriloquist affect, as if some foreign power took possession. Remember (speaking over the clip from the film, *The Exorcist*, where the girl is possessed) that at the beginning of the film this was a beautiful, young girl. How did she become a monster that we see? By being possessed, but who possessed her? A voice.[1]

This is an obscene essay. It deals with obscenity as a particular and peculiar 'traumatic dimension of voice' performed by women onto other women in the traumatized space of the Govindpuri slums. However, it is not only its subject matter that lends this essay its character. It is also in the liberties it takes to obscenely identify in these performances the potential to displace patriarchal-spatial hierarchies; an exhibitionist display of emotionality; and a well-articulated desire for love, not only as an esoteric experience but also a condensed social, sexual reality. Since at the core of every trauma lies (unfolds) a violent social, moral, physical event, the ruminations in this chapter constantly concern themselves with identifying these sites of violence the obscene performances not only claim, but also create, on its self and on the others.

Women spewing sexually explicit and violent abuses (in this context, in Hindi), toward the female body, which are traditionally reckoned to be the classic masculine expression to reiterate the hierarchy, as the particular instance of obscene 'traumatic dimension of voice', is the focus of this essay. Whilst the chapter acknowledges the broader materiality of gendered obscene-sonic exchange in the slums, this essay focuses on the particular and peculiar economy of this exchange when the obscenities are not only claimed by but are also exclusively directed at women by other women. By implicating themselves in the violence directed toward the 'real' and 'imagined' body of the self (and thus taking charge of that violence, at least rhetorically), the women create a disruptive and volatile space where gendered spaces, roles, and identities necessitate reframing. The evocation of these abuses, I argue, is a strategic act of subversion and circumvention of the patriarchal hierarchies. The landscape of patriarchal hierarchies is not an exclusive domain of masculine presence(s) and reiterations; and more often than not, it is the performance of masculinities—by both men and women—which accord it its particular characteristic. In that sense, while this essay acknowledges that the cartographic, emotional and social imaginations of the patriarchal landscapes are devised by

---

1   *Slavoj Zizek's The Pervert's Guide to Cinema* (dir. Sophie Fiennes, 2006). Emphasis added.

the dominant sensibilities, women often assume a masculine persona to institute these imaginations, especially when the exchange does not involve gendered interactions but unfolds in an apparently gender 'neutral' setting exclusively between women.

It is within this framing that the evocations—obscenities by women directed at women—are affectively employed toward several agendas: social, cultural, spatial and political. However, in this chapter I explore the evocation of these abuses to map the cartographic and cathartic experience and experiencing of love in, and within, the slums of Govindpuri (hereafter 'GP'). The essay then dwells upon the agency and extent of strategy available to the marginalized—here, women in an essentially patriarchal setting, and slums within the broader materiality of the city—to affect the designed subversion and circumvention to complicate the reckoning of the self deflected through the prism of sonic performances, emotions, identity and violence. In that, this essay, even though romantically inclined, refuses to romanticize violence by engaging with its perverse everydayness. In the discussions that follow, it is a matter of deliberation to not highlight the particular social and political considerations and consequences of voice and sonic performativity as agency in the given context. The intent is not to collapse these distinct categories. Instead it aims to unfold these obscene evocations as a complex and nuanced negotiation between the two to highlight the ruptures, continuations and displacements between different kinds of sonic permissibility available to a certain group and the resounding impact it can have.

Baby and Bitiya, two formidable women in GP, who not only allowed me to experience their experiencing of love within this schematic, but who also agreed to have their narratives exploited for broader extrapolations, are the punctuations—not as objectified entities, but as necessary instruments (in all their sensuousness)—carrying these explorations further. I, as a bearer of the feminine form, and an interlocutor-in-charge, insert myself in the text, not with a self-indulgent agenda, but to highlight the anxieties of the encounter of the obscene sorts, across myriad considerations, especially of class distinctions.

Obscenely, Yours

Beginning at the basics: the self, before I venture into the self of the other. I grew up in a setting reeking of colonial and real hangovers. Both my parents were in the Indian army; my father was part of the elite, combative commando forces and my mother a dentist in its medical forces. Over the weekends we had croquet games, long-drawn bridge games and lots of gin. We, the children, did not partake in the latter though. We grew up with smatterings of grammatically incorrect English, and our parents—mostly, fathers—exclaiming, *bloody hell*, *God damn you*, and *bastard*. That was the extent of obscene exclamations I grew up with. I never heard them swear in Hindi, but as I grew older, I got to know of abuses in Hindi: *maader-chod* (mother-fucker), *behen-chod* (sister-fucker), *chutiya* (cunt). However, it was only when I had left the security of parental nesting, acquired half-baked degrees, romanced with revolutionary ideas, drank enough dark rum and reckoned myself to be truly liberal that I started using these expletives as punctuations as the men around us did. I was not alone. I was part of a cohort who had grown up with socialist realities and leftist ambitions while assuming neo-liberal sensibilities. We, of course, like them (the men) did not mean them literally; the violence was truly displaced, or so we thought. The beginning was hesitant though, but once realizing the currency the utterance of these expletives carried in sustaining a moral and social shock, it was incorporated as part of everyday emotional and intellectual expression.

Men who found it deplorable did not see us beyond the main door. The exchange—social, intellectual and sexual—was thus mediated by a highly sexualized, violent vocabulary. This exchange, in all its liberal pretensions, not only displaced the body and site of the violence, but violence itself. However, all said and done, we never lost our moral-virginal hymens. The liminal space we had managed to carve out through these obscene performances allowed us to transgress across conflicting social-moral landscapes. I had reckoned that I was thus truly liberated from middle-class sexual mores and moral prejudices. However, when entering yet another liminal space, I was compelled to renegotiate the social-sexual-moral economies I was convinced I had claimed.

In 2004, I was appointed to assist Dr. Jo Tacchi in a Department for International Development (DFID) funded research on 'Role of Information and Communication Technologies (ICTs) in Poverty Alleviation'. The slums of Govindpuri were one of the identified research sites. Until then, even though I had lived in Delhi for almost a decade, my experience of and exposure to the slums in Delhi was through a primarily middle-class, educated, urban lens. This implied that, while I was aware of the rhetoric of displacement and resettlement vis-à-vis the slums in popular mainstream media and academic discourse, I had never experienced the space first hand. Though conscious of the discursive practices that othered the slums and slum-dwellers, I was still reluctant and hesitant when it came to setting my terms of engagement, primarily because of my limited knowledge of the space. The narratives highlighting the everyday violence, displacement and marginalization of the slums also—often, subconsciously and insidiously (as fine subtext)—included testimonies of the social, moral and sexual conducts in these spaces. These, the narratives emphasized, were different, and this difference lay in the distance from the middle-class-ness of these practices.

And thus I ventured into the slums of GP, hesitant and reclaiming the middle-class-ness I had spent years to shed off. Or at least I reckoned. At the most fundamental level, this was obvious in the deliberation of attire I chose to present myself in the slums. It was not the Westernized appearance I usually donned — T-shirt and jeans — but a more staid one reflective of the 'indigenous' culture — *salwaar-kurtas*[2] — with, of course, a perfectly draped *dupatta*.[3] However the deception went deeper and further: a heavy smoker, I did not dare light up in GP; a drinker of some merit, I refused to claim this indulgence; romantically and sexually adventurous, I definitely did not acknowledge these encounters, or even their possibilities. However, pertinent to the context of this essay, the most dramatic shift was in the presentation and performance of my sonic self in the space of the slums. The language of communication and conversation in GP was Hindi — that in itself was a shift, as I inhabited

---

2   A type of suit with loose trousers and long shirt. It is a common, everyday attire for most young women in Asia.
3   A long scarf worn with the salwaar-kurtas; in most instances it is considered essential, and not wearing it is often seen as a sign of indecency.

spaces where Indian-English was the de facto language. Moreover, the iteration of Hindi I chose as my sonic identity within the materiality of GP was chaste and definitely devoid of the obscenities, which otherwise were part of my everyday vocabulary.

It has been ten years since those early days of hesitant, deceptive encounters in GP. Following the DFID research project, I undertook to pursue my doctoral research focusing on politics of production and articulation of sound as an interface to interrogate the everyday interactions between the residents of the GP and their middle-class neighbors. The anxiety of leading an almost schizophrenic identity as a researcher overwhelmed me, and I invested in intellectual and methodological inquisitions to resolve the sites from where these split-sonic performances emanated. Not without its distressing emotional, intellectual and theoretical reckonings, I came upon the realization that central to the assumed sonic performance in GP was the internalization of the logic the testimonies (insidiously in academic texts and overtly in mainstream media) sustained: the otherness of the slums, and its residents, and this difference arising out of the distance from middle-class sensibilities. The pathology of assuming the deceptive, chaste sonic identity was premised not in witnessing the transgressive spaces women claimed in the slums (as we — the middle-class counterparts — aspired for in our contexts) by obscene utterances, but in the danger imagined in the identification of the self with that of the others. The self of the others was thus not only systematically absented from the discursive space(s), but it was also strategically demonized by affecting a distance through assumed sonic identities to assert an embryonic distance.

Once arrived at these deliberations, I agreed to put myself into as much scrutiny and observation as I took the liberties of the self of the others. Thus we — the women and I in GP — smoke, drink, discuss our affairs and political positions (with liberal smatterings of obscenities, which we anyway employ as punctuations) with truthfulness, which does not necessarily obliterate the class distinctions, but it surely does not deliberately perpetuate or deflect it. However, most significantly, we collectively acknowledge the currency of sonic-obscene performances in claiming spaces, though not without their violence, in our specific contexts, even though we necessarily do not perform them together.

Shutting Anyone's Speakers

Bitiya is a feisty young woman. By her own admission, she has done it all: got married at the age of 16 to her lover against her parents' will; had a daughter by 18; left her abusive, alcoholic husband at 19; had a raging affair with a neighbor's relative; supported her family, including getting her two sisters married off, by taking up sex trade; had a live-in lover for seven years; and presently is readying to bring up his child after they had a volatile and violent breakup. She is a force to reckon with: 'I have done things on my own terms and I have borne the consequences as well. No one in the locality can say anything to me. I can shut anyone's speakers.'

It was not long before I witnessed her *shutting the speakers*. She was in the middle of a heated argument with one of her neighbours — a young woman — when I arrived. The context or the cause of the altercation was lost to me, and I did not dare interrupt the exchange. Even though this exchange was liberally doused with obscene expletives, they were restricted to the normalized *behen-chod, maadar-chod* variety, but soon the argument picked up momentum, and so did the nature of the obscenities.[4] They became increasingly violent and sexual. By now Bitiya was dominating this sonic exchange. The choice of her expletives insinuated violence onto the feminine body, which included, but was not limited to, 'shoving things in her cunt; getting the neighbour raped by her uncles; her [the neighbour's] incestuous sexual encounters with her brother, father and any stranger who would have her; and the ultimate evocation of the sexualized violence of the neighbour's enjoying being raped'.

The young woman was thus silenced, and she agreed to take down the garland of worn-out shoes she had hung facing Bitiya's house as an insult to the latter's family.

I was not unaffected by this highly violent and sexualized exchange of obscenities between the two women, even though I had witnessed similar exchanges earlier. Noticing my unease, Bitiya offered the following explanation. 'Here, the only way to shut people up is by spewing more gannd [filth] than they can. That is the only way anyone's speakers can be silenced'. The explanation offered by Bitiya was not without its Zizek-ian evocations. By identifying the sonic performativities of another in terms of a technological-mediated object—the speakers—Bitiya in fact arrived at a proposition similar to that of Zizek's that the voice in fact can be 'coming from somewhere in between your body'. Also in this evocation, the metaphor of speakers, which can be turned off, is particularly telling, as it poignantly sums up the spaces of dominance—social and cultural spaces—the obscene-sonic performances permit. Thus in this specific performance the sonic space is dominated by the one who can silence or shut the speakers.

However, silence—both performed (being silent) and imposed (being silenced)—is not a static category of sonic being and cannot be contained within the singularity of a listening position within a specific context. Being silent and being silenced can rupture, intersect and interlude the soundscapes in a context in similar manifestations. But the resounding impact of the particular performances more often than not emanates from the spatial, social and political positionality the performer occupies. In the Indian context, the negotiations between being silent and being silenced is strongly situated within its historical, religious and political epistemologies. And these manifest themselves thus: the silence demanded of the lower-caste/classes vis-à-vis the upper-caste/classes both in their everyday, immediate encounters but also as agents of knowledge production; the deliberate silencing of the subaltern as a political category, and the exalted 'silence' of the men of cloth.

Vocal Digressions: The Cartography of Abusing and Loving

The narratives of Baby and Bitiya I discuss in this essay concern themselves with some of these negotiations: sonic dominance, silencing and displacement of spatial-patriarchal hierarchies. But they also venture into the geographies of emotionality of the self of the other as

---

4   Literally translated as sister-fucker and mother-fucker, respectively, these abuses are used in the everyday, common exchange without the direct implications and violence suggested.

articulated through the experiencing love. GP is a highly gendered space, where the mobility of women comes under close scrutiny by both the immediate family and the extended social network. Here, it is the feminine body on which the otherness is doubly inscribed, both of the structural and everyday violence. This otherness is inscribed by limiting the performances the feminine 'self' is capable of—bodily, sonically, sexually and emotionally. The being and becoming of the feminine self is situated within a hetero-normative narrative with subservience and compliance as its core ethos; digressions from this normative narrative are closely monitored—mostly by the older women—and invite social and cultural disapproval; and in extreme cases ostracization often also resulting in physical violence.

In this section I will emphasize the manner in which instances where sonic and emotional digressions by the feminine self disrupt and displace the registered hetero-normative narratives, though not without its violences and violations—to the self and others.

Both Bitiya and Baby are single parents. However, that is not the only thing the two have in common. They both left their marital homes to escape abusive husbands and since then have been the arbiters of their respective families. On different occasions and in varying circumstances, both of them have earned a decent living through sex work. Over the years both of them had several 'love' affairs outside of both their Muslim and slum community. Most of them have been clandestine, but in both their cases one love affair stands out as the ultimate experience: relationship with Dimpy in the case of Bitiya, and Baby's affair with Chand. They conducted these respective relationships openly, challenged the communal order, and had live-in relationships. Here it might be worthwhile to highlight (especially as regards responding to the issue of the encounter of the researcher's self with that of researched) that these confidences by both Bitiya and Baby were not revealed in a research encounter but were shared over a period of few years during which I, as a researcher, was in turns an object of inquisition and research to which I responded with as much truthful integrity as I expected from the researched. Over the years we transcended the sonic distance and displaced sonic performances of identities to arrive at sonic intersections whilst acknowledging the class distance, allowed us—I shared this relationship with most of the residents of GP, especially women—to share collective sonicities. The shared collective sonicities across class and spatial considerations within the broader materiality and imagination of the city are not without their negotiations, and often lend themselves to varying practices of silencing.[5]

Bitiya and Baby's romantic undertakings allow situating the intersection of these two digressions—sonic and emotional—within the specific materiality of GP, whilst complicating the position of slums in the broader imagination of the city as spaces capable of emotionality. Bitiya's relationship with Dimpy and Baby's with Chand came to stormy endings. The deliberation toward the final closure of the respective relationships involved public fights, loud obscene and abusive exchanges and physical violence. During and after the end of the relationships, Bitiya and Baby, casual acquaintances until then, found in each other unusual allies. Their open defiance of social-moral-sexual norms meant that when the said relationships ended,

---

5   Tripta Chandola, 'Listening into Others: Moralising the Soundscapes in Delhi', *International Development Planning Review*, 34.4 (2012), pp. 391–408.

they could not seek out the social support networks available to, for instance, a recently widowed or a married woman abandoned by her husband, or one who returned to her parental home on account of consistent abuse, predominantly physical. Even though in the case of both Bitiya and Baby, abuse—both physical and emotional—along with abandonment were central to their narrative and experience of an essentially patriarchal relationship, they were not extended the concessions on account of the arrogant identification of 'love' as the determining rationale for the said relationships.

Herein unfolds the intersections of the sonic, sexual and romantic digressions. Bitiya and Baby were incensed by their partners' new romantic involvements, but also for not being able to receive any social and cultural validation for their experience of love. They both agreed upon a retaliatory strategy. The anger they felt on account of the displacement was, however, not directed at their former partners, but their present lovers. And thus they decided to 'teach' them a lesson by publicly shaming them, by shutting their speakers. The negotiations for arriving at this confrontation are uncannily similar in both the instances. Both Bitiya and Baby set out to establish the everyday routines about the other woman in question, they gathered as many details about their histories and present preoccupations and the geographies of 'love' they were claiming with their ex-lovers.

One afternoon Baby was informed that her ex-lover, Chand, and his present romantic interest were spotted at a public park not very far from GP. The moment seemed opportune, and the two allies—Bitiya and Baby—set out to shut the speakers. Once the two of them were spotted in the park, Baby took to abusing the romantic interest in question, whilst completely ignoring the ex-lover, in highly sexualized and violent obscenities. The obscenities in themselves demand an intellectual inquisition to locate the violence—real and imagined—articulated by them; however, the concern of this essay is in the very performance of these obscenities rather than the cultural modalities of their production. These obscenities were marked by two prominent sets of rhetoric: first, to establish her prowess as a sexual subject by claiming the very real and imagined violation of and violence toward the feminine body inherent to these obscenities. These included evocations to the effect, 'my cunt can hold as many cocks as I want, if you had the same capacity you would not steal my boyfriend'; 'I can accommodate different cocks in different orifices at the same time'; and 'it is my cunt, what I do with it is my business'. But the effectiveness of the obscene performance as a retaliatory strategy lay in disenfranchising the other—Chand's present romantic interest—of exactly the same sexual subjectivity and control over it as Baby claimed for herself. These included calling her a randi (a whore), and projecting on to her feminine body violence of a highly sexualized nature, 'you will be gang raped' and 'hope you are fucked by your whole clan, but even that won't satisfy you', and 'obviously you are insatiable, that is why after being fucked by everyone in your neighbourhood and family, you use your cunt to attract other men'.

The woman in question—Chand's romantic interest—was taken aback, especially since Baby had Bitiya to reiterate, almost perform the function of an echo, in this obscene performance just extending the space and scope of sonic colonization. Soon a group of onlookers gathered about. Some men, including Chand, tried to intervene. However, at that moment Baby started tearing off her clothes and threatening that if anyone interfered she would file a suit of section 376 against them. Under Indian Penal Code, 1860, Section 376 is reserved to report and charge the accused for attempting or having committed rape. If reported, the police have to take action against the accused, and it remains as a recorded criminal case against the identified perpetrator until proven innocent. If Baby's retaliatory strategy relied upon making a distinct demarcation between sexual subjectivities as claimed by the sonic performances, Bitiya's strategic intervention to encounter the other collapsed these demarcations by sustaining a narrative in which the other's corporeality was held as vulnerable to the real sexual and physical violence she had encountered in her relationship. Indeed this was also a publicly performed obscene sonic moment. She, along with Baby, made an unannounced visit to Dimpy's present lover's house. Bitiya then proceeded to narrate in some detail the sexual violence—both real and rhetorical—she had endured. She evoked her body as a piece of meat that Dimpy devoured as and when he wanted; he treated her like a *randi*, often physically and verbally abusing her. She made a plea to the other to reject Dimpy on account of the shared violation of the feminine body. The climactic moment of this obscene sonic performance was inscribing the script of an imagined violence onto the other's body: 'he will fuck you as he wants; if you don't agree to what he desires, he will not shy away from raping you and talking filth about you to his friends'. Her ultimate threat to disrupt the romantic adventures was to file a complaint against Dimpy under Section 376, especially as by then she was carrying his child.

Silencing the Lover's Speakers: Muting the Self of the Other

If indeed 'voice' is to be considered as something 'coming from somewhere in between your body', then it is also laden with the potentiality of occupying other *in-between-nesses*: spatially, socially, politically and culturally. Voice as a simple act of speech and its rhetorical capacity to evoke a collective reaction (for instance, political and religious congregations, among others) is at once grounded and displaced. Voice emanates from a time-space continuum, but it reverberates across multitudinous, intersecting temporal and spatial realities resonating a reiteration of the voice, intended or otherwise. This potentiality of voice to literally, metaphorically and rhetorically extend one's domain of being is well acknowledged in GP. And thus the women are required to perform silence of sorts: don't talk too loudly; don't talk to strangers; don't retaliate; don't talk back. The women however continually perform the sonic digressions. They challenge, subvert and circumvent these hierarchies by claiming the sonic space, by performing obscenities of the nature discussed in the earlier section. However, at this juncture it is pertinent to establish that not all sexualized obscenities are registered as digressions. Some of them like *maader-chod* (mother fucker), *behen-chod* (sister fucker), *chutiya* (cunt) are normalized in the given context, and are used by both men and women as interjections and punctuations, both jocularly and in slight altercations. These obscenities are not absent of the imagined sexualized violence. However the site of the violence—the body of a mother or a sister—is still claimed (or in fact un-claimed) in its abstractions, steadfastly located within the familial and social order wherein the figures of the mother and the daughter are revered and respected, and thus beyond the realm of the 'real' violence these imaginations contain.

The sexual and social freedoms claimed and exercised by Bitiya and Baby are in no way singular instances of challenging the hetero-normative, masculine cartographies in GP. However what sets aside the narrative of these two women are the significant overlaps in their experiences—social, cultural and romantic; but also the particular manner in which both of them assumed a certain masculinity in claiming these spaces. The instance of Bitiya 'shutting anyone's speaker' is but an assertion of it. They are both constantly approached by neighbours, relatives and friends to deal and negotiate situations, especially involving local cops, goons and matters of fights in their respective streets; one of the reasons why both women enjoy this privileged position is on account of their ability to spew filth and shut anyone's speakers. As mentioned earlier, GP is a highly gendered space where the mobilities and performances of women—social, sexual and sonic—are highly restricted. The 'obscene' sonic performances of Bitiya and Baby disrupt the established hierarchies. The men—often amused—find it disconcerting because of its emasculating potential to displace them from their claimed space. The women—especially those at whom these obscenities are directed—are further disenfranchised by the peculiar encounter of gendered violence (however rhetorical and free of real violence) by other women. However, Bitiya and Baby, though performing this violence and claiming the masculine space, are not subtracted from the rhetorical and violence onto the feminine self inflicted by these sonic-obscenities. The only recourse available to them to claim the masculine spaces, as women who are *besharam* [shameless] enough to spew the obscenities, is to expose their own cartographic, emotional, sexual and sonic selves to the very violence they intend to inflict, and thus displace.

If women spewing sexualized, violent abuses are the ultimate sonic digression, the declaration of love—as an experience and desire—by them is its emotional equivalent. Love and its declaration threaten to disrupt the precariously sustained order of normative social, moral and sexual values, especially in regard to containing and controlling the feminine self. The obscenities performed by women, which do indeed register as sonic digressions and affectively disrupt the spatial-patriarchal-sonic hierarchies, are the ones in which the women directly implicate themselves and other women in the violence directed toward the real and imagined feminine self.

The Danger of the Other's Love

Love is dangerous. It resounds with social, sexual and moral possibilities and digressions. However, the pathological dread of declaration of love— especially by women—is the exhibitionist display of the self vis-à-vis an identified other. In the concluding discussion to this essay, I will situate this pathological dread of love as a peculiar instance of perverse masculinities in a marginalized setting of the slums. I shall also highlight the manner in which this perversity, and thus its depravity, of slums often evoked by the state, middle-class retort, and in cultural representation of slums is a justification to maintain a distance from these spaces and displace them. A paternalistic disciplining agenda is inherent to these narratives, which is symptomatic of the broader anxiety of the dominant structures and narratives to allow for an emotionality, and thus an identification of a well-defined and claimed a sense of self to the marginalized spaces and communities.

As discussed in the previous section, Bitiya and Baby found solace in each other to articulate their experience, anxiety and trauma of love within these negotiated cartographies. It was only within the shared experience of displaced selves that the two of them could rehabilitate their individual self, especially since they lacked any other narrative spaces to claim it. The end of their respective relationships was articulated by both of them (in collective and independent conversations where I was inadvertently present)—in different terms—as a significant moment of rupture to the projected and imagined sense of self, as within weeks of the break-up both Dimpy and Chand had assumed new romantic relationships. Socially, culturally, sonically and sexually lacking the space to locate the love as a valid category of experience within the real materiality of GP, the displacement from an imagined site—however displaced—where this experience was validated by the presence of a responsive other; both Bitiya and Baby encountered the ultimate displacement of being absented from this collective, fantastical realm by the insertion of an another—sexually active and sonically performative self. The voice of the other (Dimpy's and Chand's newly acquired romantic interests), muting their own, compelled them into undertaking matters, into shutting the other's speakers—even whilst sharing an intimate, immediate and violent identification with the other as always occupying the space of the Other within the hegemonic, masculine performativities and spaces.

Emotionality in Marginalized Spaces: The Self of the Other

Slums are heterotopic spaces in the city. They are both dreaded and desired, the former for its potential to disrupt the fundamental core of social-moral values owing to the imaginations it evokes on account of its density, dirt and digressions—social, cultural and moral. Within this dreaded potentiality for digressions lies its perverse desire. However, this desire rarely translates into a direct engagement with the space, but manifests itself in the hyperbolic interest in situating the position of the slums in the present of the city. This tension was especially exaggerated in a city like Delhi, with its ambitions to transform itself into a *'world-class, clean, green' city*. Moreover this transformation, essentially structural, also relies on the readily available, cheap manual labour from these marginalized spaces and communities. This ambition draws inspiration from following the Singaporean model, which prides itself in transforming itself into a 'world-class city' under Lee Kuwan Yew in a very short period of time. In fact, Sheila Dixit, Delhi's chief minister in her third term, got a special mention in LKY Cities in Transformation Award4 for her efforts to improve the city's environmental, civic and urban planning.[6]

With 'Delhi as Singapore', Sheila Dixit extended to the burgeoning middle-class in Delhi a model that immensely appealed to their aspirational ambitions of what Slavoj Zizek identifies as 'capitalism with *Asian values*'.[7] The scope of this text does not allow to engage at length with the problematic and politics of employing 'Delhi as Singapore' model as strategic rhetorical tool, which was affectively employed to justify violence—by the way of demolitions, displacement and resettlement—on marginalized spaces and communities (namely, slum-dwellers,

---

6 Special Mention - Sheila Dikshit, https://www.leekuanyewworldcityprize.com.sg/laureates/2010/special-mentions/sheila-dikshit/.
7 Poonam Chandra Pandey, 'Sheila Dixit: Architect of Modern Delhi, Wanted to Develop it like Singapore', https://morningindia.in/sheila-dikshitarchitect-of-modern-delhi-wanted-to-develop-it-like-singapore/'. Slavoj Zizek, 'Capitalism with Asian Values', *Al Jazeera*, 13 November 2011, https://www.aljazeera.com/programmes/talktojazeera/2011/10/2011102813360731764.html.

homeless people and migrant labour) in the city. However, it allows to explore the particular reckoning of the self as a modern, disciplined and self-governing individuated entity which has insidiously found its way into urban planning discourse as well mainstream, cultural representations. It is within this particular notionality of the self that I complicate the position of slums in the broader imagination of urban materiality by focusing on its emotionality with love as a key concern in GP.

The Oxford English Dictionary defines emotions (n.) as 'a strong feeling deriving from one's circumstances, mood, or relationships with others', and 'emotional' and 'emotionality' are defined as the states that express this 'strong feeling'. Central to this definition of emotions extending to its performance, emotionality, is a strong sense of self and the relationship of this self with an identified other. Slums are strategically denied a self as it allows to accommodate the anxiety about their otherness across political, intellectual, social, cultural and indeed, emotional manifestations. In its most fundamental aspect, it completely disenfranchises slums of any identity and thus its assertion. It systematically limits their right to the city. This fundamental disenfranchisement further extends into denying the slums and its residents the possibility to imagine an (or any) other. The denial of the self of the slums in discursive spaces, middle-class imagination and mainstream representation is then logically extended to acknowledging any emotional capacity or its performance, emotionality.

This double denial, first of the self of the slums and then the possibility of othering by the other, translates not only in immediate disenfranchisement, but also significantly allows for the displacement of the marginalized both in the historical and futuristic imagination of the urban. The peculiarity of the suspended displacement in the imagination of the state is not incidental but strategic. Owing to this suspension, the demolition, displacement or violence inflicted on the slums finds justification as it is understood that they neither have any historicity nor any future claims to the memory and culture of the space they inhabit—that until re-settled by the state, they exist in a void. And thus the ruthlessness of the violence inflicted is often masked within the rhetoric of benevolence; in that they are in fact being extended legitimate claims to history, memory and culture. The lack of acknowledgement to their emotionality is yet another strategy (though seemingly insidious and instinctive) to perpetuate their violence. For, if the residents of the slums were indeed identified as 'emotionally' capable, they would have to be acknowledged to have capabilities of individual expression, which would then extend to acknowledging their collective identities as well.

However, this denial of emotionality does not imply that their performance or expression of self in the public, or for that matter in their private spaces is not unacknowledged. In fact the performance is constantly scrutinized; however it is not engaged within the framework of expression of self but as a gross deviance from the modern, disciplined and self-governed self that is acquiring a currency within the cultures of urban transformation in Delhi. And this imagination of the self, drawing from the Singaporean model, has been affectively consolidated in the popular, middle-class aspirations, which then find resonance in urban planning projects, several of which — including the Bhagidhari system — were recognized as exemplary efforts by Sheila Dixit in the special mention she received in LKY's Cities in Transformation Awards.[8]

Love in the Times of Othering: Muting the Self of the Other

At the outset this chapter announced its obscene intent. And here, in the conclusion, wherein the narrative structure demands a closure and neatly folded resolutions, the essay performs its hyperbolic obscenity by its refusal to succumb to these compulsions in that it does not arrive at a logical culmination of the conversations initiated, but aims to leave with provocations both for the author and its reader. The deliberation to listen into the obscene sonic performances of women in GP, the identification of self, emotionality and moments of disruption of sonic-spatial and patriarchal negotiations was not a cheap attempt toward sensationalization. Instead by undertaking these listenings—not without their violence, both real and imagined—it was to precisely highlight the perversity of the available moments of encounters between the mainstream and the marginalized to recognize these pathologies: of the self of the other.

Women spewing the highly sexualized and violent abuses in GP are a perverse titillation to the dominant agents (here, men) and narratives in its real encounter with this body but also in situating these bodies as sexual subjects within the broader cartographic imagination of self and emotions. If the women are indeed articulate and claim these violence(s), it is because they desire them. But also the vocalization of this desire—a performance of the self, so to say—necessitates the imperative to discipline them. And thus the space and scope available to women to express themselves is limited to obscene performances and encounters, which are fundamentally recognized as offensive or disgusting by accepted standards of morality and decency. Even love, an otherwise exalted and celebrated emotion of being within the mainstream hegemonic discourse, is only allowed to be actualized and articulated within the discussed obscene performances of and by the women in GP. Thus love as an expression of self and emotionality is denied legitimacy to the women in GP, operable only in its hyperbolic manifestations. This particular predicament of women in GP is not only representative of the sustained marginalization they encounter as the other within its dominant, patriarchal context but also symptomatic of the othering slums (as a space) encounter within the broader urban imagination. Essential to sustain the othering—inscribed on the women in the localized context of GP, and slums as a space in its generalized projection—is then to deny them a well-articulated sense of self by dismissing their emotionality.

However, emotions indeed do abound in marginalized spaces. But making this seemingly commonsensical assertion demands qualification, and more importantly, quantification. Within the very tapestry of this necessity to qualify are woven the questions which have preoccupied philosophers, scholars across disciplines and artists: the construction of the self, the position of the individual and the intimate relationship between the self and the state, which then

---

8   The premise of the Bhagidari System (literally translated as 'participatory system') is to involve 'citizens' in the processes of governance so as to make it effective, transparent and collaborative. However, the only citizen groups that are presently involved in the Bhagidari System are the Resident Welfare Association (RWAs) of middle-class, often gated settlements and market traders' associations (MTAs).

raises further issues of citizenship and the spaces available to different and diverse selves to enact it in its complete capacity. However significant these questions are, here it is important to attempt to unveil not only whether emotions abound in marginalized spaces (in fact I begin with that assertion), but to further understand the politics of denial of emotionality in these spaces. The recognition of the emotional of the other is also plagued with a fundamental methodological and philosophical paradox. Indeed, here lies an inherent dilemma because in recognizing the emotional of the other, one also acknowledges the 'self' of the other (and in fact engages with it).

And Thus, the Savage Is a Savage, and Remains a Savage

Perhaps we need to take a step back, and before pondering on the denial of emotionality and its politics, perhaps it is pertinent to wonder why the denial in the first place. Of course, there is the entire contestation of the self-other as discussed in the earlier section, and indeed inherent to this denial is a strategic disciplining agenda. However, we, as human beings, are instinctively and intuitively aware of emotions; we know they are important and that they shape our lives in ways sometimes even beyond our imagination. We all have succumbed to them: love, jealousy, loneliness, betrayal, anger, angst, hurt. This landscape abounds in its wilderness. And only while taking a walk amid this wilderness of emotional possibilities, especially while reflecting on the self-other constitutions in this landscape, does it becomes evident that the other after all is not denied all emotionality. The emotions associated with the other, which find credence, and even sympathy, are of anger, rage and betrayal (though only if it is against the system). There is sometimes even space for the performance of these emotions by the others; though it is only recognized in its collective manifestations justified, celebrated, sympathized or dreaded within the rhetoric of the subaltern, finally rising in the long-awaited revolution.

In *Don't Ask Me for That Love Again*, one of the greatest poets from South Asia and a committed communist, Faiz Ahmed Faiz, while celebrating his lover's beauty, evokes most poignant imagery to justify his forsaking the love for a cause thus: 'There are other sorrows in this world/comforts other than love/ Don't ask me, my love, for that love again'.[9] Here, the sorrows are not of a personal nature, but a response to the plight of the poor in society whose '[…] bodies [are] plastered with ash, bathed in blood' to serve the rich who have 'cast their spell on history'. Romantic love is not for the revolutionary, perhaps an impediment to the Revolution itself? But why is love an anathema to revolution? And if the revolutionary herself cannot claim love, what about those—the others—for whom the revolutionary renounces her love? The cathartic moment in the compulsion to choose or renounce love in one's commitment to the self or the other lies in the very individuated and involved articulation of love as an experience, process and practice.

Love as a concern for philosophers, scholars, mainstream media and popular culture remains the epitome of the celebration of the self: in the surrendering, suffering, exhilaration and com-

---

9 Faiz Ahmed Faiz, 'Don't Ask Me for That Love Again', trans. Agha Shahid Ali, in *The Rebel's Silhouette: Selected Poems of Faiz Ahmed Faiz*, Amherst: Massachusetts UP, 1995, 5.

plete indulgence it demands. It is indeed almost a narcissistic indulgence. It has capacity to completely obliterate the other. When the poet, in the throes of his melancholia, announces to his lover that romantic love is not an indulgence he can afford, the loved — the other — is completely absented. The pathos and the pain of the loved are irrelevant, and it is the lover's discourse that dominates. It is this dread of the other as an individuated entity with the capacity to not only experience but also articulate a plethora of intense emotions with the potential to absent and obliterate the other of the other that propels the hegemonic imagination into catatonic paralysis to acknowledge love as a valid category of emotionality of the marginalized. And thus only spaces available to the self of the other to claim sonic and emotional territories is through either an obscene or a hysterical performance. This hyperbolic rhetoric is then strategically evoked to deny an acknowledgement of their self within broader, structural discursive spaces.

References

Chandola, Tripta. 'Listening into Others: Moralising the Soundscapes in Delhi', *International Development Planning Review* 34.4 (2012): 391–408.

Faiz, Ahmed Faiz. 'Don't Ask Me for That Love Again', trans. Agha Shahid Ali, in *The Rebel's Silhouette: Selected Poems of Faiz Ahmed Faiz,* Amherst: Massachusetts UP, 1995, p. 5.

Pandey, Ponam Chandra. 'Sheila Dixit: Architect of Modern Delhi, Wanted to Develop It like Singapore', https://morningindia.in/sheila-dikshit-architect-of-modern-delhi-wanted-to-develop-it-like-singapore/'.

Zizek, Slavoj. 'Capitalism with Asian Values', *Al Jazeera*, 13 November 2011, https://www.aljazeera.com/programmes/talktojazeera/2011/10/2011102813360731764.html.

Zizek, Slavoj. *The Pervert's Guide to Cinema* (dir. Sophie Fiennes, 2006).

4. THE SUBALTERN AS A POLITICAL 'VOYEUR'?

But it also explained that the place in which they found themselves prevented from understanding this law of domination: they were dominated because they did not understand, and they did not understand because they were dominated. Which meant that all the efforts they made to struggle against domination were themselves blind, trapped by the dominant ideology, and that only scientist able to perceive the logic of this circle could put them out of their subjection.[1]

The Rally: Politics at the Crossroads

It is a fine February evening, in more than one ways. I am at the intersection, yet again. But not a researcher, not awaiting someone to come and accompany me into the slums. There is no scheduled interview. I am not a researcher in and at the moment. I am wading along with the jubilant, intense, some inebriated crowds to celebrate the sweeping, historic[2] victory for the Aam Aadmi Party (AAP) for the 6th Delhi legislative assembly elections. I share the chorus and chants for the party's victory, and rejoice in the announcements by the residents of the slums of Govindpuri that 'this is our victory', 'it is our *sarkar* [government]', and 'now it our responsibility to ensure that the government functions properly'.

The intersection cuts across the Navjeevan and Bhumhiheen camps, on either side, and meets with the road leading into its posher-distant-cousins of settlements, Alaknanda, Chittranjan Park and further into the Greater Kailash territory. Alongside the road, on whose either side's slumming spreads out on to it, also are a few middle-class apartment blocks, Kohinoor and Konark. This road encircles the Navjeevan and Nehru camps. A trip down this road is for many – uninitiated, apprehensive and vicariously inclined – the most intimate they get with the slums. Lacking open spaces within the slums, the encircling road becomes the arena for the residents of these slums: here, the children come out to play, wares are sold, people hang about, and markets spread out. This blatant, unapologetic slumming evokes diverse reactions from the middle-class neighbours.

A lady, residents of Kohinoor apartment and a professor of political science in a women's college in Delhi, articulated it thus:

> I moved into these apartments 20 years back, the price was affordable because of there were these slums. But we were assured that they will be soon relocated. I am all for the dignity of the poor, and they should get proper houses, but does it have to be here? Never in my entire stay here have I walked this road [leading to the intersec

---

1   Jacques Rancière, *Proletarian Nights: The Workers' Dream in Nineteenth-century France,* trans. John Durry, New York: Verso Trade, 2012, pp. 31-32.
2   Sanjay Kumar, 'Interpreting the AAP Win', *The Hindu,* 11 February 2015, https://www.thehindu.com/opinion/lead/interpreting-the-aap-win/article6879316.ece.

tion, passing along the slums]. And in the last few years what with the air-conditioning in the car, I don't even have to roll down the windows. That such a relief.

When further asked had she ever been into slums and how did she reckon the residents their lived like, 'hell no, I have never been inside. And I bet they live packed sardines'. Another residents of the Konark apartments, also a petitioner in the Public Interest Litigation (PIL) which sought to remove the slums, whilst maintaining that the presence of the slums accounted for the nuisance levels (including the embarrassment it caused to the middle-class residents) admitted that, 'the presence of the slums, and its people on the roads, lends to the vibrancy in this area and also makes it cheaper for us to live here'.

The intersection then is an important landmark for both the residents of the slums and its visitors. During my initial research days, when I still was not acquainted with the geography of the inner-lanes in the camps and moved into these spaces with certain apprehension, it was here at the intersection – *maachi market waali red light* [red light outside the fish market] – that I was met with by the residents. In that, the intersection and the road leading into the slums are the main arterial link with the world of slums and slumming for those variously interested: research, activism and politics.

During the time of the elections – Municipal, State, Centre – the road assumes a renewed importance. The politicians keen to seek the voter support base of the slums without really slumming it out – venturing into the lanes of slums – to reach out to the residents. The park, adjoining the communal toilets on the Bhumhiheen camp side of the road and Konark apartment block, becomes the congregation grounds during the times of election. And thus it was not a surprise the victory rally for Avaatar Singh rode along this road.

I begin with this event to enliven the vibrant, dense and contested political landscapes the urban poor inhabit. Here, to celebrate AAP's historic victory or undertaking a catharsis of this event as a metaphor is not the intent. The centre-stage is the marginalized space of the slums in the city, and the attention steadfastly remains on the urban poor – here, resident of the Govindpuri slums as representative of that constituency. The poor as an electoral constituency remain an enigma for most political parties, commentators and pundits during elections at any jurisdictional level – national, state, municipal: why do the poor cast their vote? And what determines their allegiance? Patronage? The 'freebies'? The communal evocations? The caste rhetoric?

The literature, as well as non-poor commonsensical reckoning, abound with interjections, inquisitions and 'explanations' towards this end: why do the poor vote? However poignant and penetrating these analyses there is not an absolute answer to this question, and each election result compels a new set of questions and interjections. And thus how could not I, as an ethnographer and interlocutor of the lives on the margins for more than a decade, not feel arrogant enough to undertake the task, to once and for, answer the overwhelming question, why do the poor vote?

The Ethnographer at the Crossroads: Interrogating the Politics of the Subaltern

Politics is omnipresent, and as an atheist, it is in the realm of the political, first and foremost and fundamentally, that I locate the consolidation of one's position within the broader, intersecting matrices of social, cultural, religious, amongst others. However as an ethnographer in/of marginalised spaces, in the initial years of my forays in GP, I found myself hesitant to openly discuss the politics. Indeed: the focus of the research being undertaken then did not foreground the political lives of the poor. However, I saw politics of caste, communal, regional and gendered strategically negotiated and performed within material realities of the slums, and in turn also lending to give its particular characteristic. But also, that these very lens informed the negotiations (and relationships) of the slum-dwellers with the middle-class residents and spaces which are, more often than not, predicated on the former being allowed to occupy only a subservient position. And thus in encounters as such, complex and complicated trajectories were revealed through which the political self – manifest in one's caste, communal, gender, regional identities – were calibrated, emphasized, negotiated and/or subverted.

Baby has been working in an upper-caste, Tamilian household for the last twenty years as a domestic worker. When she first went to seek the job, she was mistaken for a Hindu widow, given the fact that her body was not marked by the symbolisms which establish the marital status within the Hindu cosmos; namely, absence of a *mangalsutra, bindi* and bangles. Her employer, a chaste, upper-caste woman, not only felt kindly towards Baby, but also hired her at a rate higher than the going one at that time. During the last twenty years, the family has looked after Baby and her extended family with some consideration, often paying when health and education needs in the family demanded investment.

Baby has immense respect for the family. In recounting the chastity of the household, she talks with certain reverence about their highly meticulous abstemious practices, especially, in regards to food. They don't eat garlic, onions, definitely no meat of any kind. Considering Baby cooks for them as well, they are convinced she shares their food-beliefs. Often at this moment of telling, she cannot help being naughty to wonder aloud, 'how the hell did these people with so much money, intelligence and education, just could not figure it out all these years'. Baby's real name is Chandbibi, who in the neighbourhood is known for her delicious buffalo-meat kebabs.

Saroj, of whom I shall speak at length later, was a formidable politician in Navjeevan camp. She hailed from a lower-caste village in Uttar Pradesh, but since her early teens had been a resident of Delhi. One hot, summer afternoon I was visiting her house. We sat on the *charpoy* in the lane, outside her *jhuggi*.[3] Through the open door I could see a house sparsely and cleanly organised, the shades were drawn and from where I was in the heat, the coolness of it was very enticing. But no such invitation was extended, and thus we sat outside, smoking (she, *beedi* and I, rollies; and often sharing each other's).[4] An hour or so into the conversation I

---

3   A bedstead of woven webbing or hemp stretched on a wooden frame on four legs.
4   Beedi is a thin South Asian cigarette made of 0.2-0.3 grams of tobacco flake wrapped in a tendu

asked for water, the throat was parched, the heat overwhelming, I was losing focus. Saroj sent out orders, and I expected a cool tumbler of water to appear in matters of seconds, after all the open door and the fridge I could see were only a few meters away. But the wait continued, and so did my desperation. About 15 minutes later, one of her young sons hurried back with the 2-litre bottle of Coke and a couple of plastic glasses. They were filled, and I was offered one. I refused, 'I don't drink Coke, and I really, really do want water, can I please just have some?'. In my breaking voice, the desperation was evident.

Another nod from Saroj, and this time the water did materialise in matter of seconds. As I was guzzling the cool water, Saroj remarked, with a slight amusement in her voice, 'but people like you, even in the slums, don't drink water or eat at our place'. The upper-caste inscription which my body carries and hard as I try, I cannot scrub it off, and surely never announce, had led to the anxiousness which it was reckoned the ultimate metonym of capitalist-consumerist celebration, a Coke, could resolve. There are more than many such encounters and instances wherein gender, caste, communal, regional distances and differences are maintained: people of different caste will not drink or eat in other's houses; sometimes they will not enter into each other's houses, having the entire social interactions at the doorsteps for years, and certain lanes are avoided on account of certain kinds of people living in those camps in the slums.

The practices in the immediate, intimate realm, whether be of culinary preferences and prejudices; the nostalgic continuation of regional traditions, even if the region (the village) had not been visited in their living histories; the peculiar sense of fashion, which both determines the shades of decency but also 'daring' (as it is articulated especially by the youth to challenge the traditional norms); the shifts in notion of leisure and utilization of time, and the anxieties about it among other sections in GP, are not merely a manifestation of the interiority of cultural identities being produced and performed in public. But, I insist, that in these everyday, 'banal', *apolitical* activities, the political selves of the residents of GP is foregrounded – inadvertently, unwittingly, and also not without a certain deliberation – and is at once a response to the material realities of being a slum-dweller, but also the broader dialectical relationships within which these are produced.

And thus to return to my own position as an ethnographer, even though aware of these complexities, I found myself unable to take the bull by its horns, so to say, to ask the residents of GP, what is your political position? What informs it? Who do you vote for? What does casting a vote mean? What sense of entitlements, rights do you expect from the government you voted in? How do you respond when the candidates, parties you voted in do not respond to your needs? And in setting these specific questions as the only ones resolving the overwhelming question (oh, why do the poor vote?) I was committing a double whammy of a research (and by extension intellectual and political) faux pas in absenting from the banal, apolitical, everyday practices of the residents of GP their political selves.

Whilst it is tempting to attribute naiveté, lack of experience to this blind spot in discussing with the residents of GP their political selves and ecologies during the initial research period,

---

(Diospyrox melanoxylon) leaf and secured with coloured thread at both ends.

the personal hesitation and unease to discuss these concerns with the slum-dwellers (as a middle-class, educated, upper-caste individual) is in fact representative of the broader and fundamental anxiety to engage with the marginalised, the identified others. In this essay, it is the others in their political presences and performances that hold the centre-stage.

But, Why Should We Not Vote?

Between late 2012 and early 2013, following up to the Municipal Corporation of Delhi (MCD) elections, I focused on the manner in which residents of GP were mobilized by different parties and the role of local leaders within the slums. As a researcher, I was more confident and confrontational in my research agendas and questions than my initial forays into GP.

Amidst the intricate, incestuous and maze-like lanes of GP, the summer afternoons are like an older relative having a nap, around whom the children uncontainable enthusiasm have to tip-toe, lest they wake them and invite their wrath. The winter afternoons, on the contrary, are like a never-ending blanket that is being woven by the old and young alike, spread out on the terraces, squat in precious corners where the sun has not died, collectively adding to its warmth. The winter of 2012 was no different, except along with the tales and talks of the everyday, the know-how about the neighbours, and what was happening in another's house, the afternoons were enlivened by the announcements by representatives of different political parties contesting the MCD elections; meetings to 'get-to-know' the candidate; and the speculative conversations about each candidate's politics and their proposed agendas.

As researcher, with a very precise focus to resolve the identified question, the matter of the different political parties, their histories, the profile of the respective candidates, the presence in the slums and their past achievements and interventions in the slums was not a concern. But the conversations in GP were replete with these discussions, more specifically targeted towards a character appraisal of the candidates from different parties. The matter of their personal fortune; their businesses; love affairs; benevolence; corruption; the arm-strength each candidate could yield via the *goons* in each of the camps, among many other facets, were discussed to threadbare repetitions. From my *then* naive position of reckoning that the political of the poor is a distinct, separate entity – almost as an astral form floating over and above - from the *banality* of the everyday, I found these conversations tiring. But I persisted, perhaps awaiting a fate like Ali Baba's to chance upon the magic words, *open sesame,* to enter into this astral political realm, where ideologies, revolutions, utopia would be discussed, aspired and designed towards. I started to suspect everyone of Morgiana's deftness and cunning to keep me out.

One of the most common refrains, after a candidate had been reproached for an action or other, or indeed praised for a redeeming act, was that after the reverie of the elections, the meetings, the rallies, the fascination of freebies and the grand promises into the future were over, and one or the other candidate had won, the jhuggi-walahs will be left to their fate, to fend for themselves and nothing was going to change. This sentiment was particularly exaggerated one afternoon in Baby's lane.

When the candidate for whom Baby had been appointed to organise a 'meet and greet' gathering did not turn up, instead sending his deputy laden with samosas and ladoos for the attending women, the disappointment and resentment was particularly severe.[5] Baby's sister-in-law, and her neighbour, have a fraught relationship. Their loud recriminations of every aspect and each member of other's lives are commonplace, followed with much interest by the neighbours for its abusive, obscene and often simply jocular affects. Since the campaigning for the elections had started, and Baby had agreed to be an agent for the candidate in question, Baby and her sister-in-law's relationship had taken a turn for the worse. Baby did not leave any opportunity to exhibit and perform her newly acquired importance as an agent, proximity to the candidate and lending a suggestive air about herself that she indeed was in the know-how of what ensues in the inner circles. And thus when the much deliberated event was a no-show, and Baby publicly shamed, how could the sister-in-law miss the opportunity to rub salt into the wounds?

The sister-in-law is a garrulous woman of bulbous proportions. When she is present, she does not only defiantly occupy the space, she indeed becomes the space. Considering not only Baby, personally, but the jhuggi-walllahs, collectively, had been humiliated by the candidate's no-show, the sister-in-law could not hurl a direct assault at Baby, instead in the manner of the 'voice, the great deep cry of [the] Fog Horn shuddering through the rags of mist', pronounced, her heaving, heavy breasts sans the *dupatta* punctuating her performance, 'we have to cast our vote, irrespective of the fact that nothing ever happens. Our fate is worse than that of the whores. We will have to fuck someone, someone will fuck us, whether we get anything or not. Well, let's vote for Baby's candidate this time, after all she is one of ours'.[6]

An otherwise unapologetic woman, Baby had shrunk becoming the corner she was leaning against. Baby was my introduction to this lane in Navjeevan camp, and I had shared her enthusiasm in getting things in order for the now no-show 'meet and greet' (if only to understand the intricate workings of political mobilization in the slums). I realised that in such a pronouncement irrespective of whether the said candidate won or lost, it would be reckoned Baby's responsibility for 'nothing happening' for the next five years and for its residents to have been yet again *fucked over.*

I intervened, and with a certain sense of permission that I could. The strict researcher-researched, self-other boundaries were already blurring. I put out the overwhelming question, in almost a manner of reproach to those present for *ganging up* on baby, which I had been yet been waiting to ask at the opportune moment (perhaps when I had in fact chanced upon the *political* of the poor), 'so, why do you vote then?'.

The question drew exclusively attention to me, and a momentary stern silence was followed by a collective question (Baby had immediately shifted sides as well) in the manner spoken to the child who had missed the basics of multiplication: 'But, why should we *not* vote?'

---

5   Indian savoury and sweet snacks commonly served at communal gatherings.
6   Ray Bradbury, 'The Fog Horn', https://archive.org/stream/TheFogHorn/TheFogHorn.txt.

'Well', I continued, sensing that I finally have to tell the others what they don't know, all of you keep on insisting that nothing happens, that the politicians just use you for the vote, they treat you nicely only during the elections, and after that no development takes places, and things don't change, then why do you vote?'. The conversation, now almost combative continued, 'but still what has nothing happening, no improvement, corrupt politicians have to do with why we should not vote?'

The Theatre of the Political and the Subaltern as Unrealised Characters

Both Baby's sister-in-law's pronouncement, and the following assertion about casting the vote among the residents of GP, set in motion an intellectual paralysis and stasis. As if all this time, my engagement with the poor had been the Rorschach test being read upside down. Of course, why ought not the poor vote? And when they in fact do, why ought their choices be put under threadbare examination in regards to their motivations, awareness and engagement with not only the democratic ideas but also the working of the systems and processes? In the analyses to address the overwhelming question – why do the poor vote - the underlying sentiment is that the unique vibrancy of the Indian democratic system (though what makes it unique in fundamental, foundational ways is never really spelled out) and the society's inherent pluralistic and accommodative character extends *hope* to the poor, even though their predicament remains more or less unchanged.

The rationale for the poor's presence, unrelenting participation and performance identifies and emotional core responding to the hope candidate, the party's rhetoric and theatrical rallies can evoke. On the other hand, the tendency of the non-poor not to vote, especially at the most local jurisdictional level of Municipal elections, is accorded to an informed decision premised on disconnect, apathy and dismay with the democratic and political systems, processes and their functioning. Of course, I am presenting a rather simplistic condensation of these analyses, poignant and pertinent in their significant ways. And the intent is not to either critique or contribute to these discussions.

The seemingly straightforward question, 'So, why do you vote then?', were the magic words to open and enter the astral realm of political of the poor I had been desperately seeking for. The question of why, how, whom and towards what end the poor vote for were all at once rendered inconsequential if they were not teased out, approached and explored within the 'particular conception of the world'[7] the slum-dwellers, the poor, those on the margins, inhabit.

The 'particular conception of world' the poor, subaltern, marginalised have, lending them their peculiarity, is not a symptom of their poverty, marginalisation and subalternity. Instead, poverty itself is the condition of concrete historical, geographical social, political processes, grounded in the broader material realities and dialectical relationships. In order to engage with the political (here, with the intent to understand why and how the poor vote) of the poor, or for

---

7   Antonio Gramsci, 'The Intellectuals', in *Selections from the Prison Notebooks,* Q. Hoare and G. N. Smith (eds) New York: International Publishers, 1971, pp 3-23.

that matter any facet of their lives which cannot simply be viewed in isolation, these processes, their historicity – however contemporary – must be foregrounded to insist on the vulnerability, precarity and unliviability as these are the axis along with which the bodies of the poor in their corporeality and their presences in dispersed abstractions (political, cultural, social) exist.

Without such an undertaking, the subaltern, the poor, the marginalised (of each and every order, category and constant calibration) shall be stuck sharing the fate of Pirandello's unrealised characters.[8] And thus I abandoned the project of once and for all neatly resolving the overwhelming question, but I also did not assume the role of the elusive author who would finally allow the subaltern as *characters* to realise themselves. In short, I became one of the unrealised characters, whose predicament and politics was not determined by the *condition* of poverty, but was nevertheless in search of a narrative (and author) which could allow for an ethical cohabitation with the subalterns, the poor, and those on the margins.

Enter the Booth: Politics without the Politics

By late December, 2012, I extensively and intimately started following the everyday of two women leaders, both affiliated with the right-wing Bharatiya Janata Party (BJP), Saroj and Saiddya. The two of them made an unlikely pair. Saroj, who passed away in 2014, was a wiry, *beedi*-smoking, lower-caste woman. Saiddya hails from a middle-caste, Muslim family. As flamboyant as Saroj was, uninhibited in making her presence felt and claiming the space, Saiddya presents herself with a demure but definite sense of self. The pair of them piqued my interest as both of them representatives of their constituencies – lower-caste Hindu and Middle-caste Muslim, respectively – are traditionally reckoned to face the wrath (the intent of a disciplining agenda) of the right-wing Rashtriya Swamay Sevak (RSS) backed, BJP rhetoric.[9]

In the task assigned to mobilise women to vote for BJP in the upcoming elections, and as I followed them, there were no speeches, pamphlets to be distributed, either an excited celebration of BJP's candidate for councilour from the area or a hectic criticism of the opposing candidates. The matters that dealt with were everyday and commonplace. The difficulties, roadblocks, the families – either visiting or who were paid a visit - were encountering whilst dealing with the different state agencies, hospitals, police, legal matters, as also domestic disputes and the manner in which Saroj and Saiddya's interventions (owing to their proximity to the candidate) mitigated these issues.

Of the two Saiddya was the more restraint and demure one; as Saroj would jocularly comment, 'of the two us she is the respectable one, that is why she goes to the schools and hospitals, I am the bloody loudmouth that is why I have to deal with the goons, sister-fucker of men who beat up their wives and the cops'.

---

8   Luigi Pirandello, '*Six Characters in Search of an Author*', trans. John Linstrum, London: Methuen Drama, 1991.
9   I wrote journalistically about the MCD elections covering the profile of Saroj and Saiddya, Tripta Chandola, 'Slum in the time of politics', *Business Standard*, 21 January 2013, https://www.business-standard.com/article/beyond-business/slum-in-the-time-of-politics-112030400055_1.html.

And indeed Saroj, weighing less 50 Kgs, held her might with aplomb. It was spending afternoons with her that I had my lessons which refined and sophisticated my engagement with the politics of the subaltern. She would command – everything she did, even a smile, gravitas of a command – space, respect and attention, and indeed got it. And I felt highly privileged to be taken under her patronage. After wandering about the lanes, a *charpoy* would be summoned, almost blocking the passage (but who could dare to complain), Saroj would spread her meagre self on it and I would be the only one allowed to sit on it next to her. The first time two glasses, filled to the brim with undiluted, dark rum, were served to Saroj and I in the afternoon, I was slightly taken aback and my hesitation was very evident. After the initial performance of chastity, I used to smoke openly, and share drinks with friends in GP, but before this had never done publicly.

In her classic style, Saroj slapped her thighs, and laughed, 'listen, I know you are like me, we are just the same, I realised this the moment I saw you. You are very courageous, and you are not a cheat, but you are definitely not one those 'nice, virtuous' ones, so drink up'.

In re-listening to the conversations, recorded during those few months, whilst drinking rum, smoking, sharing the most intimate aspects of our lives, deliberating politics, I am at once overwhelmed with gratitude for the wealth of wisdom, lived experience and insights Saroj shared with me, and taken by a child-like fancy to click my heels and dance for her approval of me. In that, this essay is a tribute to Saroj's memory, the organic intellectual and philosopher par excellence. I learned my first practical lesson in the possibilities of ethical cohabitation, as a praxis and practice.

The conversations, long and winding, often without a specific beginning and usually with an abrupt end, were uninhibited, often confusing and combative. Whilst my debt to Saroj in my engagement with the political of the poor is surmount, the voices which guided me through were many and abounded in their multiplicities. Saroj, here, is evoked as a medium, a channel, and a mouthpiece of these voices, which all did not sing in unison, there were conflicts and tensions.

On one of these afternoons, I finally raised Saroj the question which had been bothering me since I was first introduced to Saiddya and her, 'we know how BJP talks about the lower-castes, the Muslims (the demolition of Babri Masjid had been a topic of discussion between us), then how do the two of you reconcile to being associated with a party which is so openly anti-Muslims and so upper-caste?'

> Of course, we are aware of that, but is it only BJP who is anti-Muslim and lower-caste? You tell me? Everyone is, consciously, subconsciously, if not anti-Muslim definitely thinking through jati (caste), even the Muslims. I won't even blame the upper-caste of being jaati-waadi (caste-biased), even I, the bloody bhangi (lower-caste) I am, I won't let my children marry someone lower than us in jaati. When it comes to the roj-maara ki baat (everyday practices), it does not matter, but when there are long-term consequences – like, marriages – I am not going to take the chance. I know it is wrong, I suffer it. People will sit at my feet, ask me for my help, let me sort

out their lives, but they will not drink water from my house. Of course I know it is wrong, but do I have the strength, courage and will to affect change, no. Perhaps if I were rich enough, I would be more khule-dimaag ki (open-minded, liberal).

What do you mean? Should you of all the people not be standing up, fighting against everything that is wrong? What they say, about the lower-castes, the jhuggi-wallahs?

Beta (My child; even though Saroi and I were spared of only a few years in age, she commanded the space of a wizened person, and always referred to me as Beta, a term of endearment I was only glad to be showered with), what makes you think I have not been fighting my life? I had to sort out my husband, he was bloody abusive, older to me by almost 15 years and got married to me when I was about 15. Now he is hurled up in that little room, bastard scared to come out, but he beat me up. I worked in people's houses, at construction sites, I was here in the jhuggi's when it was a big, bloody swamp. What makes you think I have not been fighting my whole life?.

'Yes, I get it, the life in the jhuggi's was difficult and you have managed so much, you command so much respect, and do much for the people, but you still are associated with the BJP. They are anti- lower-caste, women, Muslims. Why?'.

Garibi se badi koi sachai nahi hoti (There is no bigger truth than poverty). You think I will stand for anyone hurting Saiddya or any Muslim family here, of course no. That time has not come here, and I will not stand for that kind of injustice and violence against anyone. But then I also do not shy from thrashing the men (and their mothers) who harass their wives, daughter-in-laws, is that OK then? BJP is in charge of the municipality, and their people at the local level listen to me, give me izzat (respect), get my work done, get me the izzat I get here. That will do for me until the time for a decision comes. If I had the monies, if I did not have to sit at the feet of the BJP people for years like the people you see here sitting, I would have had the luxury of taking sides more clearly. Garibi bhi ek dharam hota hai, beta [Poverty becomes a religion of sorts, my child].

But what about the State elections, the general elections, what is your role in those elections? Do you still remain unaffected by what each party candidate is saying?

Dekho bhai, aisa hai, [See, this is how it is], when there are the "big" elections, then we have to go, then we do take women for rallies, they get blankets, shawls, it is a bit like a picnic. That is a different game, we [as party workers] don't have much to do with it. But when the MCD elections happen, they have to come here, when the matter of concern is "here", where else will they hold the rally. Now bloody hell tell me, how many candidates want to roam the lanes of the slums, so we get their work done'.

During these winter afternoons in late 2012- early 2013, I found myself intensely engaged in the density of the everyday life of the slum-dwellers, especially the political. In these discussions I had anticipated an animated discussion about the recently concluded India Against Corruption[10] (IAC) movement (April 2011-November 2012) which had led to the emergence of a new political party, Aam Aadmi Party (AAP) from within the section of protesting leaders.[11]

'Did you organise people, especially the women, to go to Jantar Mantar[12], to take part in the protests against the whole corruption prevalent in the country?'.In asking this question, I retrospectively realise my folly to reckon that the *poor* had naturally allied to the cause; even though in my distant analyses of the movement (from Singapore) I had presented a highly critical evaluation of it in regards to the participation of the middle-classes and the framing of corruption within a cleanliness discourse.

> Of course, it was everywhere, on the TV, news, and we did follow it closely. The Gandhi-jaisa aadmi (reference to Anna Hazare) was admirable, to sit there, not eating, fighting for the cause of corruption. But, firstly, none of the political parties came here to "round us" up in the buses, with promises of blankets or lunches, as is usually the case. How the hell are we supposed to go all the way, paying for the fare, missing out on the work on our own, except when we are taken? But also, samaaj mein nahin aaya ki matlab kya tha [but we did not quite understand the meaning of the whole protest]. Bilkul, ghuskori kharab hai, galat cheez hai [yes, giving bribes is a wrong thing], but you tell me, how do we survive without giving guss [bribe]? Matlab, the thula [colloquial term to refer to the cops] who asks for a 100 here and there, is he wrong? Do you know what he earns? He is one of us, we don't think of it as ghus.

Then Saroj went to explain and implicate herself in the *danda of gusskori* [the business of bribing, and thus by that extension being corrupt].

> Beta, let me tell you this. There was this woman in the lane, newly married and had altercations with her husband and in-laws. She was a very feisty woman, I liked her for that, but she was also very quick of temper. I tried to talk her through, I even said, if she wants to leave the husband and her marital home, I will sort it out. But one day, god knows on what whim, she left her child out in the lane, closed the door and set herself to fire, leaving a message on her phone that her in-laws were setting her to fire. I know that wasn't true. I was here. The husband and the mother-in-law were

---

10 Wikipedia Contributors, 'India Against Corruption', https://en.wikipedia.org/wiki/India_Against_Corruption, accessed 4 April 2020.
11 In these journalistic articles I reported on the last day of the IAC's protest at Jantar Mantar here: https://www.business-standard.com/article/beyond-business/getting-a-rise-112080500044_1.html; and here: https://countercurrents.org/chandola090812.htm.
12 Jantar Mantar is an astronomical historical momument in Delhi. It was a prominent site for holding protests on which following National Green Tribunal ordinance was shut down in 2018. Now prior permissions are required to hold protests here, Aniruddha Ghosal, 'End of a protest: The story of Jantar Mantar as a protest site began in 1993', *Indian Express*, 26 June 26 2018, https://indianexpress.com/article/india/jantar-mantar-protests-ngt-end-of-a-protest-2011-lokpal-agitation-anna-hazare-4922867/

away. I had to palm the investigating thulas with money to not regard phone messages, and other negotiations. Don't get me wrong, I am not saying that the husband and his mother were saintly, but they did not kill the girl. At best they could be accused of harassment, but murder. That wasn't fair. And yes for the running along, pulling the strings, negotiating with the cops and lawyers and finally letting them off with a case of harassment but not murder, I charged 10,000. Of this I paid the amounts to the cops, etc., but also kept almost half as my fee. I do not see this as corruption, it is a service I am providing. The poor thulas they know everything, but have such little powers, and do you know what they earn for the work they do? I am supporting them too. What is wrong with that? How else would they got justice?

In the framing of the corruption as a social malice, the IAC movement specifically insisted on the role of the people who *give* bribes in perpetuating corruption, highlighting their immorality in this complicity. Here, then the voices intervened questioning their own participation? Is it corrupt to give money to get the child into school? To get an identity card made? What do they mean by black money, for us money is like magic, it disappears as soon we lay eyes on it, one of the congregating woman jocularly remarked. Of course, everyone agreed.

With the Municipal Corporation of Delhi elections only a few weeks away, I raised questions not about why they vote in abstraction, but the grounded practices of it: who they will vote for? Whose campaign seemed effective? Which candidate? In raising these questions, I was hoping to arrive at the epistemological, reflexive processes through which 'decisions' are made, and the manner in agency and structure were negotiated in a Bourdieu an sense.

The responses at the most fundamental level seemed frivolous to me: 'we vote because we can'. That was the most common refrain, the much touted celebration of the practice of the poor voting as exercising their right was not asserted as vehemently as I had read/expected. Of course, in my naïveté then I failed to identify the capacity to act (in the action of casting a vote) in itself an event of assertion of agency. One man, a first-time voter in the coming elections, announced, 'I will be voting for Congress'. *Who is the candidate?* 'I don't know the candidate, the family has been voting for Congress ever since, and how can we betray the legacy of Mahatma Gandhi!'. *I don't understand,* I said. 'Well, they are descendants of Mahatma Gandhi, Indira was his daughter'. *Well,* I interjected, *that wasn't the case. Indira Gandhi was Nehru's daughter, she was married to a man whose last name was the same as Gandhi.* 'She was a Gandhi, right, and of Congress, *hum tho haat ko denge* [we will vote for the 'hand', the Congress party's symbol]'.

'*Aap kisko vote dete ho?' (wh*om do vote for?), I was under the inquisition and scrutiny of those, including Saroj, whose political motivations I had until then putting under microscopic examination. I fumbled, I was embarrassed until then (2012) I had not cast my vote in *any* of the elections in the country – General, State and Municipal. In fact, I didn't even have a voter's identification to be eligible to cast the vote. I told them as much. 'So, you cannot vote. *Yeh tho bahut chutiyapa hai* [this is such a bummer]. Saroj mausi (an aunt – mother's sister, and as she was referred to by one and all) can get you made one, you know'. Saroj nodded, and added, 'no charge for you'. The *act* of not casting the vote in fact cast a shadow of doubt on my politics as event, *'tho koi party koh support kaise karte ho?' (*so, how do you show your support to any party?)'.

Political being the only terrain in and through which I negotiated my own identity, I feel ambushed. I took on to give a brief history of my political engagement with the left, my involvement with All India Students Association (student wing of the Communist Party of India (Marxist–Leninist) Liberation) as student at Jawaharlal Nehru University, the commitment to the agenda of the left, workers revolutions, instilling revolutionary consciousness, the concerns with class struggles, against caste and communal tendencies, etc. They gave me a patient hearing, until Saroj interrupted rather irritably, '*Beta,* this party, whichever it is, seems the one we should be aligning with, right? They work for us, but pray tell me one thing, why haven't we heard of them before this? Why haven't any of their representatives come to us? Where are they?'.

I was silenced in humility. The 'organic intellectual' had made a pronouncement resounding the anxieties of Ranciere's cited earlier. And thus we returned to the act of voting – not as a metaphor, or the burdens of its memory – but as an event in an asserting agency.

Yet again, evoking Saroj as the mouthpiece, the loudspeaker, the channel, the medium, for the multitudinous and multiplicities of the *voices*,

> Hum vote karte hain, koi ki kar saakte hai [We vote because we can]. A while back you were asking about people selling their votes, and even if they have committed to voting for someone, got the money, why don't they vote for someone else? Yahan pe kutch maslee hain [there are a few issues here], how many things do you think we have we can sell and ask the price we want, negotiate? Vote is a thing, which can be sold, and better still we don't lose the thing, it comes to us in another five years, at least thrice. Unlike house, jewelry we have to sell. But that does not mean, everyone sells their vote, or can simply be incited by daru [alcohol]. There is something called ethical practice of transaction, here most transactions are based on trust, and so when we do say, we will take the money and vote for you, we are honouring that trust and transaction. When we enter the booth, even though we go together in groups and usually if the party is taking us, there will be festivities, everyone is on their own. They are thinking for themselves, it could be the money they have taken, the kindness a candidate had shown, or some work they had done, or perhaps not done. You ask repeatedly, why support BJP as a Muslim? Why vote for that candidate when he has a case pending? Why not vote for the party which has said they will do something about the slum-dwellers? But, beta, when we enter the booth, anyone of us, we are not only just jhuggi-walahs, or woman, or Muslim, or bhangi (lower-caste), or garib (poor), yes, we are all of that, but in the booth, we are also absolutely alone, who is to say, eh?

A young, pretty lady, a domestic-worker by profession, an attentive audience to these conversations, one of the afternoons, amused by the fervour of the discussions, breaking the decorum of interrupting Saroj (an act which otherwise invited severe reprimand from her, had it not been for the pretty lady's youthful exuberance and infectious excitement), 'When the voter registration comes which also has a photo, it feels really nice. Taking that slip to the booth is so much fun, and when I go in I press whichever button fancies me'.

Saroj smiled at her indulgently, and said to her, '*Beta*, this time, when we are going to the booth, you come with us, we will have even more fun'.

The Subaltern as Political Voyeur

The discussions about the politics of the poor in Govindpuri in 2012-2013 highlighted the resonances of the India Against Corruption movement (IAC) of 2011 and the Municipal Corporation of Delhi (MCD) 201s amongst its residents. In 2015, I also closely followed the involvement of the residents with the Delhi Legislative Assembly elections. Each of these events as they unfolded within the ecology of Govindpuri are deserving undertakings on their own, and a reading of these three political moments in conjunctions only lends to further nuanced reading (and thus revealing) of the 'organic, political' selves of its residents.

The imagined, projected call of a clean, corruption free India did not hold much resonance here. It was, as discussed through the narratives, not on account of the idea of corruption, and thus its absences, as incomprehensible, but the linear and collapsible identification of the corrupt with immorality, greed and to a far-fetched extent being anti-national. The fact of everyday lives of living on the margins compels negotiating with the state, its authorities and the mainstream through a network of tacit arrangements and exchanges, more often than not, humiliating and disenfranchising for the poor. Do they want to continually experience it? If they had a choice, would they still do it, were the rhetorical questions raised to be answered in the negative. Of course not. Would they not want services, goods and their rightful demands to be fulfilled without succumbing to these tactics? Of course yes. But what to do? Without these corrupt practices, left to their own devices by the State, they would perish.

In their rejection of the so-reckoned 'second struggle for freedom', the slum-dwellers reveal with an astute sensibility a sociological-political reality, which a lot of commentators and enthusiast of the movement sustained an amnesia about in its celebration, that corruption is a structural and systemic concern, its practices unfolding in the social realm (caste being its pivotal and obscenest manifestation) is far more detrimental than the financial exchanges. In fact, the latter relies on the former to exact and exaggerate its benefits.

In the immediate political ecology of the MCD 2013, elections, epitomised in the two women, Saidyya and Saroj, the arbiters of political agendas of the parties within the slums, reveal political sensibilities, vocabularies and capacities to negotiate the concerns of caste, gender, amongst others categories, towards a census and/or conflict. These negotiations are poignantly revealing in more ways than one: they highlight that the slums, and its residents, are not a homogenised whole, and that to achieve the desired political end an *insider* is indeed needed as the ploy of 'empty' promises and incentives is just not enough.

During the celebrations of the Delhi Assembly Elections results on 10 February 2015, the repeated insistence of the party's victory being theirs and the responsibility to ensure good governance shared by them with the elected members, the residents of GP at once emphasized the importance of their participation in AAP's success and claimed ongoing partnership with the state. Along with these insistences the residents reiterated that they had exercised this political mandate out of their own will, and that they had not succumbed to either incentives, coercions or considerations of identity politics (all implicated in other political rallies that I have observed) to bring to fruition the '*andolan*', movement, which AAP as a party had set out to accomplish by ensuring their sweeping victory in the Delhi elections 2015. In this political performance, the residents' revealed a highly matured and assured political self.

And here, I return to the thought with which I started the essay. And to the misplaced reckoning of the 'scientist', the lot of which I am often associated with and the association I vehemently oppose, that the dominated do not in fact understand the laws and logic of domination. It is a matter of deliberation to not allow the task of meaning-making of the 'self' to the subaltern as it then allows to obliterate the 'self' of the subaltern in its corporeality, only to be engaged in its abstractions. As evidenced through the narratives here, the subaltern is not only aware of the rules of the games of domination but also knows how to subvert and disrupt it, even though only slightly and, more often than not without, any substantial impact.

In fact, through the performance of political 'naivety' – *what do we know? What can we do?* – expected of them, the slum-dwellers demonstrate an astute awareness of the experience of poverty they are expected to perform, especially when encountering State agents, civil society workers and politicians, to accrue financial assistance, subsidies and other benefits. The performance to accrue immediate and extended 'benefits' is often confused with their compromised and absent political core, a reckoning which the grounded experiences of the political of the poor puncture.

In each of these three events, India Against Corruption 2011, as *rejection* to the movement's premise; the engagement with the MCD elections 2012, *claiming stakes*; and in the celebration towards the victory of AAP in Delhi Assembly elections as an event of *political participation and collaboration*, the slum-dwellers exhibit a highly mature engagement with the political landscape of the present in its imagined, immediate and extended ecologies.

Even though these three events highlight the 'organic, political' self of the slum-dwellers, as a representative constituency of the subaltern, the tapestry of being and becoming it unfolds within is revealing of a finer, intricately woven, sometimes fragile, designs. The slum-dweller, she, is at once astute and street-smart; she knows what she wants, but sometimes is lead ashtray; she gives in to her desires with a reckless ferocity, but she also holds on to her grounds, when she wants, putting at stake her most intense desires and immediate needs. If she knows the lanes of the slums, reckoned dreaded and dark by those who have never ventured into, like a sorcerer, she is not lacking in the knowledge, desire and imagination of the highways and super-highways out there. In short, she is an argumentative, intuitive, emotional, not without the intent of self-interest, inquisitive, imaginative, deliberative whole.

Poverty is a compelling and difficult text to read, and its committed readers few and far between. In engaging with the politics of the poor, it is easier to reckon, identify the political as existing in isolation, a seductive temptation so as not to concern oneself with the messiness of the processes, structures, systems which produce and systematically sustain poverty. Moreover, in engaging with the political of the poor, detached from their diverse sensibilities and sentimentalities, it becomes convenient and commonplace to expect the commitment of the poor to the predicament of poverty to violent, loyalties; such that, the poor then can be (and are allowed) only to be poor, devoid of emotions, aspirations and desires. However: Poverty does not happen in isolation, and nor does politics and poetics. The subaltern knows, lives and experiences it well.

The State and the hegemonic narratives, deliberately deny the poor the capacity to imagine, inquire and emote. And if it is in fact extended to them, it is only within the terms of excesses, threatening to tear the seams of the social fabric. And in this identification, as definite structural and systemic tactics, the poor, the marginalised, the disenfranchised, the subaltern, is recognised as an 'imbecile', lacking a core, logic and sense of 'self'. The plans and policies that are thus envisaged for this constituency not only absent their presences – as they do not know they are present – but are always predicated on the project of disciplining them towards an evolutionary agenda of incorporating them into the normative social, cultural, political order.

And it is within this schematic that I evoke the imagery of the subaltern as a 'voyeur', seeking intellectual, theoretical and real permissions for the subaltern to be voyeuristic. The State engages with the subaltern as *voyeur* in its aimless and senseless wanderings, which it then translates as necessitating the agenda of containing, silencing and disciplining the subaltern. However, the subaltern as a *voyeur* in its second avatar is possessed of imaginations, inquisitions and emotions to draw out its own maps, where its coordinates are steadfastly located (and thus allowing it capacities to shift back, forth and sideways), and these mappings are populated with many of its selves, spaces, and histories.

Thus, in celebrating the voyeurism *of the subaltern*, the intent is to recognise and engage with the 'organic, political' self of the subaltern, with all the misconceptions, misgivings and multiplicities she possesses. This is not merely an ambitious, well-intentioned, romantic agenda; without allowing for the imaginations, inquisitions and emotions of the subaltern, the project of the realisation of a truly democratic, ethical, equitable and just social, cultural and political order remains and shall so, a distant dream.

References

Bradbury, Ray. 'The Fog Horn', https://archive.org/stream/TheFogHorn/TheFogHorn.txt.

Gramsci, Antonio. 'The Intellectuals', in *Selections from the Prison Notebooks,* Q. Hoare and G. N. Smith (eds) New York: International Publishers, 1971, pp. 3-23.

Kumar, Sanjay. 'Interpreting the AAP Win', *The Hindu,* 11 February 2015, https://www.thehindu.com/opinion/lead/interpreting-the-aap-win/article6879316.ece.

Pirandello, Luigo. *'Six Characters in Search of an Author'*, trans. John Linstrum, London: Methuen Drama, 1991.

Rancière, Jacques. *Proletarian Nights: The Workers' Dream in Nineteenth-century France*, trans. John Durry, New York: Verso Trade, 2012, pp. 31-32.

Chandola, Tripta. 'Slum in the Time of Politics', *Business Standard*, 21 January 2013, https://www.business-standard.com/article/beyond-business/slum-in-the-time-of-politics-112030400055_1.html.

Chandola, Tripta. 'Getting a Rise', *Business Standard*, 25 January 2013, https://www.business-standard.com/article/beyond-business/getting-a-rise-112080500044_1.html.

Wikipedia Contributors, 'India Against Corruption', https://en.wikipedia.org/wiki/India_Against_Corruption, accessed 4 April 2020.

5. COLLABORATIVE LISTENING: ON PRODUCING A RADIO DOCUMENTARY IN THE GOVINDPURI SLUMS

With Tom Rice[1]

It was almost midnight when we started our sojourns. We, Tom and I, were going to attend a jagran – a night long event in celebration of one god or another, of the many in the Hindu pantheon, marked by musical and theatrical performances – being held n the park opposite Navjeevan camp and adjacent to Bhumhiheen camp. Jagrans, in any context, are rarely just about evoking the gods; they are about communities coming together and such. In the Govindpuri jhuggis, there significance is elevated on account of several factors. The residents of the three camps - owing to the lack of space and resources - find it difficult to organise such collective events. The jagran, which Tom and I were going to attend, was being sponsored by a prominent politician - Chandraprakash - and not entirely out of altruistic reasons. In hosting and sponsoring such events, he meant to accrue political mileage by allowing for collective cultural indulgence which are few and far between in the jhuggis. This brief background is essential to understand what follows thereafter.

Even though the lane cutting into Bhumhiheen camp to approach the park is not very narrow, the sea of humanity that had descended upon the space made it feel just inches wide. Tom, tallish and white, stood out, and as we were trying to hurdle our way through this densely packed human layering, we encountered drunk young men, who were keen to mark their territory by hurling obscenities and cackling at their performance, especially when it evoked a reaction in the crowds, namely the women. The women were trying to make their way in too, there were young girls - either in groups or accompanied by an elder - equally keen to indulge in the rare occasion of collective, cultural event. However, the space, the experience and performances were essentially masculine in nature.

Tom, who had arrived in Delhi for the first time only hours back, was overwhelmed. And not surprisingly; I did not let it be known then, but even I was. He insisted we go back, and we did. At the corner of the intersection, we stood, his sense of unease apparent. I rolled a smoke, whilst Tom regained his breath. We agreed to make our way back into the park; in retrospect, I am not sure whether Tom remained overwhelmed, but as soon as the tents acting as makeshift entrances into the park opened up, he was at his sonic best: listening, recording, catching sounds as they were hurling about. The expansiveness of the park, replete with all the props for the theatrical night to follow - a stage, children, men and women dressed in the attire of different gods and bright lighting - was a relief; even to me.

---

1 Tom Rice is a Senior Lecturer (Anthropology) at the University of Exeter, http://socialsciences.exeter.ac.uk/sociology/staff/tomrice/. Tom Rice, 'Govindpuri Sounds', *BBC*, https://www.bbc.co.uk/programmes/p02hm1rx. The documentary was commissioned by BBC for its The Documentary program and was aired on 2 February 2015. More information here: https://ore.exeter.ac.uk/repository/bitstream/handle/10871/34775/Tom%20Rice%20Govindpuri%20Sound%20REF%20document.pdf?sequence=4&isAllowed=y.

And thus wetting his ears in this deep end Govindpuir jhuggis soundscapes, we set out over the period of next three weeks to record for the BBC radio documentary on Govindpuri Sounds.

The next three-weeks were a sonic indulgence at its loudest. Tom soon acquired a fan-following among the residents of particularly Navjeevan camp, especially the children. The association being immediately established on account of the Tom-Jerry cartoon, and Tom was often referred to as Tom Tom. During the three-weeks, we followed the lives of women who had gone through difficult circumstances; we listened into women filling water; we arrived early in the morning to listen into the jhuggis wake up; we often stayed late nights.

It was an exhilarating experience for me; even though I realised how demonic my laugh is when Tom would playback the day's recording. This was on several accounts. It was the first time that I sharing the ears, so to say, with someone else such that we listened into similar notes and modulations; this practice of collaborative, shared listening which at once validated my own listening but also compelled me to tune into someone else's as well. Here, a point needs to be made. I did share listenings with the residents of the jhuggis, especially the women. By the time of recording the documentary, almost a decade and so after my initial entries into Govindpuri, we had arrived at our own 'collaborative' practice of listening. By now, I was so tuned into Govindpuri that I had almost instinctively learned how to 'block' certain sonic manifestations.

The manner in which the lived, almost everyday collaborative listening with the residents of Govindpuri was different from the experiences of sharing the ears, so to say, with Tom was on account of the fact that he was as much an outsider as one can be. We had first met in the quietness of Cambridge where we discussed listening, soundscapes and strange fictions. For me, the collaborative listening with Tom then was a validation of sorts of my own 'ears' in that sense. I had pursued my doctoral research in another staid, quietness, that of Brisbane. Though I did not live in Brisbane for prolonged durations whilst conducting the research, I spent almost nine months at a stretch there to finish writing my thesis. The exhausted silence of the city had a very disquieting impact on me. Away from the multiplicities of sonic manifestations of not only Govindpuri, but also the city of Delhi, I would often find myself wondering and worrying whether what I was not 'making up' the listenings. This is not only a mere admission of insecurity in oneself (though as a third-world academic one's work is rarely taken seriously if not validated by one or another 'first world' scholars), but is symptomatic of more structural and systemic concerns of production of knowledge when it is relying on modes outside of the established 'verifiable, legible, visual' practices.

The collaborative listening, which the recording towards the documentary compelled, thus only lend to further tuning my ears into the considerations of soundscapes as a valid social, cultural, political artefact, particularly for those on the margins? As there are teaching modules to acquaint those eager with nuances of visual cultures, could there be a similar possibility with soundscapes or aural practices? In what ways to think about listening not only as a matter of auditory compulsion or even 'engaged hearing' but perhaps 'privileged hearing'? In what ways to understand, decode, call out these 'privileges'? Can we think about listening as a valid, without concerning ourselves with its verifiability or not, methodological undertaking? In what ways then do we refine that reckoning?

Tripta Chandola (TC): I listened into the everyday of the slums in Govindpuri. Retrospectively, it is a tempting proposition to posit this 'intent' as an intellectually driven project but the fact of the matter is that it was an purely instinctive, responding to an impulse -political, poetic, intellectual and theoretical - to distance myself from the manner in which 'slums', its residents were framed in both academic and mainstream discourse. I listened, not because I was either all too familiar with the rich, interdisciplinary theoretical, intellectual contributions to sensorial anthropology, sound studies or even the explosive potential, possibilities which soundscapes allow to engage with the lives, histories and testimonies especially of those on the margins, outside the literate, hegemonic space.

Tom Rice (TR): Yes, I think this an interesting point about the listening being instinctive. I had never been sure when reading your work why you started listening to Govindpuri in the first place, but I think in the end that probably the soundscape made an impression on you, and drew attention to itself (there is a real sense on which sound has an agency of its own in this respect, and theory from STS on non-human agency can be applied to sound quite successfully I think). After the sound environment has made itself noticed, the more intellectual attention, by which I mean 'deliberate thought about sound and reading relevant literature from the social sciences', perhaps began to take over in your thought process. I remember you saying that you do not think of yourself as a particularly auditory person, which is interesting. Clearly the sounds of Govindpuri were rich, intriguing and powerful enough to make you devote a very great deal of time and energy to their study (talk about possessing agency!). I myself have always had an interest in sound. I don't know exactly where this came from, but by the time I went to university I knew I wanted to work in radio and to document life and explore ideas in a sonic medium. In the final year of a degree in Social Anthropology I was given the opportunity to write a dissertation on a subject entirely of my own choosing, I decided that I would write about the radio station at the Edinburgh Royal Infirmary (situated very close to Edinburgh University and to the flat where I was living at the time). I was working as a volunteer there in order to try to accumulate skills and experience in radio with the aim of applying for a job in radio later on. I was also working in student and community radio around then. My initial intention for the dissertation had been to look at the way the DJ's on the hospital radio station used music and techniques of speech to try to create a sense of unity among patients, a sort of imagined community of people brought together temporarily in the hospital because of ill health. One of my jobs at the station, which was called Red Dot Radio, was to go around the wards and to gather music requests from the patients which would be played on the evening's programme. However, many of the patients to whom I spoke drew attention to the sonic environment of the ward and the generally negative ways in which it affected them - preventing them from sleeping, waking them early, provoking feelings of irritation, disgust, exposure, embarrassment and so on. They used the hospital radio as a way of temporarily escaping this unpleasant sound environment. I say temporarily escaping because the fact that they were hospitalised meant that they were unable to escape it fully until they were discharged. They were to a large extent a captive audience, and had little real choice but to exist within the hospital and its soundscape. It was only really at this point, and through the instruction and direction of the patients themselves, that I began to listen to the sound environment of the hospital, noticing its qualities and being surprised by their variety and intensity. This was the start of the project that began with the dissertation and culminated in my monograph which you mention - Hearing and the Hospital. But ever since that listening with patients I have been drawn to researching sonically rich and intense environments.

TC: I listened, intently and attentively, first on the account that I as an ethnographer had to 'mute' my own position-premised hearings into the jhuggis. This 'tuning of the ear', so to say, opened up journeys and experiences of the self and the space of jhuggis as I had never heard in the academic, mainstream discourse, at least not so loudly and definitely not so assertively. Of the aspirations, romances, heartbreaks, deceit, negotiations, politics beyond the narratives of 'lacks, deprivations, misery and marginality'. I was at once seduced and humbled. And following from this, I listened, even more intently, because it was this un-listened present, past and futures of and from the jhuggis which I wanted to insist on.

TR: I think that one thing an ethnographic approach does, or rather, one thing one is aiming to achieve using an ethnographic approach, is to educate oneself as to the way in which others attach meaning or importance to particular sounds in their day to day environment. One then hopes to relay something of that way of listening - be it in a written text, radio programme, audio essay - whatever the medium. It's not so much about muting one's own hearings in my experience, but about changing the way one hears and documenting that change. That was what Govindpuri Sound was about I would say. Describing the sound environment but also the way that people live in relation to it.

That expression 'tuning the ear' is interesting. One can certainly become more knowledgeable skillful at listening to an environment. One can notice sounds and qualities of sound one didn't before, and one can become better able to judge the kinds of feelings and associations a sound might evoke in a listener or group of listeners. I guess it's important from my point of view not to think about 'the ear' in a reductive way, but to recognise that 'the ear' also involves the integrated brain/mind/body and is bound up with the position one occupies in social and geographical space, with postures, technologies (most obviously the microphone in *Govindpuri Sound*), attention, mood and so on.

I certainly felt while we were making Govindpuri Sound, that, as you say, what one heard was at odds with the mainstream academic and public discourse surrounding the slums. Almost continually there were snatches of romantically charged music drifting out of houses, and people listening and singing along to these. When they saw us walking around with a microphone many people were understandably curious. Often they wanted to sing into the microphone and and be recorded, usually singing romantic or wistful songs. As I say in the programme, people we met were often more ready to sing than be interviewed. There could be interesting political implications to this observation. There seemed to be a convention that the microphone should elicit performance rather than comment. Perhaps this would have applied less to people who understood themselves to occupy a higher place in the social hierarchy and who possessed different levels of education, confidence in the value of their own opinions and so on, though I am speculating here. Negotiations and arguments were also noticeable too: there was a lot of back and forth, sometimes at high energy and volume levels, though didn't understand the subject matter here so can't comment as to what it was really about. I was quite surprised by how much laughter I heard, though again, I'm can't be sure I understood the subtleties of the spirit in which people were laughing. I got the laughter, but I'm not certain I got 'the joke'.

I relate to what you are saying about aspects of the slum experience not being listened to. Listening in this sense - as a kind of focused and empathetic engagement - is very valuable where it has not been done before and where it occupies a space that has been neglected by more established modes and techniques of attention and attending.

TC: I listened because within this ontological engagement with the residents of Govindpuri, I was able to present their lives, sense of spaces, self, negotiations as articulated and claimed by themselves within their own grammar and using their vocabularies. I was allowed possibilities to engage with the everyday of the jhuggis besides/alongside the logic or experiences of poverty, deprivation and marginalities (even though not losing sight of it in a broader, structural sense). The poverty, the deprivations, the limited infrastructural availabilities were not a secret that had to be unraveled. These are obscenely obvious, and from my political, intellectual position, it was a bloody affrontation to the intelligence of the residents to ask them to spell it out. And to overlook the need to 'verify', 'document' and 'validate' these experiences of the marginalities - the seduction of triangulation - which captures the imagination of so many, especially when engaging with the lives of the poor.

TR: Yes, I don't disagree with anything you have said in the paragraph above. It may not be appropriate for me to say this in this piece, but I suppose I tend to encourage people to be realistic about their claims. It's not as if you spoke to all the slum residents (this would be impracticable) and I don't think you are claiming to represent all of them. Rather during a very long period of being a researcher in GP on a range of projects, establishing close and long-lasting friendships with particular people there, and speaking to a great many other slum residents over time in a wide variety of contexts, you have developed a detailed and nuanced understanding of life in GP, one which is not present in the impersonal and generalising discourses used by researchers in Development and Urban Studies, for instance. I am just riffing here...

TC: In thinking through this exchange, I read your book - *Hearing and the Hospital* - again. I am not sure in what frame or from what vantage point I was engaging with your research earlier, but in this re-reading (whilst thinking about re-listening into Govindpuri), I can draw very definite parallels to my own research.

The position of the patient in your research - particularly those in post-operative and intensive care units - immobile and incapacitated to give their testimonies of their state of well-being within a particular knowledge praxis (here, medical sciences) nevertheless do not cease to be, so to say, asserting themselves through their 'sonic bodies'. And in the attentive 'sethoscopic listening' - I will return to the this conceptual framing, which in the moment I am absolutely titalted and excited by - which these 'sonic bodies' demanded, you also locate/identify significant developments in medical sciences, technologies, modalities in making meaning itself.

TR: Yes, again I don't disagree with anything you say in the paragraph above. I guess I'm not sure how to relate it back to GP at this point. I guess we need to remember too that the readers are unlikely to have come across Hearing and the Hospital or to know what is in it.

For me, the position of the patient and the residents of the jhuggis share a certain incapacitated predicament. Is that too much of stretch? In both instances, the 'body' in question lacks a definite agency to penetrate the very hegemonic, discursive spaces and knowledge practices which in return locates/ensures its 'well being': in the case of the patients within the historiography of medical sciences itself and for the residents of 'slums' within the legal, development, urban planning discourse. However the 'sethoscopic listening' which extends palpability, evidencing the living which merely the 'seeing' might miss, to the patient in the case of the hospital, and listening as a political, methodological tool in the case of Govindpuri which compels engaging with the everyday beyond and besides the framing of 'poverty, etc'., is potent with the possibilities of accommodating, acknowledging on their own accord the records, histories, experiences of those on the 'margins'? Here, I am locating the patient's body (and the agency she can assert) within Sontag's problematisation in Illness as Metaphor.

I think you have really got to the heart of why, for me, listening is important as an ethnographic technique and also just as a way of being in the world. It's about 'evidencing the living which merely the "seeing" might miss'. It's also about attending to something that is widely dismissed as superficial and unimportant.

To continue that idea, a common attitude I encounter is: "why are you so interested in sound when (in the hospital context) people are undergoing serious operations/need to be protected from hospital acquired infections/there is a funding crisis in the National Health Service" etc. In GP it might be: "Why are you so interested in sound when there are serious problems with things like access to water". My response to this is to feel: "Well, there is a lot going on in this soundscape that evidences the things you are concerned about (for instance, exposure to noise seems likely to affect patient sleep and rest and so to affect recovery rates, which means longer patient stays in the hospital and makes the hospital less financially efficient, and the busyness of the soundscape reflects the complexity of the contact that is taking place on the ward and so reflects the difficulty of controlling infection), but there is also much going on acoustically in the ward to which you are oblivious because you don't perceive it (for instance the patients reacting with disgust and embarrassment to their own and other peoples' body sounds which are audible in the enclosed and densely occupied space of the ward, and which have profound implications for the experience of hospitalisation). In GP you could say, for instance, that the presence of water sounds in the soundscape is reflective of water scarcity and wider scarcity of vital resources, but that, as you suggest in your research, you also miss the gossip, teasing, flirtation, abusing, shaming etc that is going on if you don't listen, and these kinds of exchange are vital to the experiential fabric of life in GP.

TC: As a sound anthropologist, do you think that soundscapes [as social, material, cultural, political artifacts and listening - in different ways - as a methodological praxis] have this inherent 'disruptive' potential to disturb the hegemonic practices of knowledge production? Have the possibilities been exhausted? What are the possibilities - methodologically, intellectually, theoretically - of exhausting these potentialities, if in fact these resound with it? Or am I leaning towards romanticisation of positing visuality vis-a-vis aurality as binaries?

TR: This is a huge question or set of questions and realistically I probably can't answer them at all fully. I think on the whole that trying to set up visuality and aurality in a binary is unhelpful and tends not to work. In real life situations where the senses can only be decoupled in very temporary and somewhat artificial ways, and technological is increasingly blurring the boundaries between what is heard and what is visualised (see Ingold and also Sterne on these issues). That said, I think it can be helpful to consciously place emphasis on the aural and de-prioritise the visual at times in order to pursue particular research aims, and that this act can be disruptive to hegemonic practices of knowledge production. I don't think listening is 'inherently' disruptive, but it can be used in disruptive ways. I do not think we are even close to exhausting the disruptive possibilities of listening as a way of producing knowledge, and actually I think that in the social sciences we are only at the beginning of this journey. What the possibilities are 'methodologically, intellectually, theoretically - of exhausting these potentialities' is a big question and might need a different article.

TC: In your conclusion, whilst taking the Perspective Tour of the permanent collection at the Wellcome Museum in London, you make the point to the attendee of 'requiring imagination' to attend to the 'cacophony' which would be at the heart of the 'acoustic archaeology of medicine'. In the similar vein, I would like to stretch this call for 'imagination' to engage with the sounds of the everyday of the jhuggis, all relegated to all encompassing and overwhelming 'noise'. However, what would be the task - as anthropologist/ethnographers invested in listening, in soundscapes - to enliven the imagination of those not so 'sonically tuned'?.

TR: I suppose what's needed here is a direct provocation to listen to the jhuggis and their history (if one is taking an acoustic archaeology approach). I remember when we were making GP sound you took me to what is now a rather nice public park, a large green space near Nehru place. You pointed out that this had once been a very large slum settlement, set up by people who came to work on the buildings that became Nehru place itself, and catering for the needs of all the workers. Then, to cut a long story short, once the building project was finished the slum was cleared and replaced with the park. I have good audio of you, actually sounding quite emotional, as you explain that there is no longer any trace of the slum and that no one in the years to come will know that a slum ever existed there. You can hear the sense of loss and anger in your voice about all the traces of human life that are now gone. This would be a good point at which to provoke people to reimagine what that place might have sounded like. You could even do an installation in that park where you urge people to remember these people whom you suggest public discourse does not regard as worth remembering. Or you could gather interviews from people who lived there and then play them to visitors to the park over headphones as part of a site specific installation. That could be interesting and, as you suggest, enlivening to the imagination.

I feel that one thing the hours of recording for GP sound we made might do is represent an archive of what sounds could be heard in that particular place at that particular time. This could be very valuable for some GP residents if (and when?) the slum is removed and its inhabitants are ever relocated. Or it could be useful as a sort of public record or cultural resource. Then again, you have to wonder who would want to take the time to listen - but there may well be people one day who would have an interest. The recordings could be catalogued and given to an institution like the British Library Sound Archive (though there might well be an Indian equivalent).

I was speaking to someone recently about the GP sound documentary, and he suggested that the sounds could be edited into a package of 'sounds from a Delhi slum' and that permission to use them could then be sold to people who might be interested in making films, audio pieces, video games etc using them. It raises questions as to who really owns these recordings (the people of GP? You as the researcher? Me as the recordist? The production company? The BBC as the commissioning body and funder of the recordings even though not all of them were used in the programme? No one?). It might be an interesting project to consult GP residents on this question and find out what they feel as well as to ascertain the legal position. I doubt the sale of permission to use these recordings would ever make serious money, and it may not be worth the labour of editing the package together, but the idea does raise interesting questions as to who should have what rights over the soundscape and recordings of it.

References

Rice, Tom. 'Govindpuri Sounds', *BBC*, https://www.bbc.co.uk/programmes/p02hm1rx. The documentary was commissioned by BBC for its program The Documentary and was aired on 2 February 2015. More information here: https://ore.exeter.ac.uk/repository/bitstream/handle/10871/34775/Tom%20Rice%20Govindpuri%20Sound%20REF%20document.pdf?sequence=4&isAllowed=y.

6. I WAIL, THEREFORE I AM

The Wall

On 31 March 2008, 1,000 slum dwellings were razed to ground in the GP slums in Kalkaji extension in South Delhi:

> Construction of a five-foot wall to divide a slum cluster from neighbouring middle-class colonies is wreaking havoc in south Delhi's Kalkaji Extension [...] bulldozers razed down more than 1,000 small shops and homes to make way for a wall that will encircle all three camps in the slum cluster: Bhumiheen, Nehru and Navjeevan. Four hundred metres of the proposed 2-km wall are already in place, under construction by the Delhi Development Authority (DDA) since December. "We are acting on an order from the High Court", says DDA's executive engineer K K Khanna. And the High Court was responding to a petition filed by Arsh Avtaar Singh, former president of Kohinoor Apartments Resident Welfare Association, in May 2005. The petition sought a solution against encroachment of roads and services by slum residents.
>
> Neighbouring middle-class colonies support Singh's efforts. A flat-owner from nearby Konark Apartments, who does not want to be named, says: "All my life savings have been used to purchase this flat. For 22 years I have lived with the stink from open defecation, and constant over-crowding from blocked roads".
>
> Residents want slum dwellers to be relocated in pukka housing. "I feel bad for them", says Singh, whose own domestic help lives in Bhumiheen Camp. "They should be given an alternative home immediately".
>
> But the DDA claims it needs time to relocate the slum dwellers. "The wall is a temporary arrangement to offer protection to flat owners", Khanna says. In the interim, Daliwal, a resident of Konark apartment, thinks the wall should be built higher. "It should be at least eight foot high, and built either with bricks, or grills and mesh. There should also be fewer outlets". The camp's residents, though, are fuming. "We were given no warning", says Sagar. She claims to have bought her grocery shop for Rs 20,000 rupees 13 years ago. "I make Rs 50 a day, through which I cook for my family. We have nothing to eat today without my shop". Trying to salvage broken chairs and cutlery from his former confectionery store, Izhar Ali asks, "What should I do to earn? Can the government give me an alternative?"[...] DDA's Khanna, meanwhile, insists there will be several entry and exit points in the wall. "There are more than 17 gaps in the 400-metre stretch built so far", he says.
>
> DDA has a May 21 deadline for building the wall.[1]

---

1   Preeti Jha, 'Great Wall of Kalkaji', *Indian Express*, 5 April 2008.

A notice of planned demolition was circulated amongst the residents of GP camps through pamphlets and announcements in the last week of March 2008. The scheduled date for the demolition was 3rd April. When the announcements were made, resident groups, political organizations, and NGO's convened to contemplate a course of action to impede the demolitions. One of the resident groups in collaboration with a leading NGO in the area filed a petition to demand a stay order for the proposed demolitions. The hearing of this petition was scheduled for 2nd April.

On the evening of 30th March, the residents of GP slums began noticing surmounting police presence in the area. When inquired about their presence, the police personnel informed the residents of the demolition scheduled for the next day. Early in the morning on 1st April, an area of three kilometers around GP was cordoned off by police forces including anti-riot squads. For the next few hours, the demolition squad systematically razed the defined slums and shops to the ground.

However, unlike other demolitions, the primary agenda of demolitions carried in GP slums was not to evict illegal squatters. As the local press presents it, through this act of enclosure, the authorities consider that they will be able to curtail the movements of the slum residents on the roads, parks, and other spaces shared by the slums and nearby middle class residents, providing respite to the latter.

The wall is justified by the state authority on the grounds that it will protect the 'flat owners' (the middle-class population) in the area. By implication suggesting that slum-dwellers pose a threat to this section of society. The slums have co-existed with the middle-class settlements in this area for over twenty years. There are no recorded incidents of violent outbursts and attacks perpetrated by the slum-dwellers towards the middle-class population, according to a search of police records and media reports. Instead, the middle-class homes offer employment opportunities to slum dwellers as domestic helps, cooks, guards, and drivers.

Following the demolition and prior to the erection of the wall, I conducted interviews with both slum-dwellers and residents of nearby middle class settlements to understand the perception of 'threat' in the everyday context.A significant proportion of the slum's population work in this way, and in discussions it became clear that they would be unlikely to jeopardize their livelihoods by violence or any other form of direct conflict with their employers and vice-versa. The latter simply want to assert their claims and rights to not endure the assault - smell, noise, dirt, filth - which the presence of the *jhuggis* unleashes on them.

The demolitions at GP, the authorities later claimed, were peaceful. In the present, the outlines of the wall are barely visible as it has been innovatively woven into the architectural structures of the jhuggis. The matter of whether the wall could or could not contain the slum-dwellers for the safety of the middle-class neighbours of the apartments is not of consequence, what matters is that the middle-class neighbour's claims, owing to their position on the social-cultural-political matrix, of desiring sanitized spaces were acknowledged and legitimized by the courts and other state authorities.

The 'Noisy' Other

From where they are, what they hear of GP slums (hereafter, 'GP') is only noise. In this reckoning, sounds in GP have no intent or imagination; they emerge out of nowhere, conflate and contradict with other sounds sharing the same predicament, to disappear into another nowhere-ness. To these outside ears, the noisiness of GP has only the singular and absolute purpose to invade and disrupt their deserved silences.

That the heard noisiness of GP from the outside—namely, the middle-class residents—is not a matter of decibel levels, but is a 'particular trope of experiencing sounds is significant in defining a 'sense of the self,' which is effectively employed to create social, moral, and political exclusion[2]'. In the liberties with listenings I evoke here, the politics of production, performance, and articulation of 'noise' as a specific instance of sonic engagement to highlight the broader processes of othering in the city as a sonic premise to further complicate the reckoning of noise—politically and philosophically—in itself. In that, the listening attempt here aims to rehabilitate noise within the sonic triad of 'noise-sound- silence', wherein sonicity linearly moves from a state of chaos, through certain validations to an absolute state of calm. I will tease out these negotiations by attempting the biography of a sound—wailing—in the immediate context of GP, and then extrapolate it onto the broader materiality of the sonic capacities available to others in the city.

Slums are marginalized spaces in the materiality of a city. And in a city like Delhi, with its hyperbolic transformative agendas to become a 'world-class, clean and green city', these spaces, more than ever, represent the perversity of a past desired to be conveniently lost: poverty, violence, unstructured growth, over-population, dirt, filth, and noise[3]. Acutely aware of the particular and predicament of the sustained, strategic and everyday violence of the marginalization the slums, and its residents, encounter, the space, its sociality, and cultural politics have their own modalities to internalize this violence; and in that process deliberately define the boundaries of their own margins and locate their own others. One section of society in GP on which this violence of othering and marginalization is inscribed is its women. Gender,

---

2   I have unpacked the tensions of social and morally determined listening into the slums in Tripta Chandola, 'Listening into Others: Moralising the Soundscapes in Delhi', *International Development Planning Review* 34.4 (2012): 391–408 and in my doctoral research. Here, I establish the manner in which this listening not only affects the everyday interactions between the residents of the slums and their middle-class neighbours, but also the manner in which it frames the slum-dwellers as others within the imagination of the city, and its impact on urban policies that strategically exclude the spaces of slums and its residents.

3   In the Indian context, these constructions have a historical, social, and cultural continuity, deeply embedded as they are in the practice of caste discrimination, which are essentially sensorially ordained. However, the evocation of these categories to justify the transformations of the Delh into a world-class, global city attempts to neutralize these negotiations by rendering onto them an ahistorical, modernist agenda. This Iidentify as 'sensorial re-turn in urban planning policies' which I argue is, '[...]continuation of the elitist agenda to contain bodies and conquer spaces. However, the manner in which it is being executed is outside the praxis of caste, class and religion in the name of progress and development, thereby lending it a secular character, which denies it historical continuity and complexity. The sensorial re-turn is acquiring not only a political rhetoric and mainstream support, but also legal sanction'.

however, is not the sole category of othering, and its associative social, cultural, and political disenfranchisement. The considerations of caste, class, communal affiliation, and political loyalties are equally determinant in these processes, however for the sake of the listenings proposed here, it will be the voices — or lack thereof — of the women in GP that will form the focus of our attention.

The soundscapes in the neighbourhood of Govinpuri, including the slums, are dense and intense. It is indeed thick. To be heard here—literally, metaphorically, and politically—necessitates employment of effective sonic, technological, and social interventions. Given the space of GP is highly gendered, the women are denied these techniques of being heard, and thus their entry and assertion into its soundscapes often remain, at best, muted. To then extend masculinity to GP's soundscape as an over- arching characteristic is not an attempt at simplification of its listenings, but an invitation to hear into it from a gender-specific trope. One sound—more accurately an instance of sonic performance by women in GP—however, has the potential to disrupt the intersecting sonic, spatial, and gendered masculine hierarchies, however temporarily: it is that of a wailing woman.

An emaciated, sickly woman is sought, and quickly found. It is an early, cold, January morning in 2012. The Municipal Corporation of Delhi elections are a few weeks away. I am accompanying, listening to, and interviewing a group of women mobilized from the three camps in support of a local candidate contesting the elections. On the said day, there is a scheduled rally in support of the candidate. The atmosphere in the room where the women congregate is tense, only easing when the required—emaciated, sickly—woman is identified. Preparations are in order—often hasty, tense, and leading to heated exchanges. I am told these are for the rally due in a few hours, but the specifics of the plan are not discussed and there is no room for interrogation of that sort. The emaciated, sickly woman is the hero of the moment; deliberations about her attire, where to get the desired at such a short notice, and assuring, and hushed consultations with her are taking place in a corner. I continue to listen. Eventually we set out.

The stage for this setting is an intersection leading from the camps to the main road. The intent by now is obvious; the group of women intends to block this intersection so that the visit of the opposing candidate into the camps can be stalled. The execution of the intent—the plan, now in motion—is not without its ingenuity and strategic planning. The emaciated, sickly woman, dressed in white, is laid down in the middle of the road on a bamboo plaque usually reserved to carry the dead to the cremation ground. She is covered with a white sheet with her face partially covered. It is evident by now that the role assigned to the emaciated, sickly woman in this planning is to play dead. And she does it quite convincingly. The women congregate around her in semi-circle, completely blocking the intersection. The imminent arrival of the opposing candidate is anticipated, and the women surrounding the un-dead dead woman start wailing in a collective, synchronized and sincere manner. It is not a cry, it is not a shriek, it is simply a 'prolonged high-pitched cry of pain, grief, or anger'; it is indeed an inarticulate 'high-pitched sound'. And, this sonic intervention has its desired effect. The candidate from the opposing party, and his cohorts, try to circumvent this sonic blockade, so to speak: they try to initiate a conversation with the group of wailing women; they try to placate them; they extend promises of justice delivered—without really knowing what the act of criminality or the grievance is being mourned over. The women, however, refuse to relent, and continue with the wailing. The threat of seeking police intervention to remove this sonic blockade was unimaginable: an assault on a group of wailing women, apparently mourning the death of one of them, would have ruined any moral respectability for the concerned candidate in the community.

Eventually, the opposing candidate leaves without holding the scheduled rally, and the women disperse as effectively as they had claimed the space, sonically. The undead finally awakens, walks alongside the others to the murmurs of applause and admiration, though not without a hint of envy. She—the emaciated, sickly woman—is after all the silent punctum of the incisive and effective sonic intervention: wailing.

If sound in its singular manifestation is to be reckoned as a particular and peculiar intersection of its spatiality and temporality in the site of its origin, then soundscapes are the simultaneity of these intersections. A spatial-temporal matrix can contain more than one sound, thus complicating not only the Cartesian notionalities of space and time, but also of the sonicities it contains. Thus, a sound is not just a moment of insular and individuated instance of utterance, but derives its momentum from the collusions with the multiplicities that abound these matrices: spatial, temporal, sonic, social, cultural, and political. A listener, not unlike a cartographer, traverses through these matrices to 'make sense', to hear, to map not by accompanying each sound (or in the case of a cartographer, venturing into every crevice) but by deliberately, unintentionally, and inadvertently leaving most un-listened into. And thus the ears, as appendages which can never be 'closed', become the libraries where these listening intos are archived.[4]

But unlike a library, and an archive, with its robust physicality and Deweyian, almost clinical sensibilities, an 'ear' remains a highly individuated, and thus an ambiguous site of production of knowledge. Lending anxiety to this ambiguity and identification of 'listening(s)' as a knowledge base is not only the technical matter of ears that cannot be closed, but also sounds that cannot be contained. And thus the individuated hearings are not so much a matter of the ears as itself, but a more insidious and astute question of 'but whose ears?'. The strategic, systematic, and deliberate privileging of hearings of, and by, certain ears— with political,

---

4   Aside: is there a technical, clinical and, even perhaps, a cynical term for storing and sorting listening without reliance on a visual paradigm? Its reliance on a doctrine visually inclined? But then Borges was blind after all? The insertion of a blind Borges (a story-teller par excellence, but most fundamentally a custodian of knowledge in his avatar as a librarian) is to at once reveal the visual-centric bias in acknowledging and classifying experiences as knowledge cultures and practices and to emphasise that there are indeed other modalities of experiencing—evolving a 'sense of self'—arrived at through a melee of sensorial explorations. Alberto Manguel who in his youth read to Borges when he started losing his sight, renders the experience of *experiencing* libraries, stories, and their classification with Borges as 'memories of memories', inadvertently displacing the visual bias in *With Borges*. The Western, Cartesian, colonial agenda of the visual bias was not without its deliberation to deny of a 'sense of self'(by disregarding the knowledge cultures premised on a sensorial reckoning) of the encountered others—the natives. The 'sensorial re-turn' is but a particular and peculiar manifestation of this kind of othering.

social, cultural, and moral currencies—then assumes the role of listeners selectively identifying sounds to situate it within the sonic triad of 'noise-sound-silence'. These listening(s) of course do not (and cannot) contain sounds permeating into ears and spaces; instead, they weave sounds together into logic of those that are contaminated, the ones that are sanctioned and others that are sanctified thus deliberating, and setting limits, to the permissible spatial-temporal-sonic intersections in a space, moment, and its memory. The ears that dare to hear otherwise, and the spaces where sounds, which disrupt the precariously listened-into spatial-temporal sonicity, abound are either silenced, deliberately un- listened into or identified as sites of sonic contamination.

It is within this schematic that the outside listening into of GP is collapsed into a cacophony of contaminated sounds collectively identified as noise. This reckoning has implication both in the real and rarefied imagination of the slums and its residents—the ears and the space: they exist in a perpetual state of chaos, lacking potential and imagination to move towards a validated, and eventually, a state of calm; the chaotic predicament is not conducive to conversations; thus they deserve un-listening and deliberate silencing; they are deemed unfit to participate into the listenings of and in the city; they are all but noise, a distraction; this chaos emerges not out of structural, social, and political marginalization of these ears and spaces, but from its inherent moral and ethical corruptibility; they are beyond redemption, and thus, not unlike an erring child punished to stand out of the classroom, they are denied recognition as citizens of the state.

The slums and its residents therefore perpetually reside in the twilight zone of being un-citizens, loud-uncouth-noisy.

But. However. Nevertheless: the city passes. Listen. The city passes. Lend your ears to the sound that refuses to die, dissolve and indeed disrupts; let us then revisit the sound which got us here in the first place: the women wailing an undead-dead, an existent non-existent. Wailing is a sound that, in its singular utterances, colonizes the spectrum of the triad 'noise-sound-silence' triad in its entirety, and thus its highly disruptive potentialities.[5]

Crying and shouting as distant cousins of this sonic performance are not without this disruptive potential, however, these acts inherently extend an invitation for a negotiation: either a complicity in the act, situation, or moment responded to by crying or shouting; or, a desire to seek redemption and retribution, and often even an acknowledgement of guilt and penance.

---

5   Here, the disruptive potential of wailing as a sonic performance by women in GP is identified as '[...] a scandal with the sudden intrusion, the unanticipated agency, of a female 'object' who inexplicably returns the glance, reverses the gaze, and contests the place and authority of the masculine position. The radical dependency of the masculine subject on the female 'Other' suddenly exposes his autonomy as illusory'. See Judith Butler, *Gender Trouble,* London: Routledge, 1990 (1999), pp vii. This performance further displaces the male gaze (and hearing) which Zizek identifies as '[...] endeavors to counter the fundamental hystericity (lie, lack of a firm position of enunciation) of the feminine speech' by laying claims to the very vocabularies which are reckoned to render them incomprehensible, thus divesting the male gaze (and its hearings) of its autonomy. See Slavoj Zizek, *Organs without Bodies: On Deleuze and Consequences,* London: Routledge, 2004 (2012).

Wailing is a non-negotiable sonic performance. Seemingly inarticulate in its "prolonged high-pitched cry of pain, grief, or anger" or just as a 'high-pitched sound', it is in fact unapologetic, resilient, and assured. In its so-heard incoherence, it carries the currency of being a contaminated sound, noise; in its effectiveness to demand attention of the ears, it is a validation of an emotion intensely felt, a sound; and, in its transcendental potential to silence by demanding complete hearing, it also manifests the calmness of silence. In that: wailing comes to haunt the hearings, it disrupts the spatial-temporal-sonic matrices as in its sonic performance its potency to contain "noise-sound-silence" all at once. Women as systematically muted agents—historically, politically, and sonically—performing the wailing further lends to the anxiety: if the silenced finally start speaking in tongues that cannot be contained and demand complete reverence, one only wonders the wrathful gods they will evoke. The imagery of a group of women in GP wailing onto the body of an undead-dead uncannily evokes the predicament of the slums in the city, here in the city of Delhi.

Superimposing the masculine/feminine binary to the cartographic reality and imagination of the spaces in the city, slums most definitely embody the *feminine*, and the sustained, systematic, and everyday violence that it entails. Here, the intent of evoking the binary of masculine/feminine to situate the real, imagined, and desired engagements between the slums and the city is to complicate these reckonings instead of reinforcing them[6]. In their encounters with the city in different capacities—for example, as employees, voyeurs, and consumers—the men from the GP feel emasculated, especially in their interactions with middle- class women as employers and objects of desire. In these encounters, it is required of them to perform *femininity*, exaggerated by the *silence* they have to maintain. This silencing is instituted by the expectation of non-negotiable subservience in the case of former, and its almost-negligible possibility of actualization in the latter. These displaced (never disrupted though) masculinities, however, are rehabilitated by its exaggerated, perverse hyperbolic performance within GP's spatiality and sociality where their position, especially vis-à-vis women, is one of dominance. However this performance, with all its violence, does not dissipate uncontested, remaining an exclusive domain of the men. Women, both as individuals and occasionally, as a collective, challenge it, whilst others (who either by the virtue of their social position—mother-in-law, for instance—or by enjoying a certain political legitimacy) not only embrace and internalize its vocabulary but execute its violence on other women and weaker men. The identified *feminine*, not necessarily a biological entity contained within gendered qualifications, continues to be a site (both in its pathological situation of a space and a body) where the perverse desire to

---

6   The reactions in the Indian media and the middle-class rhetoric to the brutal Delhi Gang Rape case of 2012 are symptomatic of these negotiations. The fact that the perpetrators were residents of a slum settlement in the city distracted attention from the fundamental violence and brutality of the act of rape to the specific case being evoked as particular pathology of slumming. The materiality of this space was identified by most commentators as a breeding ground for rape. It is overpopulated; the people uneducated, and by that stretch uncouth; people here do not experience sex as a personal, emotional act, but perform it publicly; men are drunk and women lack morals. And, of course, these spaces are swarmed with those alien things: the migrants. The media was replete with such elaborations, with Sheila Dixit, the Chief Minister of Delhi then, even managing to push her deca- de long agenda of restricting the entry of migrants in the city in the kitty. See also: http://www.abc.net.au/am/content/2013/s3683181. htm; http://www.theguardian.com/world/2013/sep/07/gang-rape-fear-anger-delhi-slums

discipline, destabilize, and de- stroy can be melodramatically performed. The anticipation lending tension to the punctum moment accruing the *masculine-feminine* dramatics (in either its rendition of space or body) is not a resigned deliberation of the sustenance of the status quo, but the palpable *dread* of a conversation.

The deliberate compulsion to collapse all and every sound of the slums in its hearing by the dominant ears—namely, the middle classes—as contaminated and relevant only in its noisy manifestation is merely an attempt to deny the potential of mutable sonicities. And thus to keep the slums suspended in perpetuity as un-heard, silenced, un-dead, and un- existent in the circus that makes the city.

However. Nevertheless: *the un-heard do wail; the un-dead do not just cremate themselves into ashes; and the un-existent continue to move across the spatial-temporal-sonic matrices.* In their wailing, they haunt.[7]

Postscript

Saroj, the protagonist of the essay *The Subaltern as a Political Voyeur*, the organic intellectual, was the undead, the hero of the hour. She set her eyes on me as she woke up, commanding a smoke. As we walked into the lanes, she inquired, 'white does not really suit me, does it?'. I wanted to but hesitated in saying it aloud, 'neither does being dead'.

References

Butler, Judith. *Gender Trouble,* London: Routledge, 1990 (1999), p. vii.

Douglas, Mary. 'The Social Control of Cognition: Some Factors in Joke Perception', *Man*, 3.3 (1968): 361–376.

Jha, Preeti.'Great Wall of Kalkaji', *Indian Express,* 5 April 2008.

Zizek, Slavoj. *Organs without Bodies: On Deleuze and Consequences,* London: Routledge, 2004 (2012).

---

7   The potential of wailing — as a particular sonic performance and as a more generic manifestation of the gendered, spatial and social negotiations — is identified within its capacities to occupy/claim the position of *trickster*, 'dispelling the belief that any given social order is absolute and objective,', who demands an audience, critical and engaged, instead of silencing this performance, potent with possibilities, by a silent reception. See Mary Douglas, 'The Social Control of Cognition: Some Factors in Joke Perception', *Man*, 3.3 (1968): 361–376.

7. SONIC SELFIES: EQUALIZING THE ENCOUNTER WITH THE OTHER

In conversation with Jodi Dean (JD) and Geert Lovink (GL).[1]

GL: For many cultural critics, the selfie is a symbol for neo-liberal self-promotion. There is a constant pressure to perform, to show-off, be present. The selfie embodies the desperate attempt by the 'failed individual' to show that she (or he) still in the rat race: I am alive, don't forget me, look at me and think of me, next time you can do me a favour [...] But first, how do we deal with the selfie phenomena beyond forced participation or moral accusation, and develop ways of seeing that integrate machine readable interpretations?

It is a winter afternoon in the jhuggis. Whilst Delhi summers evoke kindness of a very particular kind, the winters bring a peculiar conviviality. And thus in one of the lanes of one of the camps, where I am also present, just hanging about, this conviviality is performed in all its loudness. However, there is a moment of rupture in the din of conversations, casual banters, conflicting musical performances, an old woman with frizzled hair rather casually lifts her arse, in full sight, and let out a garrulous fart, brrrraaaaaaaaaaaaaaar. A moment's silence followed with an equally loud collective laugh, but it was not to embarrass or make the old woman conscious. She shifted her arse back to the comfortable position, taking her time.

Retrospectively, I think that was the moment when I started thinking of sonic performances as particular 'individuated moments' of establishing and extending one's sense of self and space. This was much before the 'selfie' days, Smartphones had not yet invaded the everyday life. From my middle-class location, this public performance of a very 'private' sonic moment (which I distinctly remember being taught to curb, especially in public), I was intrigued. The slums are highly gendered space, and especially women's mobility and performative potentialities in every regards comes under intense scrutiny. However, the old woman on account of her age had accrued permissions which are otherwise limited to the young women, and thus the permission without the embarrassment. A transgressive space is thus claimed and created.

I retrospectively attribute 'sonic Selfies' as a framework to locate the individuated moments of sonic performances, particularly of the identified Others, which when located within listening as a methodological and political intervention exposes the potential to displace, disturb and disrupt the 'encounter' in the Althusserian sense.[2] And thus from my almost two decades of listening into the slums of Govindpuri, I highlight other encounters which the sonic selfies necessitated, which I later extrapolate to macro-level encounters from the everydayness of the jhuggis. The insistence on recounting the sonic selfie encounters with the slums is to disrupt

---

1   Jodi Dean, 'Jodi Dean - Selfie Communism', *YouTube*, https://www.youtube.com/watch?v=iZvvH56XqCw. Geert Lovink, 'Narcissus Confirmed: Technologies of the Minimal Selfie', *Sad by Design: On Platform Nihilism*, Pluto Press, 2019, pp. 98-107.
2   Louis Althusser, *Philosophy of the Encounter Later Writings: 1978-1987*, G. M. Goshgarian, Oliver Corpet and François Matheron (eds) New York: Verso, 2006.

the imagination of the slums, or perhaps any people, spaces and ideas on the margins, as homogenised, flattened existences.

A young girl, not a day more than 15, from a conservative family, who insist on 'controlling' her mobilities and bodily spatialities and performances. She practices the ultimate defiance by insisting on adorning a pair of jeans, a forbidden epitome of 'modern' ways reckoned unbecoming by her family. She is beaten, abused, threatened with dire consequences by her mother and brother, but she asserts her 'sonic selfie' by a stoic muted, silent response. She does not retort. When hit, she does not even cry, even though the tears streaming down her face evidence to the momentum of the movement of the hand that landed on her frail cheeks. But neither her silence or the jeans she is wearing can be taken away from her. After a while, the family members relent. And in the days, months, years, as I saw that young girl accumulating years, her styling of her jeans just got better.

I can go on to list such moments in some length, but those are replete in the other essays in the book. I want to return to GL's evocation of the 'moral accusation' and 'failed individual' which the creation and circulation of 'sonic selfies' via mediated technologies, smartphones to be precise, brought on to the residents of the slums as a constitutive representative others in the broader urban imagination.

Sonic selfies as a moment of individuated performative sonic selves and claiming of spaces by the others, here the residents of the jhuggis, induce anxiety, particularly when performed in the shared public spaces, which within the hegemonic imagination needs to absented of the presences of these others. When the 'sonic selfies' were merely limited to bodily presences and performances, there were adequate strategies of silencing, disciplining and absenting these performances from these hegemonic spaces.[3]

The mediated sonic selfies, particularly the extensive usage of the smartphones to listen to music, have 'loud' conversations over the phone in public spaces - malls, metro, amongst others, and the performative presence of the others of using the 'same' kind of technology, namely the Smartphones, exacerbated newer forms of 'anxiety of proximity' with the others. Unlike the 'second visuality' of selfie communism which images produce, as JD insists, these mediated 'sonic selfies' are not as easily to be ignored, absented and silenced.

Before proceeding with the transgressive capacities of the 'sonic selfies', a pause is in askance to locate these tendencies in the broader context of the bureaucratic-technocratic imaginations of locating the other.

In 2013, the Government of India released a report, 'Housing Stock, Amenities & Assets in Slums—Census 2011'.[4] In this report, along with the access to potable water and sanitation

---

[3] The bodily presences of the *others* itself reckoned loud, uncouth and immoral, and thus even in their 'silent' presences, these bodies are not desired.

[4] Office of the Registrar & Census Commissioner, Ministry of Home Affairs, Government of India, 'Housing Stock, Amenities & Assets in Slums - Census 2011', http://censusindia.gov.in/2011census/hlo/Slum_

facilities to the slum dwellers, it accounts the 'number of households availing banking services and number of households having each of the specified assets'. These assets include, amongst others, mobile phones. I wrote an article responding to the media coverage, particularly focussing on the usage of mobile phones in the slums.[5] The manner in which articles in mainstream media articulated these data sets is quite revealing of the popular perceptions of 'slumming' in the cities. They were nothing short of being virulent. Consider these: 'Amenities in slums match up to urban homes [...] India's first-ever census of household amenities and assets in slums has revealed that slum dwellers are also spending more on TV sets, computers and mobile phones rather than sanitation'[6] in one, and the following in another: '34 per cent in slums have no toilet, but 63 per cent own mobile phone [...] Depending on how one looks at it, "slumming it" may just have acquired a whole new meaning — either most Indian towns live the life of slums or the quality of life in slums is improving'.[7]

In both these articulations the tension to reckon the slum dwellers as 'consumers' is contemptuously palpable. The first blatantly overlooks the structural factors leading to the systematic lack of sanitation facilities in slums, which in fact is a state responsibility, by shifting the onus on to the slum dwellers for not tackling these issues; it is also clearly disapproving of the fact that the slum dwellers spend more assets clearly meant for 'entertainment' than investing in 'improving' their everyday conditions. The second articulation, more subtle in its tonality, at the outset sets out the anxiety of sharing the same 'consumerist-cultural' space with the slums.

I juxtapose these reckoning with my experience and involvement from the early 2000's in the Open Source Movement in India and ICT4D project, the heydays of the obscene celebration of new media technologies with perverse potentials. Interestingly, in those days my issues (and eventual departure) with the ICT4D movements and projects was not a response far from my more recent articulation. Then, it was reckoned, and I loosely articulate my own perspective on these initiatives, 'seek out the poor, marginalised people and spaces, equip them with one or the other fancy new media technologies - computers, phones and such - and teach them life skills, and lo behold, their lives will improve'. In both these reckoning of the 'poor' - the eternal other - are denied any foundational sense of 'self' wherein they can make 'informed' choices, whether it be about what life skills and technologies might be most useful or in their capacities as 'consumers' who in fact make an informed choice about spending their own money on technologies, particularly smartphones, just to have *fun*.

The issue I had with such a reckoning that the sole and singular mandate of these initiatives leaned towards a 'utilitarian' use of the new media technologies for the poor and thus further

---

    table/Slum_table.html.
5   Tripta Chandola, 'Dumped through Technology: A Policy Maker's Guide to Disenfranchising Slum Dwellers', *Journal of Creative Communications*, 8.2-3 (2013), pp. 265–275.
6   Moushumi Das Gupta, 'Amenities in the Slums Match up to Urban Homes', *Hindustan Times*, 22 March 2013, https://www.hindustantimes.com/delhi/amenities-in-slums-match-up-to-urban-homes/story-krqsZjcilVd7pb7vsCl8iP.html.
7   Uma Vishnu, '34% in Slums Have no Toilet, but 63% Own Mobile', *Indian Express*, 22 March 2013, http://archive.indianexpress.com/news/34—in-slums-have-no-toilet-but-63--own-mobile-phone/1091573/.

'rendering technical' the terms of these engagements, such that, '[f]irst, they reposed political-economic causes of poverty and injustice in terms of amenable to a technical solution. Second, they highlighted only those problems for which a technical solution in fact be proposed'.[8] These initiatives were beyond the concerns of the fact these were a strategic way for the State to absolve of its own responsibilities by outsourcing them to these funding organisations and, more importantly, these were insidious ways for the capitalist agendas (which usually also inadvertently served the purposes of the funding organisations) to enter into erstwhile unidentified, untapped markets and to impose a certain form of governmentality.[9]

In the aforementioned article, I argued, and I quote at some length for its set the backdrop to 'develop ways of listening' into the 'sonic selfie' phenomena.

> Official records as the 'Housing Stock, Amenities & Assets in Slums—Census 2011' (GOI 2013) are testimonies of, and by, the State to report on the 'reality'—the transformations and progress; often reckoned as staid these testimonies, in fact, are ways in which the State not only 'reflects on the real', but also strategically sustains the idea of 'the real' it wants to purports. Considered on its own the report in question projects a 'reality' of the slums that is totally divorced from the 'real, everyday' experience of slumming. The media response to the Census 2011 report then can be identified by the State to mask its inadequacies (lack of inclination), as well as justifying the market-logic of development, by insisting on the 'increased purchasing' power of the slum-dwellers. In celebrating the dense penetration of mobiles the analyses fails to take into cognizance that for the first decade following the opening of the economy (1991)[10] and the subsequent telecom policies (1994[11], 1999[12]), slums and other marginalized spaces, were not part of the network and remained 'disconnected'. These were essentially meant to cater to an urban, middle-class population. Indeed the penetration of mobile networks in the slums (facilitated by cheap hardware and competitive call rates) have introduced 'new' cultures and practices of communicating, but these are not dramatic ruptures and, in fact, in most instances either a continuation and convergence of existing practices, replete with their social and cultural discrimination, prejudices, politics of control and access. While it is of significance to highlight how the everyday of the residents in marginalized spaces is transformed by the use of mobile phones, these practices ought to be situated within the backdrop of whether these technologies allow for residents of these spaces to become 'empowered, engaged' citizens with capabilities and capacities to make informed choices

---

8   Tania M. Li, *The Will to Improve: Governmentality, Development, and the Practice of Politics*, Duke University Press, 2007, p. 126.
9   cf. James Ferguson, *The Anti-politics Machine: 'Development', Depoliticization, and Bureaucratic Power in Lesotho*, Minnesota UP, 1994.
10 Wikipedia Contributors, 'Economic Liberalisation in India', *Wikipedia*, August 2014, https://en.wikipedia.org/wiki/Economic_liberalisation_in_India, accessed 1st April 2020.
11 Department of Telecommunications, Ministry of Communications, Government of India, 'New Telecom Policy, 1994', https://dot.gov.in/national-telecom-policy-1994.
12 Department of Telecommunications, Ministry of Communications, Government of India, 'New Telecom Policy, 1999', https://dot.gov.in/new-telecom-policy-1999.

about participating in the democratic processes. Mobile penetration and its cultures of consumption in marginalized spaces is affected by the market forces or government and non-government interventions to 'incorporate' the residents of the slums as 'citizens' by illicit participation in initiatives designed to exhibit 'model citizenship' patterns; any digression from these narratives causes anxiety, as is evident from the media reportage to the Census 2011 report.

The anxiety-inducing tendency has to be located in the broader context of the position of the others - in their corporeal presences but also in imaginative potentialities. But when the other announces herself in fully glory, the summer causally swaging in her hips, singing a song she desires - however out of tune and unharmonious - walks the same paths as the hegemonic self, the latter quite literally loses the plot. And sets about to imagine other ways to summon, discipline the other.

I thus propose 'sonic selfies' as a conceptual framework, in all its loudness and corporeality, as moment of displacing, disturbing and rupturing the aspirations and imaginations of the tapestry of the hegemonic self whilst also dislocating the sites where power, control and violence could be exerted. In that, the 'sonic selfies' compel an equalising moment, however momentarily, in the encounter with the other. I also remain astutely and cynically aware, and thus do not overemphasis on these practices to compel structural changes, set in motion a revolutionary momentum, and I am not averse to admitting that these 'equalising moments of encounter' might only be compelled by matters of compulsions. However, the encounters with the Other does not need to be predicated on the premise of 'love thy neighbour' but a mutual, mutable respectability to not silence them. The 'sonic selfies' have compelled such an encounter wherein the Other cannot be muted, and the hegemonic self has to listen, however grudgingly. Because, the ears, they never close and thus insisting on a collective listening project of the selves of the others.

GL: The object watches us: the selfie is watching back [...] Selfies can be read as proofs of utter presence, not as evidence of electronic solitude, let alone a symptom of a personality disorder; they do not exemplify who we are but show that we exist, at this very moment.

JD: We should take this point to its logical extreme, selfies are a communist form of expression, social products appropriated by capitalism, now of course the critical reflex is to dismiss selfies as yet another indication of a pervasive culture of narcissism, I disagree. The narcissism, the narcissism critique approaches the selfie as if it were analysing a single photograph, it views the person in that photograph as the photograph subject. Selfies though should be understood as a common form emerging out of the communicative practices of secondary visuality. Understood from within this practices, the selfie has a collective subject, the many participating in the common practice, the many imitating each other, the figure in the photo is incidental. So, a selfie is a photo when makes of oneself using a mobile phone in order to share the photo on social media, it exists digitally in that weird in between of instant and forever, it's not meant as a commemoration, it doesn't memorialize what we've done, it's a quick registration of what we're doing.

A confession is in order: compared to most, I am a novice when it comes to the use of Smartphones. I only acquired one, and that too as a gift from a friend, in 2017. Until then, I carried a Nokia 1100, which cost as much, and had none of the 'smart' capacities. I carried the phone 'un-smart' phone, almost as a chip on my shoulder, an announcement of a counter-cultural statement: I refuse to participate in the obscene, perversity of over-connectedness, indulgence in the 'self', and resigning myself to the diktats of the market. I would often remark, and not without a certain self-congratulatory moralising, partronizing tone, that integral to the identities of the young girls, with whom I shared momentary space whilst traveling in the ladies compartment of the Delhi metro, are the three *S's: Skinny jeans, Smartphones and Selfies*. I was both intrigued and exasperated with this project of having 'oneself stare back at itself'. I am the child of socialist India, where acquiring a landline was a bureaucratic battle, and its usage permitted none of the immediacy, intimacy, privacy and unimaginable connectedness (or perhaps dis-connectedness of connections) which the smartphones allow.

The pervasive takeover by the Smartphones in Govindpuri also amused me, though perhaps I was gentler in my critique. But, there was one. I remember returning from Australia in early 2015, and as had become the habit over the years, one of my first visits would be to the jhuggis, carrying gifts and presents not from some distant lands, but often the 'non-place' sites of the duty free shops. Amidst the catching up, the food, celebrations, I found the 'gang of girls' - all in early 20s, more or less - with whom I shared more personal and intimate relationships, huddled and having hushed conversations in the corner. I interrupted and inquired whether another of their assignations was being plotted, and feigned irritation at being left out. Seethu, whom I had first seen as a young, confident teenager, had by now acquired a job in a fashion merchandising firm and who regaled all by her 'out-worldly' adventures, said, 'well, Didi, no, no, there is nothing we are planning of that sort, and if we were, we would need you. But this is something different, I hope you don't take it any other way, but we were planning to pool in money to buy you a proper phone. We think you might be having some money issues'. I was tad bit amused, but mostly flattered by their attention. I told them, I was perfectly happy with my non-smart phone, I had no use for it. I used the phone for what it is meant to do, and not everything else. These 'smartphone' toys were for the young ones.

And over the years, I was fascinated by the increasing use of the Smartphones (hereafter, SPs) in the jhuggis, particularly the young girls. I was not engaged so much in their agendas and projects of 'presenting and performing' themselves, but identified the usage of smartphones as emerging sites of 'feminine' assertions – in terms of romances, venturing into external networks, etc. – especially as cyber cafes, when they were really prevalent and popular were essentially masculine spaces. And, secondly, the manner in which the inherent capabilities of the smartphones was allowing to circumvent the text based, literate modality of engagement which the non-smart phones did not allow.

On every visit to GP, I found myself more and more intricately seduced into this world of non-text, verbal, visual mode of ways of being, making meaning the residents of the slums, particularly women, were venturing into. What was most fascinating for me was the manner in which a certain kind of de-colonization of the erstwhile otherwise reckoned-democratic, but still elitist, space of the Internet was being achieved by the constant and consistent presence the others were etching onto it. Through the various social media platforms, these others - the mostly illiterate, lacking technical skills and technological tools, residents of GP - were inserting their 'footprints', so to say, on this uncharted territory to become producers in their own right, instead of merely consumers. These others silenced and absented in this space were making their noises, without inhibitions and much aplomb, and like how!

One particular aspect of the claiming of these uncharted territories, modes and modalities of being, performances was the use of WhatsApp voice messaging feature in the smartphones which caught my imagination and intrigue. Within the scope of the retrospectively attributed framing of 'sonic selfies' whose canvas, so to say, is much broader, here I want to insist on the practices of using this particular feature to respond, and perhaps even modestly further the disruptive potential of 'selfies' as 'communist form of expression' and 'as proofs of utter presence'.[13]

I also draw on my experience of producing, creating and consuming 'sonic selfies' - via the WhatsApp voice feature - which has exploded my relationship with the 'field', already firm and solid, into a sonic constellation of a kind of commoning which could not be performed earlier. And it is in this capacity of commoning is that I locate the possibilities of 'communist form of expression' to be sophisticated. Most of my closest and oldest associates here have never received formal education and autodidacts in their own rights; in fact, it is to these I owe the hacks into a lot of applications and their potential to which I remained blissfully unaware. Until I was not available on the WhatsApp, the communications had to have a certain preparedness: what time, missed calls, low credit balance and other such considerations. The WhatsApp voice feature, a gesture which in its physicality requires a flattening, has disrupted, displaced and ruptured the matrix of the spatial-temporality-physicality of our encounters. And I insist on this particular feature of the WhatsApp to emphasise on 'sonic selfies' because in my encounters with my middle-class, educated, mostly upper-caste, rarely Muslim collegiate (a slice of the hegemonic self, perhaps) via WhatsApp, this feature is rarely, if never, used. Our exchanges are text-based and visually orientated.

And thus: a young woman, with no formal education, ensues a romantic liaison with a man - who knows of what age - whom she met surfing one of the social media platforms by sending him voice messages. Sometimes he would send text, which she would rush to her friends who could read to be translated. And recorded an adequate response. He was, as she found out, an engineer, living in a not so far off middle-class settlement. He never questioned her intent to not respond by text messages, because when he did send her a text to say he was busy or could not talk, she would compensate the 'silence' with an emoji reflecting her reaction: sad face, its OK face, thumbs up! She sustained and circulated an idea about herself, a mirror reflection, akin to Narcissus but unlike him not succumbing to it even to be the golden flower, and thus allowing herself simultaneously to announce her presence but also transcend it.

---

13 Here, I have to extend my sincere acknowledgements to Geert Lovink. It was only after hearing his talk, even though I had read the text earlier, at the Kochi Biennale, 2017, that the idea of sonic selfies' as conceptual framing began to hum a tune in my head, which I hope to have put together in symphony here.

And is not transcendence the fundamental essence of claiming the 'self' in most fundamental Marxist sense towards a collective, unalienated Utopia? Perhaps the deception was dually performed, he was not who he said, but does it matter? This medium - an equalising encounter with the Other - activated by 'sonic' exchanges allowed both of them to go 'beyond the given reality, the world as it is, overcoming it practically, conceptually and ideologically'.[14]

In the essay, *An Obscene Calling*, I called out the tendencies of the hegemonic self to deny 'emotionality' to the other. Without extending too much importance solely on the WhatsApp voice message feature, I evoke it more in an illustrative sense to highlight the manner in which this feature allowed a 'voice' to the emotions which otherwise remained unactualized. Baby, of whom I also spoke in that essay and another essay, *Subaltern as a Political Voyeur*, in the present has finally left the services of the Tamil Brahmin household she had been with for the last twenty years. She articulated her decision thus:

> Over the years, I have bitten my tongue on all kinds of humiliations they pelted on to me. Because it suited their interest, they presumed me to be Hindu, and such was their indifference, but also authority, that I had no choice to play the game. I am not complaining, they did a lot for the family. But I am talking more about the humiliations at the everyday level. Of course, there were no prescribed days of leave or off, and god forbid, if I chose to take one day off, the bloody Madam would make feel like a worm, and then giving me stale leftovers and me having to show gratitude for doing so. I had to constantly be grateful. But one day I just had enough, perhaps it is also a matter of age, and the fact that the family is doing well and maybe even 5 years back I wouldn't have been able to take the decision, but that day the camel's back broke. So, one of my relatives passed away, I called the cunt of the Madam in the morning to say I won't be able to make it today as I had to attend the funeral. Bloody behenchod (sisterfucker) of the Madam, first she was obviously angry and then she had the bloody gall to tell me, could you not have informed me about it yesterday? What the fuck, I thought, as if I knew that the relative was going to die on me; as if everything in my life should be aligned just so she doesn't have to fucking do her own dishes one day. I hung up. But, bloody hell, was I fuming? So I took out my daughter's one, and sent a voice message to hers with the bloody choicest of abuses, letting her know how pathetic her existence was, the passes her husband had made at me at least in the initial years, but also the little thieving I had done in her house, and the ultimate fucking bomb was to say, you fucking whore, you think you are very chaste, right, for the last twenty years you have been eating food cooked by a Muslim who makes the best buff kebabs. She also had Rukshar's number, so she must have known who it is, but after a while I saw that she indeed listened to the message, the two ticks established that. I felt so relieved for finally letting all of it go.

The 'voice' that the said feature allows to the unactualized emotions are not limited to only the encounters with the hegemonic self as the other of the Other, the residents of the jhuggis find ingenious ways to use this feature to express their emotionality within their own life worlds.

---

14 Jaroslav Krejci, 'A New Model of Scientific Atheism, *Concurrence,* 1.1 (1969): 87.

Whether it be in regards to communicating displeasure over a lover paying undue attention to another by sending a 'silent' recorded message, or to tell an estranged brother that in spite of the loud, brutal recriminations and altercations, the love is still there.

Perhaps Baby's instance sets up a notion that all encounters with the other of the other are tense and acrimonious, and the WhatsApp voice feature allows to perform and exert one's presence whilst subtracting 'real time' implications. There are enough instances to illustrate that these 'sonic selfies' - mediated via the WhatsApp voice feature - allow, in my reckoning, an equalising (not necessarily always translating into equitable, ethical co-habitational spaces) plane for the other to assert their 'presences' to announce that they are in fact 'present' in the same space-time continuum, that they in fact cannot be absented. Of course, the same WhatsApp voice feature which enables this 'equalising encounter' also comes with the capability to 'block' or 'unlisten' to these 'sonic selfies'. However, that conditions is predated by the fact that the 'presence' has been inserted and performed.

In that, I find myself seduced by the possibilities of an 'equalising encounter' of the voice feature of WhatsApp, whose imagined and intended usage has been extended in its appropriation to be claimed to announce 'presences', form 'collectives' and practice commoning erstwhile unavailable on the same technological platforms to the identified others. In this essay, whilst the inspiring anchor remains the everyday negotiations of and with the residents of the GP, the other I evoke is the constituent group of people who are denied, structurally and systemically, to participate in knowledge production, consumption, circulation, recalibration and disruption processes. In that the 'voice' that the said feature allows has implications more far reaching than just matters of utterances, it opens possibilities of a collectivization which has been denied to this group. The denial of the self to the others, of course, is the foundational premise which does not even permit this group to participate in the 'pervasive cultures of narcissism'.

Within the hegemonic project, the self of the other is a muted entity. It refuses to recognise among the others the otherwise celebrated contours and curvatures which the hegemonic self so callously either claims, disrupts or denies as a matter of right and choice (my own resistance to Smartphone being a pathetic testimony to this tendency). The hegemonic project does not want the others to be complex entities, but static receptors without the capacities to transmit.

And thus I evoke 'sonic selfies', one of its particular manifestation - the use of WhatsApp Voice feature in Smartphones - as an illustrative instance which has evidenced the transcendental, transgressive potential to sustain ruptures in the anxiety-ridden distancing, silencing absenting agenda of the hegemonic forces with the encounter with the other.

The task at hand for those of us who listen, but also have the capacities - however limited in the broader schematic of insidious capitalist subordination - is to activate these sites of 'equalising encounters', even at the cost of disrupting, displacing and disturbing our own positions within the comfortable womb of the hegemonic self we so often find ourselves curling into in foetal positions when the encounter with others becomes too real, too anxious, too neurotic.

JD: One does not replace or subordinate the other, they intermix mash and mingle, such that neither alone can be said to be the repository of truth, because images circulate as conversations, we find ourselves engaging in a new communicative form where the originality or uniqueness of an image is less important than its common generic qualities, the qualities that let it circulate quickly and easily that make it contagious [...] It marks a contagious intensity, something about which people have strong feelings, crowds in squares and in media are generally diverse and tumultuous, imitation, repetition, contagion do not imply agreement.

There are days, whilst visiting Govindpuri, even at the cost of not making appointments at the said time, I often find myself sat on the road under the Govindpuri metro station, the closest one to reach to the jhuggis. It is an overhead metro station, and the road over which Delhi metro's tentacles spread is one of the main arterial roads leading to dense industrial areas of Okhala and further edges of the city. I sit here in my quietness, sipping a tea, rolling a smoke, revelling in the 'intermix mash and mingle' of the 'sonic selfies' which are reckoned to render this moment in space-time continuum a 'noisy' bearing.

Here, a pushcart with his frail attendant cries out to have his way cleared; a man in a SUV, with rolled up windows and AC on full blast (whose heat can be heard from a distance) keeps his hands on his horn, because he cannot hear the din he is making; a public transport bus in which many a lives will perhaps lose a dime or an opportunity because of the delay, announces a rather masculine sonic intervention of its desire to have its way; in the same bus, perhaps there is a young couple, I find myself hoping, who are only finding out they are in love, and which they know is forbidden, indulge in silent, slight touches amidst the demonic dances of the 'sonic selfies'. Here, the possibility to 'shut out' is absent, and thus 'shutting out and absenting' of the Other itself not an option. The multiplicity of the 'sonic selfies' - whether they be the frail cries, or amplified horns, the clanking of the cycle rickshaws which itself creates its own moment, the music that plays from someone having a conversation on speaker mode on their mobiles, or just using their mobiles as transmitter of songs of love and longing, or simply lust. Or even those who lend to this 'intermix mash and mingle' in their silences - necessitate a moment, however momentarily, to cohabit, to acknowledge the 'presences' of the others, however unpalatable it might be to their sense of selves, to respect the logics of the collectivization that compels an accommodation which otherwise would be negotiated, distanced and/or silenced.

The poetics of the moment burst me into raptures of an equally poignant political possibilities. And I want to shout out to no one in particular and everyone in general, a spectre is haunting the world, the spectre of othering. Let us abandon our seats as silent spectators in this theatrics of the world drama wherein an identified other is maimed, raped, burned, silenced without an apology in full view. Let us make the noise.

References

Althusser, Louis. *Philosophy of the Encounter Later Writings: 1978-1987*, G. M. Goshgarian, Oliver Corpet and François Matheron (eds.) New York: Verso, 2006.

Chandola, Tripta. 'Dumped through Technology: A Policy maker's Guide to Disenfranchising Slum Dwellers', *Journal of Creative Communications*, 8.2-3 (2013): 265–275.

Das Gupta, Moushumi. 'Amenities in the Slums Match up to Urban Homes', *Hindustan Times*, 22 March 2013, https://www.hindustantimes.com/delhi/amenities-in-slums-match-up-to-urban-homes/story-krqsZjcilVd7pb7vsCl8iP.html.

Dean, Jodi. 'Jodie Dean - Selfie Communism', *YouTube*, https://www.youtube.com/watch?v=iZvvH56XqCw.

Ferguson, James. *The Anti-politics Machine: 'Development', Depoliticization, and Bureaucratic Power in Lesotho*, Minnesota UP, 1994.

Li, Tania M. *The Will to Improve: Governmentality, Development, and the Practice of Politics*, Duke UP, 2007, p. 126.

Lovink, Geert. 'Narcissus Confirmed: Technologies of the Minimal Selfie' in *Sad by Design: On Platform Nihilism*, Pluto Press, 2019, pp. 98-107.

Vishnu, Uma. '34% in Slums Have no Toilet, but 63% Own Mobile', *Indian Express*, 22 March 2013, http://archive.indianexpress.com/news/34—in-slums-have-no-toilet-but-63--own-mobile-phone/1091573/.

Krejci, Jaroslav. 'A New Model of Scientific Atheism, *Concurrence*, 1.1 (1969): 87.

8. REVISITING THE HOUSING QUESTION

The breeding places of disease, the infamous holes and cellars in which the capitalist mode of production confines our workers night after night, are not abolished; they are merely shifted elsewhere! The same economic necessity that produced them in the first place, produces them in the next place. - F. Engels in The Housing Question, 1872.

I was told about contractual jobs at BSES to take meter readings, and I was assured a position by the cousin sister who also works. I thought, I am going for an interview, I should dress up, and I did! I got matching suit and nail polish, and washed my hair, and put on makeup. However, when the official saw me looking so stunning and realised where I was from, he said in front of everyone, you are from the Jhuggi Jhopdi colony and want a job, you think you will be selected if you are looking so 'hi-fi'. I felt very humiliated. - Bharti, long-time resident of the Ghevra JJ Resettlement Colony

We like living here, we have made this settlement what it is, this is our home. It has been for the last 30 years, we all have been part of turning this [spreading her hands around to suggest the settlement at large] into what it is now. We are proud of living here, just don't call us the bloody jhuggi-walahs, slum-dwellers. - Praveen Bhaaji, long-time resident of Navjeevan Camp, Govindpuri.

I often wonder, these apartment-people keep saying move us, they complain about us, call us dirty and drunks, and treat us so badly...but if we are not there, who is going to wash their dishes, take care of their babies, do all the bloody menial work for them... - Nagma, long-time resident of Navjeevan Camp, Govindpuri.

We do not want to have a city with slums [...] We're working toward this goal, which is something that has to be achieved both on humanitarian grounds and in terms of beautification of the city. First, slum-dwellers have no place in a modern city and must often be moved so that new infrastructure can be built; second, destroying slums is a humane act. - Sheila Dixit, former Chief Minister of Delhi, 2002.[1]

Reading these evocations in conjunction, it becomes evident that there is an obvious need for new concepts, methodologies and frameworks to capture the complexities of the newer forms of selves, inscriptions of marginalisation and its disenfranchising impact the newer forms of urbanites are producing. The Housing Question in the cities raised by Engels in 1872, at the turn of the century, is still as relevant and urgent, if not more, to ensure that both the idea of the city and the reality of its experience continue to be sites of transformative resilience and perhaps even propel towards the actualisation of the 'right to the city', as called out by Lefebvre, at the cornerstone of which is a highly-evolved sense of participatory and emancipated sense of 'self' of the urban citizens, including the urban margins.

---

1   Amelia Gentleman, 'Poor Lose Homes as Delhi Clean up for Games', International Herald Tribune, Paris, 2 January 2007

In The Housing Question, Engels further insists that the significant improvement in the working-class tenements in the 19th century industrial towns was not on account of making living conditions for this class better, but in fact to allow them just adequate sustenance levels so as to assure their continued contribution to the exploitative processes:

> Capitalist rule cannot allow itself the pleasure of creating epidemic diseases among the working class with impunity; the consequences fall back on it and the angel of death rages in its ranks as ruthlessly as in the ranks of the workers [...] As soon as this fact had been scientifically established the philanthropic bourgeois began to compete with one another in noble efforts on behalf of the health of their workers.[2]

Sheila Dixit, who reigned Delhi's 'Clean Delhi, Green Delhi' campaign to put the city on the world map as a 'world-class city', particularly towards hosting the Commonwealth Games, 2010, was Delhi's Chief Minister between 1998-2013. It was during her tenure that the city witnessed the highest number of slum demolitions in the city particularly towards the cleaning drive. Her justification of these demolitions on 'humanitarian' grounds resounds with the *'philanthropic bourgeois'* attempts that Engels insists on; furthermore, the grander agenda of the 'beautification of the city' which justified these demolitions are in alignment of the tendencies highlighted by Engels in 1871 instead of being an aberration. The 'politics of aesthetics', invisibilizing the undesired bodies and spaces and the disciplining agendas that were subsequently instituted were not a particularity of the Indian neo-liberal urban spaces, post 1991 when the Indian economy was opened, but in fact characteristic of the very mode of production of capitalism.

The body of the slum dweller, or any identified urban marginal group, in the city is considered to inhabit illegal spaces. The notions of a 'sacrilege centre' inscribes on the bodies of and from the 'vulgar margins'. These, in turn, systematically produces an anxiety about the 'peripheral bodies' in the urban imaginations thus impacting and effecting the entries of these bodies in otherwise reckoned democratic and open spaces. By employing overt, subtle, and insidious strategies, the imagined 'peripheral bodies' is subjected to civilizing and disciplining agendas. This violence (on these bodies) at an everyday level not only limits their agency to negotiate with the urban systems, but also lend to perpetuating and sustaining *similar* body politic of control and surveillance within their own contexts. And thus *spatial agency* as a basic right towards equitable urban futures to calibrate *space in the city remains un-actualized* when *space of the body* – as a fundamental assertion of one's identity in the city – itself becomes 'heterotopias of deviation'.

And here, the testimonies of Bharti, Praveen Bhaaji and Nagma, and similar accounts, which inform my position, further complicates the methodological approaches and interventions in addressing the housing concerns for the urban margins. The predicament of those on the urban margins - the slum dwellers, the residents of the resettlement colonies, the migrants, the homeless - is caught in the cul-de-sac of their bodies' labour desired for the task that goes into the 'beautification of the city', and in fact in running the meticulous, exploitative

---

2   Frederick Engels, *The Housing Question*, 1872.

machinery of the city, however the presence of these bodies evokes disgust. Thus: the space of the body of those on the urban margins and the body of the space (by the way of the sight of the slums, the homeless squatters and similar spaces) both are haunted by the spectre of precarity, vulnerability and illegality. Without taking into cognizance the lived experience and realities of the urban poor, the methodologies and approaches informing the housing policies and plans for the same will continually and cyclically endure the fate of Engel's prediction of being 'merely shifted elsewhere'. Bharti's testimony from a resettlement colony is but an affirmation of this finding fruition.

Housing is not merely a matter of infrastructural concern. Particularly for the urban poor who are amongst the most marginalised and precarious constituent groups in the cities, the ease, access and availability of adequate housing is determinant in not only shaping their present but also securing their future and long-term aspirations. The existing approach is limited by the very *limited* manner in which it engages with the 'real housing conditions' for the in the cities. The future research design and focus needs to consider the capacities existing and needed to ensure sustainable, livable futures (with focus on housing demands/needs/conditions) in the city among the urban poor. And the manner in which housing issues impact not only the present but also actualisation of future aspirations for the informal sector in the workers. One of the key ways in which these research can contribute to policy discussions is by generating data sets, insights and understandings to inform and define parameters for what 'livable and inclusive' cities for this constituent section of the population in the city means. A key lacunae in understanding the 'livability' for the urban poor is the lack of, or very limited, insights available to capture the overall 'well-being' - social, cultural, psychological - encountered by the urban poor as articulated by themselves.

The lived experiences of the urban poor, more often than not, fail to find way into policy framing and considerations. The fault line lies not so much in the 'intentions' but the methodological and conceptual approaches which inform these studies. In my doctoral thesis, drawing on a five-year long ethnographic research in the Govindpuri slums, I proposed *listening* as a methodological intervention to engage with the everyday negotiations of its residents. It recounts the experiences and encounters of the slum-dwellers in relation to the space they inhabit. The fulcrum to engage with these narratives was the practice of *listening*, privileging what, how, when and why the slum-dwellers listen in and into. The matter of agreeing upon *listening(s)* as a trope of engagement with the slum-dwellers about their everyday was not intentional and strategic; instead whilst 'hanging around' the slums the intent, urgency and anxiety amongst the residents to articulate their sense of selves employing their own referential vocabulary was realised in their listening practices.

In my doctoral thesis, drawing on a five-year long ethnographic research in the Govindpuri slums, I proposed *listening* as a methodological intervention to engage with the everyday negotiations of its residents. It recounts the experiences and encounters of the slum-dwellers in relation to the space they inhabit. The fulcrum to engage with these narratives was the practice of *listening*, privileging what, how, when and why the slum-dwellers listen in and into. The matter of agreeing upon *listening(s)* as a trope of engagement with the slum-dwellers about their everyday was not intentional and strategic; instead whilst 'hanging around' the slums the intent, urgency and anxiety amongst the residents to articulate their sense of selves employing their own referential vocabulary was realised in their listening practices.

In that sense: in my research I was not only keen on what the residents of the slums were *listening into,* but also – both as a methodological and political position – to privilege the 'ears' of the slum-dwellers.

These *listening(s)* of the slum-dwellers into their everyday practices also allowed insights into the wider social, cultural, spatial, emotional, sensorial and political cosmos of the slum. The importance is exaggerated as these insights about the slum-dwellers rarely find their way into the official *sarkari or* bureaucratic records. The *listening(s)* of the slum-dwellers then not only complements the readings of the official records but also complicates them. It does so by inserting and amplifying the *voice* of the marginalized, disenfranchised poor by considering and recognizing their position in the city, its broader urban planning policies and socio-cultural fabrics, as actualized, appropriated and critiqued by them. Insisting on these *listening(s)* also lends to a broader political mandate by extending a self-reflexive agency to the slum-dwellers, allowing them a platform to comment on what they make of *what* (by which I mean policies, popular middle-class imaginations, public discourse) is done to them. In short, whilst we know enough about what is done to the urban poor, these *listening(s)* in fact allow us to hear into what the urban poor do about what is done to them. The importance of these *listening(s)* is paramount in extending a 'voice' to the marginalized to identify and articulate their own demands depending on the lived experiences which continually expose their vulnerability of systemic, structural and immediate concerns.

The methodological framework of listening allows for these lived realities become a key focus on how poor communities organize and navigate precarity shape existing governance capacities and alter urban poverty as a way of life towards resilient, inclusive and sustainable futures. Towards truly achieving the mandate of 'Right to the City', it is essential to develop critical insights into whether spatial 'access' translates into the constituent population being able to accrue long-term material, social and cultural capital for a more consolidated 'well-being' in the city. The policy framing, actionable investments and future research needs to direct its efforts towards meeting the housing and living conditions for the urban poor in a holistic manner, such that this constituent group of city's residents can also claim these spaces as their 'homes' with pride, dignity, self-respect and assurance.

The last two decades have witnessed the landscapes of the Indian cities undergoing significant transformations. For both the long-term residents and the newer-arrivals, these urban landscapes are at once sites allowing possibilities for realities and aspirations erstwhile unimaginable to be actualized and spaces where social, structural and systemic violence and discriminations are strategically reproduced and reinforced. The re-calibrating sites, processes and manifestations of violence, disenfranchisement and marginalization in the transforming urban landscapes also necessitate theoretical, methodological and political interventions towards the project of democratic, just and equitable futures for the city as spaces and sites of ethical cohabitation.

To end, perhaps at a polemical (and also pessimistic) tone, considering a disruption in the capitalist mode of production, which as Engels identified will only continue to reproduce the question of the housing for the urban poor, is not an imminent reality and which thus also limiting the actualization of the 'Right to the City' and thereby possibility resilient urban futures. After all, if there is an ongoing contestation of claims to spaces, identities and sense of 'self' for the urban poor in the manner in which they never really become 'urban', as identified by Lefebrve, in that, 'they come to see participation not as speaking at a public hearing or serving on a citizens' panel, but as the living struggle for a city that is controlled by its inhabitants', how does one truly envisage extending the capacities to the urban poor to empower them into resilient futures?

And, here methodologically, I want to make a rather bold intervention: whilst it is of utmost significance to *listen into* the lived and experienced realities of the urban poor and to constantly employ innovative methodological tools to inform policy, there is also an urgent need to add another constituent group in the city in the endeavours of educating them: the middle-classes. Resounding through Nagma's prescient question, *what will they do without us*, the middle-classes need to be made brutally cognizant of the fact that their modern, clean, sanitized, world-class claims and desires for the city will in fact remain a distant dream if the urban poor are not given dignified and equitable presence in their imagination, encounters and reality. It is only when everyone in the city is recognised as its *inhabitants* that urban resilient futures will be actualised.

Lastly, in revisiting the housing question which is yet to be realised, one cannot overlook the first, foremost and fundamental question: *for whom and towards what futures* are the Smart, World-Class, and Resilient cities being imagined?

The spectres that haunt the very livability of the urban poor are yet to be resolved, and which then compels the reckoning that instead of propelling towards smartness, beautification and resilience what is of urgency is to recognise across registers the complex and delicate manners in which conditions of precarity are intertwined such that the burden of resilient, ethical co-habitational spaces is a collective endeavour and responsibility.

References

Engels, Frederick. *The Housing Question*, 1872 (transcribed Zodiac, June, 1995), https://www.marxists.org/archive/marx/works/1872/housing-question/.

Gentleman, Amelia. 'Poor Lose Homes as Delhi Clean up for Games', *International Herald Tribute*, 2 January 2007.

9. TO WHOM DO YOU 'BEAUTIFULLY' BELONG? THE SLUMS' RESPONSE (IF INDEED THEY WERE ALLOWED THE TONGUES): OR, THE RITE OF PASSAGE TO THE RIGHT TO THE CITY: BUT, WHERE IS THE SELF OF THE SLUMS?

I begin with a poetic evocation:
'Their relationship consisted in discussing if it existed'
- Thom Gunn, *Jamesian*.[1]

After almost two-decade of slumming, so to say, it is in these two brief lines that I am finally able to locate (and articulate) the relationship between the city and the slums. The core of this cathartic relationship is not defined by the existence of the slums or the manner in which the slums come into existence, but is in fact determined by negotiating the modalities of dealing (or in fact not dealing) with the *existing* of the slums in the city. Central to these discussions - one-sided, and deliberated by the hegemonic voices with both control over the means/modes of production and determined intent of maintaining control over the expropriation of resources - is the strategic, systemic and structural denial of the sense of self to the slums. This denial of self to the slums manifests in varied ways in the everyday negotiations to the imaginative accommodation of these spaces in the future of the city. The denial of the self of the slums is not always predicated on intent of design or deliberation but informed - overtly, insidiously or subtly - by the processes of estrangement, alienation, dehumanisation and depersonalisation central to the capitalist machinery and reducing the labour as its living appendage.

In this essay, I draw attention to the manner in which dehumanization of the slums (and its residents), with particular insistence on denial of its emotionality, is and will remain a crucial impediment to the actualisation of the call of the 'Right to the City' until significant discursive shifts are compelled. I will also highlight the manner in which the 'anxiety of proximity[2]' with the slums in the everyday interactions, in urban planning processes but also in academic and activist undertakings, however well-intentioned, further lends to reducing and relegating the slums to an 'infantile, perennially peripheral and an abnormality' reckoning. Lastly, towards the mandate of actualising the 'right to the city', as Lefebvre envisaged in the manner of an ongoing, urgent utopian project whilst not succumbing to the tendencies of 'unimaginative realism', the essay insists the need of the hour is to discursively shift from the 'moral, humanitarian, communitarian, paternalistic' evocations whilst engaging with the concerns of the slums to collective, ethical responsiveness and democratic participation in the urban futures by both sounding and responding to the clarion call for a revolution which shifts its focus to, as Lefebvre emphasises, 'defined either in terms of the political change at the level of the state or else in terms of the collective or state ownership of the means of production'. He further insists,

---

1   Thom Gunn, *Jamesian*, http://psa.fcny.org/psa/poetry/poetry_in_motion/atlas/atlanta/jamesian/.
2   Slavoj Žižek, 'Human Rights and its Discontents: The Logic of the Stalinist Show Trials', Olin Auditorium, Bard College, 16 November, 1999.

that 'such limited definitions of revolution will no longer suffice. The transformation of society presupposes a collective ownership and management of space founded on the permanent participation of the "interested parties"' with their multiple, varied and even contradictory interests. This revolutionary project, Lefebvre continues, 'whether utopian or realistic, must, if it is to avoid hopeless banality, make the reappropriation of the body, in association with the reappropriation of space, into a non-negotiable part of its agenda'.[3]

Lefebrve's call for the 'right to the city' is a theoretical, philosophical and political project toward an ongoing, dialogic negotiation which involves inhabitants engaging each other in meaningful interactions, interactions through which they overcome their separation, come to learn about each other, and deliberate together about the meaning and future of the city. These encounters make apparent to each inhabitant their existence in and dependence on a web of social connections. They come into consciousness of themselves as inhabitants, as embedded in a web of social connections, as dependent on and stewards of 'the urban'. As they become conscious in this way, they recognize the need to struggle against the industrial capitalist city and for the urban. They come to see participation not as speaking at a public hearing or serving on a citizens' panel, but as the living struggle for a city that is controlled by its inhabitants.

In responding to the discussions about the right to the cities, the symptomatology that presents itself are two-folds: why does the 'right to the city' still remain an un-actualized project, particularly within the Lefebrevian intent and as David Harvey articulates towards 'the greater democratic control over the production and use of surplus'?[4] And, why do the existence of the slums deliberate the discussions (or, the lack thereof or when in fact undertaken in skewed and stunted) and sustained anxiety? The prognosis of this diagnostic examination is that the denial of the 'self' of the slums is a conditioned impediment which perpetually defers the moment and momentum to accrue the critical threshold essential to actualise the first and overcome the second symptomplogy.

I begin with a personal admission of my initial encounter with the slums. Even though now I claim and demand intimacy, embedded relationships and investments in and with the slums, the first couple of years were nothing less than fraught with anxiety. I was adequately acquainted (and sincerely) believed in the 'right' left politics of the rights of the marginalised, the politics and violence of displacement and disenfranchisement, but left to my own devices of having to spend hours into days in the lanes of the slums, I found myself ill-equipped to deal and negotiate with the emotions the intensity of the slums materiality, pervasive everydayness of the denial of internalised – which the residents encountered merely on account of being slum-dwellers. But my anxiety was far more insidious (in response to my own limited experiential encounters with the slums but also responding to the popular/mainstream reckoning of the slums). In short, at times I was scared, at other times, violently angered by

---

3 Henri Lefebvre, *The Production of Space*, trans. D. Nicholson-Smith, Oxford: Blackwell, 1991 (1974), p. 422.
4 David Harvey, 'The Right to the City', *New Left Review,* September-October 2008, https://newleftreview.org/issues/II53/articles/david-harvey-the-right-to-the-city.

gendered, communal, caste practices within the slums, and at still other times found myself deeply drawn to a few and took a strong dislike to others.

In the essay, *In Search of the Slums Never-Lost*, I discuss these encounters at length. However, here, I want to insist on the *knot in the stomach* that I perpetually felt during my early days of forays into the slums. This sense particularly heightened to intensifying crescendo - which often left me debilitated, emotionally, politically and intellectually - when I started pursuing research towards my doctoral research. I no longer had the convenience of a project's mandate to hide behind (which initially brought me into the slums); I had chosen to be here. I had written an impassioned proposal, 're-drawing the lines' about the engaging, exploring and eventually 'revealing' the selves of the slums which not only most did not want to acknowledge, let alone encounter. Among my middle-class cohorts and friends, I chided them, I accused them of classist positionalities, I was quick to make a judgement: 'what the fuck do you know, I, only I, know the reality, I have ventured into the lanes, I have broken bread with "them", they are my friends', and so on and so forth. For performative purposes, such anguished cries from a bleeding heart often got me the attention I was precisely evoking it to achieve attention, a shoulder to cry on, and sometimes, a long embrace into a dark night.

But, when the mornings beckoned and I had to set out to the slums, the *knot in the stomach* gripped the being of me. I felt hollow and hypocritical, the embraces and attention from the nights pungent. I theoretically knew enough about working the hyphen to speak of the knotty entanglements and messiness poetically and politically. However in the 'now and present' of conducting research, I found myself in such knotty entanglements that the 'selves of the other' presented themselves more as hauntings from far-distant shores.

I begin with an intensely personalised account my own encounter with the slums to insist that (and particularly to the group of aspiring academics, activists, or fundamentally as the collective custodians of urban futures) that however well-intentioned, politically sound, theoretically rigorous one's position is, the 'encounter' with the other – here, the slums – irrespective of its essentiality (either traumatic or otherwise tantalising) demands reflexivity. Because 'as such, the encounter constitutes the link between stability and change, determinacy and contingency, theory and practice. It is therefore one of the key elements to unlock a new materialist understanding of political transformation. The encounter is also the connecting thread between politics and aesthetics'.[5] But there are more fundamental implications lending and leading to the 'denial of the self of the slums'. Masking one's own anxiety – as a researcher, activist, and an academic - particularly when it is from the vantage point of privilege at the intersectionality of class, caste, gendered, and communal affiliations only goes as far as to suffices as not dealing with the *knot in the stomach*. But these anxieties nevertheless find their ways of accommodation in academic texts, policy documents, activists interventions, and thus the insidious task of obliterating the self of the slums is set in motion. If the other does not have the agency to evoke a response, stir an emotion, does the other even has capacity to emote?

---

5   Louis Althusser, *Philosophy of the Encounter Later Writings: 1978-1987*, G.M. Goshgarian, Oliver Corpet and François Matheron (eds) New York: Verso, 2006.

And if the other in fact cannot emote, how can the other be trusted or even recognised to have the ability to make decisions, determinations unto themselves?

I sought out guidance from the non-state actors both working with the slums of Govindpuri and those involved in broader concerns of the 'rights of the slums'. I took recourse to academic texts to if not find a 'guide' - *a kunji* - to this slumming, but at least a hint of the similar anxiety experienced and articulated by other researchers and academics. I was left wanting from both of these engaged groups in the concerns of the 'slums'.

The overarching tendency of the non-state actors and activists was [and continues] to situate the slums as a draining resources of the state: 'demented; lazy; and prone to avarice and indulgences of the morally compromised sorts'. The more well-intentioned of the sorts, among this group, treated the same constituent group in a highly, paternalistic, patronising manner: 'but, they don't know really know what they want, they have all the wrong priorities'. And, 'of course, you cannot discuss politics with them, particularly when you find their views problematic, do not 'antagonize them; they don't know better', was the advice given to me by a very senior slum activist in the city, when I was in the midst of pursuing my research on political formations within the slums of Govindpuri and which finds it way in the essay, *The Subaltern as a Political Voyeur.*

> Of course, I recognise and do stand for the rights of the slums, but do they have to live so close to us. I am a single woman, I bought this flat for the peace, solitude it offers and now this filth, I feel scared […] I have never walked the arterial road connecting her apartment block through the two camps of the slums to the main road, and thank god for the aircon in the car, I have never rolled down the windows, that way I can not only avoid the noise but also the smells.

Thus reckoned a self-proclaimed left-leaning political scientist living in the apartment block across the road from Navjeevan Camp about her neighbours in Govindpuri. During my doctoral research, in response to my question about why the residents of the slums where in fact allowed in the intimate, domestic spaces of the middle-class households in the capacity of drivers, house-help, nannies and such, the usual refrain was, 'our houses are civilized […] left to their own whims, it then they get the crazies; it is actually not their fault, it is where they live'.

In the academic texts, I felt even more fraught, I could not relate to the 'researcher' venturing about the slums in these accounts. The lanes, conversations and the experiences of the slums for the researchers in these texts were bereft of the 'anxiety' I found myself engulfed in. Here, the position of the ethnographer is eulogized vesting in her unlimited and unrestricted access to venture into a 'site' with the 'subjects' more than eager to reveal their histories, experiences, and lives. And the fact of the matter is that, and recounting from my own personal encounters in the slums of Govindpuri, but also in other marginalized spaces, yes, indeed, as a middle-class, educated person embodying structural privileges, I (and most other researchers) have unlimited, or at least unquestioned, access into these spaces. But this admission is very rarely made. And even rarer is the acknowledgement that if the positions and spaces

\of research and researched were reversed, would the middle-class researcher in fact allow herself to be researched; and particularly if the interlocutor came from the margins?

The answers to this question are difficult to find, not because the answer is easy, but because the gated community of academic scholarship on slums has collectively agreed on never allowing these questions to be raised.

These reckoning of the slums – and their representations – at the most fundamental level set the tonality, and thus the practices, of the 'denial of the self of the slums'. Here, even whilst high-pitched calls for the voice and agency of the slum-dwellers is made for, the manner in which they are 'represented' the slums come across in monochromatic, passive and 'not fully evolved' entities in the Marxian sense. Thus, if both the 'needs and there fulfilment' of the 'other' in fact can only be identified and met with by their benefactors', can the 'other' than be reckoned to have any capacity of 'self-determination'? The flattening of the anxiety of the researcher's - their *knot in the stomach* never really acknowledged - thus also lends to the *knotty entanglements* on the field and the multiplicity of the selves of the other being flattened out.

The otherwise 'harmless' practices which are commonplace (and deeply embedded in class, caste, gendered, and communal prejudices) in middle-class households, are enacted in different and varying manners across activists and academic engagements with the slums. The most commonplace of these are: more often than not *not* acknowledging the residents by their names; very rarely deconstructing, or at least discussing, the mandate and agenda of the project at hand in its entirety (to make explicit the web of connections, etc.); to discuss the arguments drawn from these engagements, to attempt to 'deconstruct the space of theory and politics' for the otherwise celebrated residents of the slums as collaborators. The framing to 'mobilise, engage and involve' the residents, more often than not, is in the vein of 'we are conducting this research/campaign for you? We will fight for your rights'. And almost always, the researcher never returns to the 'site' to discuss how far he travelled with the 'insights' and the tales he wove, the argument he made and the publications accreditations he got.

In my doctoral research, I conducted an ethnography of everyday interactions within the slums of Govindpuri and with their middle-class neighbours through the politics of sound. The research highlighted the nuanced practices and processes of 'othering' the residents of the slums enacted both within the slums (across class, caste, gendered and communal vectors) but also that the middle-classes are reckoned as 'immoral, corrupt and repugnant' as the latter views them. Over the years, I have closely followed the lives of sex-workers, domestic-workers (both, men and women in different capacities) and manual labourers, among others.

Of course the residents of the slums – in different capacities of the permissible encounters – with their *others* are well aware of the *othering* they are subjected to and it is recognised as stripping them of their selfhood, requiring them of performances of passivity, invisibility, unbecoming and unlistening. The residents of the slums are very well aware of the 'benefits' that can be accrued from their encounters with non-state actors - activists, researchers, and academics, and thus the residents are also well-versed in 'performing poverty, helplessness, and speaking of oneself only in vocabularies of lackings'. These performativities of dehumanising themselves in repressed and perverted ways extends in not only in their interactions with the state agencies and in accessing infrastructural and fundamental services – banks, hospitals and schools.

The residents have their own strategies to deal with this 'othering' - there is Baby who had worked in a Tamil-Brahmin household for past twenty years and who on the first 'encounter' with Baby assumed of her Hindu, widowed status for the lack of adornments maintained thus with them not revealing her identity as a Muslim woman, well aware that she would be asked to quit. Babita, the sex worker, who to maintain associations with a regular client who pays for her rent, sometimes afford her children's fees and other necessities to 'bathe with filtered water' - using the expensive water filter which he installed – so as to maintain his 'purity'. She chides behind his back, that not only does she not use the filtered water for herself but also not whilst preparing a bath for him as well, and thus adulterates him. The men who work as drivers for middle-class *madams and their daughters'* share very intimate space and are privy to their intimate ongoings and discussions admit to performing 'unlistening', find it particularly amusing that these women assume they don't understand English, and in doing so discuss the details of their 'ongoings' in salacious manner. In particular when it is regarding the young women from nearby apartment blocks, it often leads to the said young women being targeted in rather unbecoming ways, but also leads to these men exercising far more control over their women so that they do not start emulating those way. The women in the slums find it particularly difficult to find redressal for domestic, sexual and other kinds of abuse, or assert their claims or articulate their emotions. Until 2012, when the Indian state ruled attempt to suicide not a criminal offence, it was not an uncommon 'threat (and at times put in effect) of 376'.[6] However, since it has been ruled that 'attempt to suicide' is decriminalised but not abetment to suicide, the practice of , 'drinking just enough phenyl, calling in 100 number [the national helpline number to call the police authorities] and negotiating whilst or before the cops are summoned for testimony with those harassing' has become a popular manner in which the women seek redressal. The sex-workers in Govindpuri, who during India Against Corruption, 2011, and following Demonization, 2018, had to extend their 'services' not only to the local police personnel threatening them with consequences but also to local shopkeepers for their daily upkeep, and used to effectively to maintain their work, ensure their children's education and maintain the household upkeep.

Whilst it is seductive to reckon these acts as performance of the assertion of the self of the slums, these assertions accrue any currency of recognition when performed across two registers – either by being violent or by implicating themselves – however imaginary – in the acts of violence. The ruthlessness of the violence inflicted is often masked within the rhetoric of benevolence; in that they are in fact being extended 'legitimate' claims to history, memory and culture. The lack of acknowledgement to their 'emotionality' is yet another strategy (though seemingly insidious and instinctive) to perpetuate their violence. For: if the residents of the

---

6   Section 376 under Indian Penal Code is punishment for rape, which if reported by a woman - particularly after the 2011 Delhi Rape incident, the police authorities have to take immediate action against the accused

slums were indeed identified as 'emotionally' capable they would have to be acknowledged to have capabilities of 'individual' expression, which would then extend to acknowledging their 'collective' identities as well. However this denial of emotionality does not imply that their 'performance' or 'expression of self' in the public, or for that matter in their private spaces, is not unacknowledged. In fact the performance is constantly scrutinized; however it is not engaged within the framework of expression of 'self' but as a gross deviance from the 'modern, disciplined and self-governed' in their infantile, delinquent manner demanding disciplining.

The self of the other is only permitted as much space as the capitalist modes of productions can accommodate, and that is the fundamental impediment in the actualisation of the 'right to the city' as envisaged by Lefebvre at the centre of which is an inhabitant who has a solid, undeniable core which then facilitates 'encounters' of democratic, dialogic, participatory negotiations. To state the obvious, it is not an easy task, intellectually, culturally, theoretically, socially, to engage in a discussion about 'slums or their right to the city' because most of these calls are made within the very system – the capitalist modes of production and negotiations which produce them in the first instance as Engels pointed in 1872 and which remains still relevant.

This was particularly revealed when during the course of my doctoral research, my intent and presence was particularly found disconcerting when I was categorical about the fact that I was not interested in knowing about their poverty levels but just about themselves; anc in all truthfulness, it was in these encounters and hanging about that *listening as a methodological framework* had its genesis. Whilst pursuing the DFID research to examine 'The Role of ICTs in Poverty Alleviation', armed with an questionnaire, I would venture into the *jhuggis,* with entitlement and no regard for the personal, political, poetic, privacy positions of the residents to fill out details of their financial profiles - how much you earn, where do you spend, how much, why, why not - to essentially determine whether they in fact qualified as poor enough or not. The poverty - as imagined to be experienced within the mandate of the project - had to be validated by the poor, and as always in review discussions later there were doubts raised about the *authenticity* of their claims, what were they under-reporting, how to really 'expose' them.

Needless to say when I was allowed an opportunity to pursue my own research intent in the *jhuggis,* even though the questions evaded me, I was determined in the resolve of not discussing *poverty* with the poor. The poverty, the deprivations, the limited infrastructural availabilities were not a *secret* that had to be unravelled. It was obscenely obvious, and from my political, intellectual position, it was a bloody insult to the intelligence of the residents to ask them to spell it out.

Instead I decided to just *listen* into the manner in which the given conditions and manifestations of deprivations lend and lead to the experiences within the broader political, emotional, social, aspirational cosmos which the residents could claim, denied to and subverted. In and through these acts of everyday practice, I wanted (and still continue) to insist on that the diverse experiences of *poverty* - social, financial, political, emotional - impact on the capacity to claim and enact citizenship as a rightful, legislative, constitutional right.

The material form in these inquisitions was never-absented, its roofs, corners, crevices (or lack of thereof) became one of the ways in which everyday was experienced living in conditions that mark the infrastructural, emotional, political and social landscape in and within the lanes of the *jhuggis* in Govindpuri in my works. However, I reflect now, there was a matter of deliberation and intent - though not conscious and well articulated - to not insist on the anatomy of the material form, per se, as its presence was one of the most obvious and bearing manifestations of the *poverty* that specific discourses and practices insisted on.

Perhaps it was the keenness to *listen* that also confounded me regarding the participation and claims of the residents of the slums in the city that was dramatically transforming towards the Commonwealth Games, 2010, whilst I was pursuing my doctoral research. The academic texts and activist discourse were singularly intent on highlighting the manner in which the transformations were unleashing new politics of middle-class aesthetics in the city, and in which the slums and its residents had no place. In retrospect I acknowledge my naivete to reckon these accounts with absolute veracity of absolute truth. And thus I approached the residents of the Govindpuri slums with precise critique and assumed collective indignant response to the devastating fate our city was being held hostage to. I was *silenced* and *sidelined* on several occasions, more than a few residents took immense pride and delight in how their city would become one of the world-class ones, that there will be roads and infrastructure, and new airports and other similar facilities to showcase to the world. One of the camps of the Govindupuri slums, Navjeevan camp, has a very robust market catering to the construction industry, mostly the scaffolding that is essential in these enterprises. Commonwealth Games provided them the boost as never before, both the retailer and the workforce from the slums were not only proud but announced themselves as significant 'contributors' to the changes the city was witnessing. I am yet to come across any such assertive expressions of claiming participation in the transformation of the city from the residents of the slums in the texts, which in fact rely on ethnographic accounts to make statements about the manner in which the very slum-dwellers appear as passive agents.

There are tactics of complicity, duplicity and possibilities of 'inter-liveability' on which these relationships are precariously and delicately balanced. Here, the conceptual framing of 'people as infrastructure' by AbdouMaliq Simone while discussing the inner city of Johannesburg in the context of racial tensions in a volatile, transforming city holds particular relevance. In this formulation:

> Ways of doing and representing things become increasingly 'conversant' with one another. They participate in a diversifying series of reciprocal exchanges, so that positions and identities are not fixed or even, at most times, determinable. These 'urbanized' relations reflect neither the dominance of a narrative or linguistic structure nor a chaotic, primordial mix.[7]

---

7   AbdouMaliq Simone, 'People as Infrastructure: Intersecting Fragments in Johannesburg', *Public Culture*, 16.3 (2004): 407–429.

In mapping the diverse, overlapping and intersecting networks, modalities and landscapes of living precariously, there is an urgent need to engage, expose and arrive at the 'traumatic core' of the tensions underlying it. This is not merely an ambitious, well-intentioned, romantic agenda. In my reckoning, only the task of revealing these densities, connections and intersections of living with conditions of precariousness will highlight the real, banal of the 'other' which is systematically absented and invisibilized by the state and other hegemonic narratives. The absence of such engagement often leads to these communities being caught in another kind of totalizing Borgesian–Kafkaesque narrative without any scope of liberation. The image of the 'other' as precarious can only be disrupted by demolishing the myths and representations of the distancing and othering it is predicated on. The demystification of the 'other', by highlighting the structural, systemic and material conditions which produce the conditions for this othering in the first place, then announces itself as the political project which researchers across disciplines ought to align themselves to.

Slums are representative spaces of what the city 'ought not to'. However, an equally persistent, subtle threat is of the city turning into a colossal slum, given the rate of development, population increase, and lack of infrastructural facilities. In that sense, slums stand out as a demonic, prophetic instance of *'what could be'* but *'ought not to be'*.

A paternalistic disciplining agenda is inherent to these narratives which is symptomatic of the broader anxiety of the dominant structures and narratives to allow for emotionality, and thus an identification of a well-defined and claimed sense of 'self' to the marginalized spaces and communities. Slums are heterotopic spaces in the city. They are both dreaded and desired. The former for its 'potential' to disrupt the fundamental core of social-moral values owing to the imaginations it evokes on account of its density, dirt, and digressions – social, cultural and moral. And it is within this dreaded potentiality for digressions lies its perverse desire.

However this desire rarely translates into a direct engagement with the space, but manifests itself in the hyperbolic interest in situating the position of the slums in the 'present' of the city. Slums are strategically denied a 'self' as it allows them to accommodate the anxiety about their 'otherness' across political, intellectual, social, cultural and, indeed, emotional manifestations. In its most fundamental aspect it completely disenfranchises slums of any 'identity' and thus its assertion. It systematically limits their 'right to the city'. This fundamental disenfranchisement further extends into denying the slums and its residents the possibility to imagine an (or any) other. The denial of the 'self' of the slums in discursive spaces, middle-class imagination and mainstream representation is then logically extended to unacknowledging any 'emotional' capacity or its performance, emotionality. This double denial, first of the 'self' of the slums and then the possibility of othering by the other translates not only in immediate disenfranchisement, but also significantly allows for the displacement of the marginalized both in the historical and futuristic imagination of the urban. The peculiarity of the suspended displacement in the imagination of the state is not incidental, but strategic. It owing to this suspension that the demolition, displacement or the violence inflicted on the slums finds justification as it is understood that they neither have any historicity nor any future claims to the memory and culture of the space they inhabit. That until 're-settled' by the state, they exist in a void.

The right to the city for those on the margins ought to manifest in their capacities to reject the city without the fear, threat and/or violence of being expunged. For this relationship between the hegemonic forces and the marginalised to be premised on a non-negotiable pact of neither imposing or nor insisting on displacement. To reckon of this relationship as a love affair wherein the lover and the loved with, without, besides and in spite of any disruptions have and do accommodate the other. Accommodation has to be the critical factor here, to be able to throw a sulk, hide in a corner, turn your head away but not throw the tantrum of expunging the lover (or loved). In this analogy at varying times, the loved one is representative of the hegemonic forces, and whilst the lover retains the power to alleviate the status of the former, its position is still shrouded in precarity. For the marginalised to walk recklessly the streets with the swagger in the hips of the confidence that none can halt us.

And thus, if indeed the self of the slums were recognised, and if in the hegemonic forces in the manner of an entitled lord in *The High Bid*, the play from which the title of this talks draws from, inquires of a valet he fancies, 'to whom do you "beautifully" belong?'[8] And thus divesting the valet in the play and the slums in the city of any sense of 'self' and only acknowledging them as propertied entities to be exchange hands, one imagines slums respond resoundingly:

Do I contradict myself?
Very well then I contradict myself;

(I am large, I contain multitudes.)[9]

References

Althusser, Louis. *Philosophy of the Encounter Later Writings: 1978-1987*, G.M. Goshgarian, Oliver Corpet and François Matheron (eds) New York: Verso, 2006.

Gunn, Thom. *Jamesian*, http://psa.fcny.org/psa/poetry/poetry_in_motion/atlas/atlanta/jamesian/.

James, Henry. *The High Bid*.

Harvey, David. 'The Right to the City', *New Left Review,* September-October 2008, https://newleftreview.org/issues/II53/articles/david-harvey-the-right-to-the-city.

Lefebvre, Henri. *The Production of Space*, trans. D. Nicholson-Smith, Oxford: Blackwell, 1991 (1974), p. 422.

Simone, AbdouMaliq. 'People as Infrastructure: Intersecting Fragments in Johannesburg', *Public Culture*, 16.3 (2004): 407–429.

---

8 Henry James, *The High Bid*.
9 Walt Whitman, *Song of Myself,* 51.

Whitman, Walt. 'Song of Myself, 51', in D. McKay, *Leaves of Grass,* 1900.

Zizek, Slavoj. 'Human Rights and its Discontents: The Logic of the Stalinist Show Trials', Olin Auditorium, Bard College, 16 November, 1999.

10. THE SHRIEK: A POETIC INTERLUDE

> A man was nothing but a continent of ideas. Whereas a woman lived on shifting grounds. - Katie Kitamura, *Gone to the Forest*.

A not-so-young woman lives amongst tight lanes and crowded lives.

There is nothing singular about this not-so-young woman. She is but that, and could be anyone of them, one who lives the slumming. She is loud. She is dirty. She has desires to be devoured, but never gently. Living harshly, she desires it hard and harsh. She always does not say thus; she has no tongues.

But you, from where you are, can hear her murmurs.

You enter the slums cautiously, dark, dreaded and crowded as they are; or more confidently, if you grew up on its frail roofs. The not-so-young woman, more often than not, cannot be slight on her feet or heavily announce her arrival here. She rarely leaves. She imagines though, of the sounds she has not heard, the cinemas, the metros and the rails, the mechanical malls, and such. But also of love. The not-so-young woman wading through the din of dens wonders, does love have a sound? Will she know it when she hears it?

You enter the not-so-young woman always confidently, never cautiously. You are ensconced in the hearings that always hears you, and let her sounds wander about aimlessly. You do not even have to silence the not-so-young woman; she is taught not to speak. She has no tongues. You laugh, while thrusting your idiot in her. All the not-so-young-woman is hearing is your resounding, raucous laughter and the pain in her groins.

The not-so-young woman does not know yet whether love has a sound, but she knows now that pain does.

The not-so-young woman desperately desires the din of the dens, which on other evenings and in-between afternoons leave her with a murderous instinct. Where are the pathetic children? And why haven't the ones doused in alcohol and singing songs of a loss they have not felt, arrived? And where is the old, farting woman, always in the corner, always hurling obscenities? Perhaps they cannot hear her, the silently screaming not-so-young woman reckons. And then even the silent screaming comes to an abrupt stop: they hear her, silently.

The not-so-young woman knows now she has to find her own sound, a sound which will silence the pain in the moment which is never-ending. The idiot unrelenting. She agrees upon a sound which she has never heard, that of love. She has also never been to the mountains, she has heard that they are tall, still and never leave. The not-so-young woman hears love as the sound of the mountain standing still.

The not-so-young woman is still hearing the sounds of love, the tall mountains she has never visited, or have been paid a visit by, when the idiot relents. You let it die on her when you see her smile, but you do not hear her hearing the sounds of love. It tickles the idiot, yet again; the not-so-young woman, the idiot reckons, wants it.

These days the not-so-young woman, with nothing singular about her, wades through the din of the dens like an amused child. Some even notice her smile. She suddenly stops in the middle of taking hasty steps and stares at the door. Often she has to be pushed out of the way because she is staring at the pathetic children. Or letting the old, farting, woman in corner caress her hair while hurling the obscenities.

The not-so-young woman feels the idiot in each of these sounds. Only when the not-so-young woman can wander to the sound of the mountains does she smile.

The nights are different though, the not-so-young woman needs the din of the dens to wander to find the sound of love. But the not-so-young woman has been taught to contain the cacophony brewing within, and thus white noise becomes of her. She screams as she did, as she is taught, silently.

But one night, the not-so-young woman's body betrays her, and a shriek awakens the dens.

Many-of-you appear: some in reality, others as apparitions. You ask.

The not-so-young woman, finally having an ear to her disposal, tells: of the idiot, of the sounds, of the sound of love, of the mountains – tall, still and never leaving, of the smile, of the idiot, yet again.

Many-of-you grimly silent at first, break into a resounding, raucous laughter in harmony. The many-of-you perform a little demonic dance:

But you wanted it, you did. You smiled, you did. You did not shout, why did you not, did you? If the shriek is so loud, and the pain was so bad, how do you still live? There is a tree nearby. But, you do, you wanted it, you did. You say, your insides hurt. Why are they still inside? Did many-of-us pull it out? Why did you not pull them out yourself? You wanted it, you did.

Now the not-so-young woman wanders about the lanes wearing frocks, that many sizes too small for her, lifting it, revealing her swollen, rotting sex, shouting and singing out of tune, but I wanted it. I did. The many-of-you, your idiots still eager and unrelenting, throw stones at her, demanding her to shut up.

Coda:

The not-so-young woman, here, is the perennial, but not the static other. She is the woman in the slums. Slum in the city. The lower-caste, lower-class man beaten up on a whim of a middle-class woman. The transgendered person. The Other's body is always an identified feminine.

The You is the City. The Violence-ordering middle-class woman. The Hegemonic discursive space and its practices. In its perverse masculinity, the You demands silence as a right, and practices silencing with its desire to contain, denying a becoming and voice to the Other.

But the You, in its arrogant unhearing forgets, that on certain nights, the not-so-young woman can and does shrieks, even if you momentarily silence her.

In her shrieking, the sound she finally finds, the not-so-young woman establishes she has a voice, which one fine morning, when she is not the only, will drown: The Many-of-You.

References

Kitamura, Katie. *Gone to the Forest,* UK Edition, Clerkenwell Press, 2013.

BIBLIOGRAPHY

Ahmed, Waquar. 'Neoliberal Utopias and Urban Realities in Delhi', *ACME: An International E-Journal for Critical Geographies,* 10 (2011).

Attali, Jacques. *Noise: The Political Economy of Music,* Vol. 16. Manchester University Press, 1985.

Althusser, Louis. *Philosophy of the Encounter Later Writings: 1978-1987*, translated by G.M. Goshgarian, edited by Oliver Corpet and François Matheron. New York: Verso, 2006.

Calvino, Italo. 'A King Listens', translated by William Weaver, in *Under the Jaguar Sun,* pp. 31-64. San Diego, New York, London: Harcourt Brace Jovanovich, 1988.

Claus, Peter J., Sarah Diamond, and Margaret Ann Mills. *South Asian Folklore: An Encyclopedia: Afghanistan, Bangladesh, India, Nepal, Pakistan, Sri Lanka*. Taylor and Francis, 2003.

Bradbury, Ray. 'The Fog Horn', https://archive.org/stream/TheFogHorn/TheFogHorn.txt.

Benjamim, Walter and Asja, *Journal de Naples*, 1925.

Borges, Jorge Luis. *Collected Fictions*, translated by Andrew Hurley. New York: Viking, 1998.

Butler, Judith. *Gender Trouble*. London: Routledge, 1999 (1990).

Butler, Judith. *Notes Towards a Performative Theory of Assembly*. Cambridge, MA: Harvard UP, 2015.

Certeau, Michel De. *The Practice of Everyday Life,* translated by Steven Randall, pp. 93-105. California: University of California Press, 1984.

Chandola, Tripta. 'Listening into Others: Moralising the Soundscapes in Delhi', *International Development Planning Review* 34.4 (2012): 391–408.

Chandola, Tripta. 'Slum in the Time of Politics', *Business Standard,* 21 January 2013, https://www.business-standard.com/article/beyond-business/slum-in-the-time-of-politics-112030400055_1.html.

Chandola, Tripta. 'Getting a Rise', *Business Standard,* 25 January 2013, https://www.business-standard.com/article/beyond-business/getting-a-rise-112080500044_1.html.

Chandola, Tripta. 'Dumped Through Technology: A Policy Maker's Guide to Disenfranchising Slum Dwellers', *Journal of Creative Communications*, 8.2–3 (2013): 265–275.

Classen, Constance. *Worlds of Sense: Exploring the Senses in History and Across Cultures.* New York: Routledge, 1993.

Connor, Steven. 'Michel Serres's Five Senses', Birkbeck College, May 1999, http://www.stevenconnor.com/5senses.htm.

Das Gupta, Moushumi. 'Amenities in the slums match up to urban homes', *Hindustan Times,* 22 March 2013, https://www.hindustantimes.com/delhi/amenities-in-slums-match-up-to-urban-homes/story-krqsZjcilVd7pb7vsCl8iP.html.

Dean, Jodi. 'Jodi Dean - Selfie Communism', *YouTube,* https://www.youtube.com/watch?v=iZv-vH56XqCw.

Douglas, Mary. 'The Social Control of Cognition: Some Factors in Joke Perception', *Man,* 3.3 (1968): 361–376.

Engels, Frederick. *The Housing Question,* transcribed by Zodiac, 1995 (1872), https://www.marxists.org/archive/marx/works/1872/housing-question/.

Faiz, Ahmed Faiz. 'Don't Ask Me for That Love Again', translated by Agha Shahid Ali, in *The Rebel's Silhouette: Selected Poems of Faiz Ahmed Faiz,* Amherst: Massachusetts UP, 1995, p. 5.

Ferguson, James. *The Anti-politics Machine: 'Development', Depoliticization, and Bureaucratic Power in Lesotho.* Minnesota UP, 1994.

Fine, Michelle. 'Working the Hyphens' in *Handbook of Qualitative Research.* Thousand Oaks, CA: Sage, 1994.

Foucault, Michel. *Politics, Philosophy, Culture: Interviews and Other Writings, 1977-1984.* Routledge, 2013.

Gramsci, Antonio. 'The Intellectuals', in *Selections from the Prison Notebooks,* translated and edited by Q. Hoare and G.N. Smith, 3-23. New York: International Publishers, 1971.

Gentleman, Amelia. 'Poor Lose Homes as Delhi Clean up for Games', *International Herald Tribute,* 2 January 2007.

Gunn, Thom. *Jamesian,* http://psa.fcny.org/psa/poetry/poetry_in_motion/atlas/atlanta/jamesian/.

Harvey, David. 'The Right to the City', *New Left Review,* September-October 2008, *https://newleftreview.org/issues/II53/articles/david-harvey-the-right-to-the-city.*

Marcus, George E., and Michael M.J. Fischer. *Anthropology as Cultural Critique: An Experimental Noment in the Human Sciences*. Chicago: University of Chicago Press, 2014.

James, Henry. *The High Bid*.

Jha, Preeti.'Great Wall of Kalkaji', *Indian Express*, 5 April 2008.

Kitamura, Katie. *Gone to the Forest*, UK Edition, Clerkenwell Press, 2013.

Krejci, Jaroslav. 'A New Model of Scientific Atheism, *Concurrence*, 1.1 (1969): 87.

Kumar, Sanjay. 'Interpreting the AAP Win', *The Hindu*, 11 February 2015, https://www.thehindu.com/opinion/lead/interpreting-the-aap-win/article6879316.ece.

Lefebvre, Henri. *The Production of Space*, translated by D. Nicholson-Smith. Oxford: Blackwell, 1991 (1974).

Li, Tania M. *The Will to Improve: Governmentality, Development, and the Practice of Politics*. Duke University Press, 2007.

Lovink, Geert. 'Narcissus Confirmed: Technologies of the Minimal Selfie' in *Sad by Design: On Platform Nihilism*. Pluto Press, 2019.

Nancy, Jean-Luc. *Listening*, translated by C. Mandell. New York: Fordham, 2007.

Nigam, A. 'Industrial Closures in Delhi', *Revolutionary Democracy*, 7.2 (September 2001): https://www.revolutionarydemocracy.org/rdv7n2/industclos.htm.

Pandey, Ponam Chandra. 'Sheila Dixit: Architect of Modern Delhi, Wanted to Develop it like Singapore', https://morningindia.in/sheila-dikshit-architect-of-modern-de hi-wanted-to-develop-it-like-singapore/.

Picard, Max. *The World of Silence,* vol. 6067, H. Regnery, 1952.

Pirandello, Luigo. '*Six Characters in Search of an Author'*, translated by John Linstrum. London: Methuen Drama, 1991.

Rancière, Jacques. *Proletarian Nights: The Workers' Dream in Nineteenth-century France*, translated by John Durry. New York: Verso Trade, 2012.

Rice, Tom. 'Soundselves: An Acoustemology of Sound and Self in the Edinburgh Royal Infirmary', *Anthropology Today*, 19.4 (2003): 4-9.

Rice, Tom. 'Govindpuri Sounds', *BBC*, https://www.bbc.co.uk/programmes/p02hm1rx.

Roy, Ananya. 'Urban Informality: Toward an Epistemology of Planning', *Journal of the American Planning Association*, 71 (2005): 148.

Sacks, Oliver. *Seeing Voices: A Journey into the World of the Deaf*. Pan Macmillan, 2009.

Schafer, Murray. 'Open Ears', in Michael Bull and Les Back (eds) *The auditory culture reader*, 25. New York: Berg, 2003.

Simone, AbdouMaliq. 'People as Infrastructure: Intersecting Fragments in Johannesburg', *Public Culture*, 16.3 (2004): 407–429.

Soto, Hernando De. *The Mystery of Capital: Why Capitalism Triumphs in the West and Fails Everywhere Else*. Civitas Books, 2000.

Spivak, Gayatri Chakravorty. 'Can the Subaltern Speak?' in C. Nelson and L. Grossberg (eds) *Marxism and the Interpretation of Culture,* 271-315. Urbana: University of Illinois Press.

Spivak, Gayatri Chakravorty. 'Scattered Speculations on the Subaltern and the Popular', *Postcolonial studies* 8.4 (2005): 475-486.

Stoller, P. *The Taste of Ethnographic Things: The Senses in Anthropology.* University of Pennsylvania Press, 1989.

Vishnu, Uma. '34% in Slums Have no Toilet, but 63% Own Mobile', *Indian Express*, 22 March 2013, http://archive.indianexpress.com/news/34—in-slums-have-no-toilet-but-63--own-mobile-phone/1091573/.

Whitman, Walt. 'Song of Myself, 51', in D. Mckay, *Leaves of grass*, 1900.

Wikipedia Contributors, 'India Against Corruption', *Wikipedia,* https://en.wikipedia.org/wiki/India_Against_Corruption, accessed 4 April 2020.

Zizek, Slavoj. 'Human Rights and its Discontents: The Logic of the Stalinist Show Trials', Olin Auditorium, Bard College, 16 November, 1999.

Zizek, Slavoj. 'Capitalism with Asian Values', *Al Jazeera*, 13 November 2011, https://www.aljazeera.com/programmes/talktojazeera/2011/10/2011102813360731764.html.

Zizek, Slavoj. *The Pervert's Guide to Cinema* (dir. Sophie Fiennes, 2006).

Zizek, Slavoj. *Organs without Bodies: On Deleuze and Consequences*. London: Routledge, 2012 (2004).

ACKNOWLEDGMENTS

The task of writing the lives of others demands humility, integrity and honesty. The lives and the spaces I write about are outliers in more ways than one, the temptations to sabotage these lifeworlds for one's own displaced fantasies (of projecting hurt, anger, jealousy) are alluring. I am grateful to the people in my life who, whilst enveloping me in generous love, listening, support, did not let me indulge in my fantasies or encourage my cleverness. ndira Ramesh, the beacon of uncompromising principles and politics, who stood up for me when I had not the courage, and not because of her generosity because it was the matter of principle. Jo Tacchi under whose supervision and with whom I learned to listen, and who has given me the confidence, the courage, and the solidness of celebrating the families which are borne out love, respect and deep caring outside the bounds of shared genetic pools. And who brutally shot down by her one assertive 'nah' any attempts to fictionalize the lives. I am eternally grateful to her for that. Nishant who is equally unwavering in his commitment as a comrade in times of crisis as he is in the pursuit of pure theory and practice of politics and who led me to finally escaping the trappings of the capitalist mode of production of the self. Rrishi Raote whose thinking, writing, editing and living have the delicateness and finesse of the finest China is my moral compass, and with the revelries and time spent with the Raote household I am allowed the indulgence of a highly eccentric, loving, respectful gang of people who call themselves a family.

In the recent years, I have been bestowed by love and support from those younger to me by several years, and in and with whom I still can revel in hope and optimism for the collective futures in these dystopic times. Katharina Wischer for her loyalty, keen intellect and pursuit of Proust and Marx, not always at the same time. Seema Sharma for resilient sense of self. Shruthi Chittoor for her commitment to the 'field', an ethnographer par excellence and from whose patient listening of the others I draw inspiration. Adya Thakur for the years she has accumulated with dignity and poise, and for always being with the promise of a fantastic holiday in wayward places. Kunal Bandapodhya with whom talking cricket, politics and shared ideas of love and living follow ceasely, and with whom watching the T20 final at Eden Garden was as invigorating as talking to people in rural Bengal about politics.

In my intellectual meanderings, I have had the privilege to find guidance from scholars who in one or another have greatly shaped my writing and thinking. Christy Collis, who patiently bore the grammatical assault I unleashed on her as my co-supervisor, and who gently guided me to be excited about space and geographical imaginations, or thinking beyond them. Ursula Rao for her unrelenting desire and demand for nothing but committed and thorough research practice to be matched with equally rigour theoretical pursuits, and for being the listener who allows me to 'externalize' my crisis; AboudMaliq Simone with whom a walk around Govindpuri and other neighborhoods on a hot Delhi afternoon rejuvenated my loving for the city; Tom Rice with whom I literally shared ears and a sonic extravaganza in Govindpuri; Tania Lewis who is unparalleled in her kindness and generosity to encourage intellectual pursuits; Kathi Kitner for allowing her research practice to be open for scrutiny; Georgina Born with whom the interactions have been few and far between in the last years but who has always encouraged my listening; Christine Guillebaud for shared listening. The essay 'Subaltern as

Political Voyeur' saw its completion with encouragement by Alf Gunvald Nilsen to commit to enliven te lives of the subaltern within their grammar and vocabularies. My special thanks to Jim Skyes and Gavin Steingo for allowing me all the concessions and missed deadlines for my essay to be included in their collection.

In the love and friendship of a few I have learned and held steadfast that warmth of hearth and home can be nurtured in spite of distances and differences. Jinna Tay with whom the love of cities, food, wanderings, stories of love realized and unactualised is acutely shared and felt. Aashish Kaul for the many afternoons and evenings where we measured our lives with the stories we shall tell. Swaroop Dev whose commitment to uncertainties is compelling, almost hopeful. Jonathan Benny for being an outlier of sorts, and thankfully so.

To Zaheer Abbas, Ananya Dasgupta, Abhik Samata with whom conversations left on some courtyard in JNU decades back are picked where they were without hesitation, and to be bemused by and at our younger selves and allowing each other to be archives of eahc other's younger ways.

To the memory of Alison Milner who made me feel at home whilst I was struggling to finish the thesis, and to Rohan McCarthy in the hope of continued conversations.

A special thanks to Rama and Rosy for accommodating my eccentricities in my endeavors to claim B 44 as my own transient home which includes, but not limited to, stripping the living room of its essentials to turn into a boxing arena. To Abhishek Vasudeva and Gaurav, boxers and trainers passionate and unrelenting about the art form in their own ways, who helped me to sharpen my punches, balance my footwork and make me appreciate the 'sweet science' of it all, again.

To the houses at whose entrance hung a robust green, metal plaque announcing - 'Home is the place where, when you have to go there, they have to let you in' - in colonial settings across the country in which I lived with mother, father, brother, mother's brother's two daughters, books, copious amounts of gin, dogs, little garden, once a cattle, bridge and croquet afternoons was as quintessentially an unhappy family as Tolstoy envisaged. To each of our differences, demons, discords, eccentricities, strange loves and stranger lives, I owe ultimately the unrelenting quest for escape, explorations and seeking solace in and with strangers with whom I've managed to nurture my own families.

I still remain uncertain of my listening, but I owe it to the space and crew at Sarai in the early 2000s where the initial, wayward wanderings in romancing and romanticizing the city were given patient audience, a validation, a license, a legitimacy to continue in these voyages. To Monica, the coolest of them all in her red boots, Shuddha, Jeebesh, Shweta Sarda, Pankaj Kaushal, Parvati Sharma, Ritika Shrimali, Mary and the many others with whom in the glassed walls of the Interface Zone we drank dark rum, wrote bad poetry, typed in 'Hello World' and shared the love of our cities in our own ways. For bearing on me to think, reflect, and mourn about the 'burden of listening', Sadan Jha, who continues to be a distant, but firm intellectual anchor and sounding board in times of of conundrum, which new ideas and experiences throw at me.

In some ways that is where it all started, and most of all I remain indebted to the Interface Zone for the friendship, companionship, confidence and belief of Geert Lovink and Patrice Reimens. They believed in the book even before I could imagine it. It is not a matter of exaggeration but practical realities that this book would not have been possible without Geert Lovink's persistence and refusal to give up on me, even when I had no faith in myself or my listening. Patrice for indulging all my fantasies, stories and always taking seriously my fallen loves and not so sharp punches.

I cannot thank enough for the keen, astute and patient editorial inputs of Sepp Eckenhaussen which finally compelled the essays in the book to take the form they have; needless to say, all the shortcomings are solely mine.

Lastly, I asked people in the lanes of Govindpuri, so how do you want to be acknowledged? 'For what?', I was asked. Well for sharing the lives and the book is finally done and so on, people do that. 'So you are thanking us for sharing our lives, is it?' Yes, I think so. 'But that seems like "the end" of sorts, like now we won't anymore or we only did for the book.' Of course not. 'Then don't remember us like that as if we are already forgotten (abhi kyon yaad karna jab bhulaye hi nahin hai).' Thus to the many more afternoons into evenings, loves, lives in the lanes of Govindpuri to whom I owe my political and poetic education, I hope one days those lanes and lives are flowing with the reds, the colour of revolution, *laal salaam*!

ABOUT THE AUTHOR

Tripta Chandola is an ethnographer based in Delhi, India. She completed her doctorate from Queensland University of Technology, Australia, in 2010. She has held research positions at NUS, Singapore and RMIT, Melbourne. She has also worked as a research consultant for several international and national projects. One of her long-term, sustained research engagement has been with the space and its residents of the slums of Govindpuri in Delhi. Her particular focus is on the everyday encounters, social, cultural, political, emotional and sensual, which inform the identity, rights and claims which the residents of the slums can assert in the broader materiality and imagination of the city.

The politics of everyday encounters of marginalisation, disenfranchisement and rights the poor are the key focus of her research. She has published in international peer-review journals and contributed to edited book collections. In 2015, BBC World Service commissioned radio programme based on her doctoral research titled Listening into Others.

Tripta Chandola is a Research Fellow at the Digital Ethnography Research Centre, DERC, RMIT, Australia.

www.ingramcontent.com/pod-product-compliance
Lightning Source LLC
Chambersburg PA
CBHW020427220526
45464CB00002B/603